From Furs to Farms

Early American Places is a collaborative project of the University of Georgia Press, New York University Press, Northern Illinois University Press, and the University of Nebraska Press. The series is supported by the Andrew W. Mellon Foundation. For more information, please visit www.earlyamericanplaces.org.

ADVISORY BOARD
Vincent Brown, *Duke University*
Andrew Cayton, *Miami University*
Cornelia Hughes Dayton, *University of Connecticut*
Nicole Eustace, *New York University*
Amy S. Greenberg, *Pennsylvania State University*
Ramón A. Gutiérrez, *University of Chicago*
Peter Charles Hoffer, *University of Georgia*
Karen Ordahl Kupperman, *New York University*
Joshua Piker, *College of William & Mary*
Mark M. Smith, *University of South Carolina*
Rosemarie Zagarri, *George Mason University*

From Furs to Farms

The Transformation of the Mississippi Valley, 1762–1825

JOHN REDA

NIU Press
DEKALB

© 2016 by Northern Illinois University Press
Published by Northern Illinois University Press
DeKalb, Illinois 60115
Manufactured in the United States
First printing in paperback, 2017
ISBN 978-0-87580-786-7
All rights reserved
Cover by Yuni Dorr

26 25 24 23 22 21 20 19 18 17   2 3 4 5 6

978-0-87580-499-6 (cloth)
978-1-60909-193-4 (e-book)

Library of Congress Cataloging-in-Publication-Data
is available online at http://catalog.loc.gov.

For Steve and John

Contents

	Acknowledgments	xi
	Introduction	1
1	The Colonial Eighteenth Century in the Illinois Country	14
2	The Louisiana Purchase, Territorial Government, and Contested Lands	42
3	From Tippecanoe to Portage des Sioux: The Wars of 1812	75
4	Statehood for Illinois and Missouri	99
5	After Statehood: Indian Removal, the Fur Trade, and Slavery	123
	Conclusion	144
	Notes	149
	Selected Bibliography	177
	Index	195

Acknowledgments

Writing history is an odd mix of the solitary and the collaborative, and I am pleased to reach the point where I can thank the people who have helped this project progress from a proposal to a dissertation, and finally to a book. I must begin with Richard John, who, first as an instructor, and then as an advisor, mentor, and friend, challenged me again and again to raise my game and showed me again and again how I might do so. Andrew Cayton and Peter Onuf took an interest in a pesky graduate student and read various versions of the dissertation and book chapters, generously providing valuable comments and suggestions that pointed the way forward at many key points.

Many thanks to Leon Fink, Brian Hosmer, Sue Levine, and Jim Sack at the University of Illinois at Chicago for the help and support they provided during the early stages of the project. Thanks also to Roger Biles, Anthony Crubaugh, Ross Kennedy, Richard Soderlund, Amy Wood, and the rest of my colleagues at Illinois State University for taking the time to answer my many questions and to chat on many enjoyable occasions about writing and teaching—and life in the world of academics.

I first met Ann Keating at a Newberry Library seminar, and we quickly bonded over a shared interest in Chicago and Illinois history. Ann was kind enough to read most of this book's chapters at least once, and her comments were invariably helpful and encouraging.

After meeting as graduate students in Richard John's reading seminar in 2001, Jeff Helgeson, Sarah Rose, Joshua Salzman, and I became friends and later formed a writing group that helped us all get our dissertations launched and eventually completed. Along with our significant others, we also formed a cooking group that was the source of many wonderful get-togethers—and more than a few odd dishes. No one could ask for better compatriots to help navigate the challenges of graduate school and beyond.

The research for this project would not have been possible without the generous support of several institutions and individuals. Fellowships awarded by the University of Illinois at Chicago, the Illinois Historic Preservation Society, the Society of the Grand Dames of America, and Illinois State University allowed me to do research at the Chicago Historical Society (now the Chicago History Museum), the Illinois State Archives and Historical Library at Springfield (now part of the Abraham Lincoln Presidential Library and Museum), the Indiana Historical Library in Indianapolis, the Missouri Historical Society in St. Louis, the Randolph County Courthouse in Chester, Illinois, and the Lewis Historical Library at Vincennes University. At each of these places I received crucial assistance from many outstanding librarians and archivists.

Many of the arguments found in this book were first presented in conference papers. Thanks to the many people who provided comments and criticism at conferences organized by the Society of Historians of the Early American Republic, the French Colonial Historical Society, the Conference on Illinois History, the Illinois History Symposium, the Newberry Library, the Mid-America Conference on History, and the Center for Legal Studies at Northwestern University. At each of these gatherings I benefited from the feedback provided about my work and also from the outstanding work of dozens of other historians at the many sessions I attended.

I would like to thank Linda Manning and everyone else at Northern Illinois University Press for their long-standing—and patient—interest in the project and for their expertise in turning my manuscript into a book. It has been a long road.

Over the years it took to bring this project to completion, I was lucky to receive encouragement and inspiration from many friends and family members. On my very first day of college many years ago, I met Debbie Avant, and she has been the most loyal and steadfast friend one could ever hope for. Lawrence Buckingham—Ocean Man—and I have been through more ups and downs together than either of us can remember. Many thanks to Dave Aftandilian, Tim Avant, Rebecca Beucher, Harriet Bloom, Michael Bloom, Matthew Bogusz, Rosemarie Bogusz, David Brachman, Craig Brooke-Weiss, Mike Butterfield, Cory Czesak, Susan

Emerick, Dan Goral, Karen Goral, Judy Hallisy, Anne Halsey, Julia Hendry, Melody Herr, Jeff Kumm, Tom Perrin, Dave Rust, Rana Hutchinson Salzman, Helene Shaevitz, Steve Shaevitz, Gigi Wernikoff, and Steve Wernikoff.

My parents Lorraine Reda and John F. Reda and my sisters Cathy Maslanka and Linda Reda have been listening to me carry on about history since my childhood and have been inexhaustible sources of love, support, and inspiration. Thank you.

During the years of writing I could always count on the feline hijinks of Bud and Dusty to keep me company at any time of the day or night. They are both gone but I have two new companions—Joey and Zina—who are now the ones who sit (or sleep) nearby when I'm reading or writing and who occasionally walk on my keyboard when they think I need a break.

Finally, it would be inadequate to say that this project could not have been completed without the love and support of my wife Phyllis. She encouraged me to pursue my dream of writing and teaching history when I had begun to think it was not in the cards, and she has since done everything in her power to support me each step of the way.

From Furs to Farms

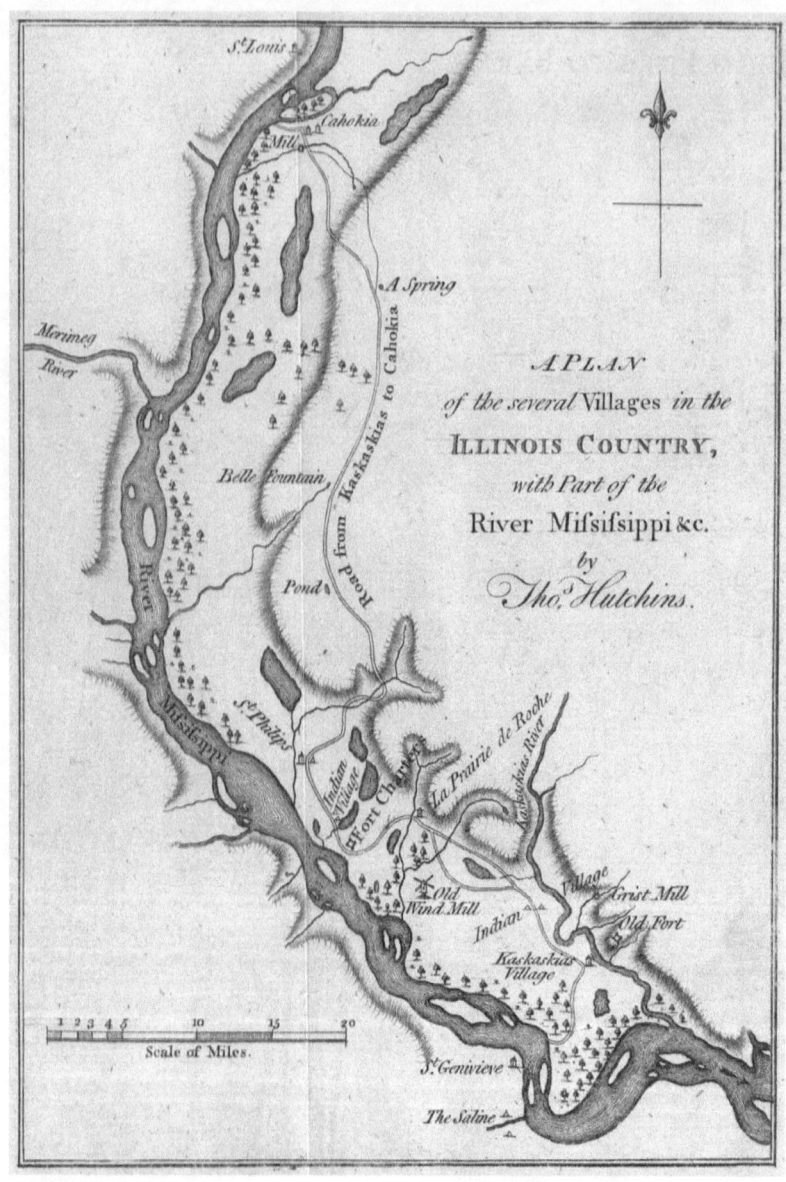

MAP 1. A Plan of the several Villages in the Illinois Country, with Part of the River Mississippi, by Thomas Hutchins, 1778. Courtesy of David Rumsey Cartography Associates.

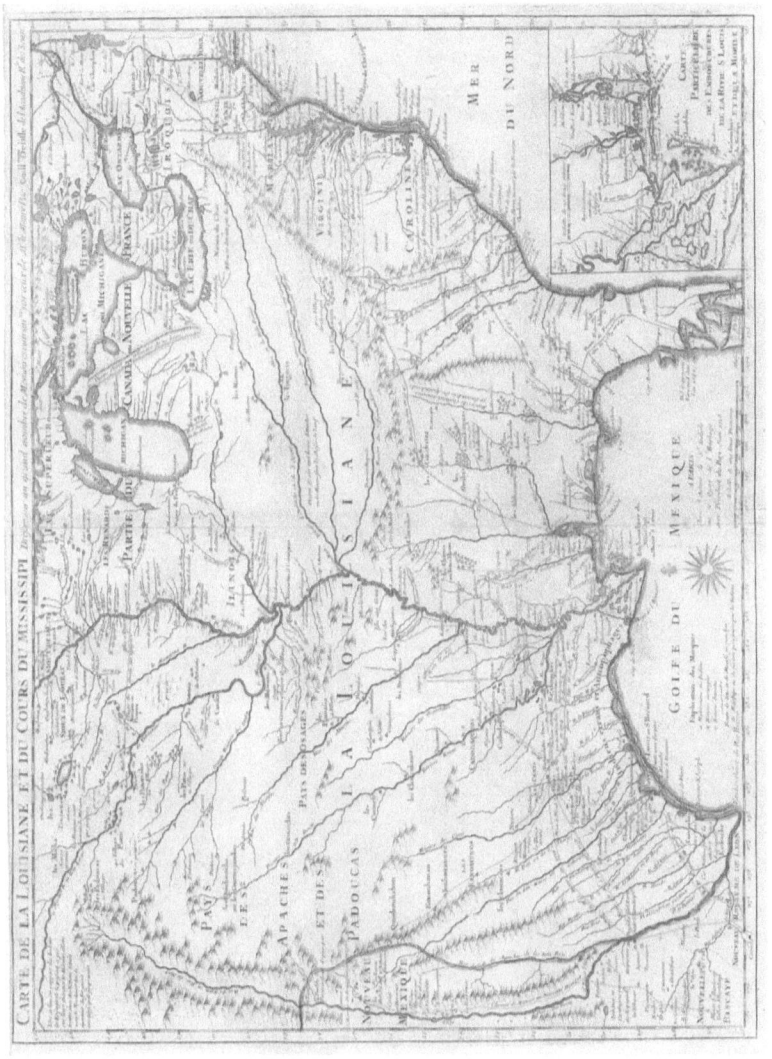

MAP 2. Carte de la Louisiane et du Cours du Mississippi, by Guillaume Delisle, 1718.

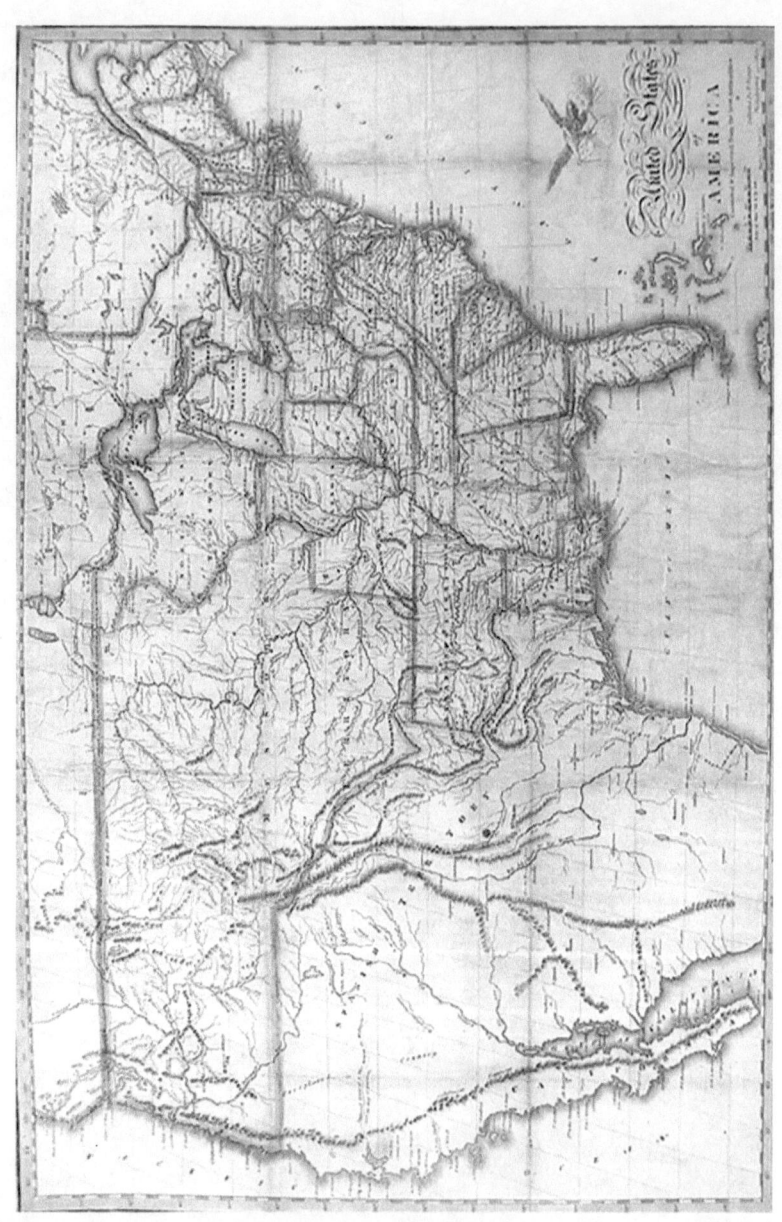

MAP 3. The United States in 1820, by John Melish.

Introduction

On the afternoon of Friday, March 9, 1804, at what is now the southeast corner of Main and Walnut Streets in St. Louis, Missouri, Carlos De Hault Delassus, last of the Spanish lieutenant governors of Upper Louisiana, addressed a large crowd in front of the Government House. "I now deliver this Place and its dependencies; the flag under Which you have been Protected for the last thirty-six years is now about to be withdrawn. You are, therefore, absolved from your allegiance to his Catholic majesty."[1] Spanish troops fired a salute and Governor Delassus and Captain Amos Stoddard, an American officer serving as France's representative, signed the formal written transfer of the territory from Spain to the French Republic. Among the three official witnesses to the signing was Meriwether Lewis, who was in St. Louis making final preparations for the Corps of Discovery's legendary expedition to the Pacific Ocean. After a night in which the French tricolor flag is said to have flown above St. Louis, Captain Stoddard, now representing the United States as the incoming military and civil commandant of Upper Louisiana, addressed a crowd that included nearly all of the residents of St. Louis. "You are divested of the character of Subjects, and clothed with that of citizens—You now form an integral part of a great community; the powers of whose Government are circumscribed and defined by charter, and the liberty of the citizen extended and secured." That evening Stoddard hosted a large party to celebrate the momentous event.[2] Thanks to the Louisiana Purchase, the entire Mississippi valley was now part of the United States.

In hindsight the two-day transfer appears to mark a transformative event in the history of the valley and its peoples: a long colonial era giving way to the promise of American democracy; the switch from subjects to citizens, to paraphrase Captain Stoddard. The ceremonies themselves seem fraught with imperial meaning, the flags being lowered and raised, representing the relative fortunes of the respective powers. For Spain and France it was a North American setback, for the United States a sign of what would soon be called its "manifest destiny." But from another perspective the treaties that caused Louisiana to change hands from Spain to France and from France to the United States can be seen as merely contributing to a transformation that had already begun, an economic transformation that had little to do with imperial politics and everything to do with the peoples of the valley and the land itself.

From Furs to Farms is a history of the part of the Mississippi valley that gave rise to the states of Missouri and Illinois. Known in the eighteenth century as the Illinois Country, it was until the 1760s in the middle of a French arc of colonial influence that stretched from the mouth of the St. Lawrence River through the Great Lakes and down the Mississippi River to the Gulf of Mexico. Like all histories, this one involves people—the things they did or tried to do—and geography. The Illinois Country was a watery world in the eighteenth century, filled with bogs and swamps but most significantly the place where four important rivers met: the Illinois, the Missouri, the Mississippi, and the Ohio. Described by historian Stephen Aron as the "American Confluence," this place was peopled by a collection of white, black, Indian, and métis peoples who were almost all connected to one or more of the "Big Rivers," and also to the fur trade: the exchange of animal skins for European trade goods.[3]

Far away, across the Atlantic Ocean, monarchs and their imperial officials in Paris, London, and Madrid at various times presumed to rule the Illinois Country. And while most would have acknowledged their failure to do so effectively, their decisions nevertheless affected their putative subjects. For that reason, a history of the Illinois Country must include an imperial perspective that involves wars and treaties and the issues of sovereignty. In the early 1760s, treaties negotiated after France's defeat in the Seven Years War transferred sovereignty over the western half of the Illinois Country (to be called Upper Louisiana) to Spain and the eastern half to Great Britain. The Mississippi River thus became an international boundary. Following the Revolutionary War the United States acquired the eastern half of the Illinois Country from Great Britain under the terms of the Treaty of Paris, signed in 1783. Within twenty years France had reacquired Upper Louisiana, only to quickly sell it to the United States as part of the Louisiana Purchase. In 1818 the eastern half of the Illinois Country was admitted to the Union as the state of Illinois, and in 1820 the western half became the state of Missouri.

No Indian signatures, however, appeared on any of the many treaties that granted sovereignty to one imperial power or another. This omission, however, did not cause the same outrage and resistance among Indians in the Illinois Country as it did in places farther east. The reason is that sovereignty did not much matter in this area, where the economy was based on the fur trade. Europeans had learned through experience that attempts to exercise authority over Indians in the Illinois Country were both bad for business and dangerous. For most of the eighteenth century the Osage Indians were the single strongest military group in the Illinois Country. Trading with the Osage was both profitable and strategically preferable to having them as enemies. By the last decade of the 1700s, however, the Osage faced competition from incoming settlers—both Indian and white—who coveted the lands along the western bank of the Mississippi River. Sorting out this competition and limiting the violence that accompanied it would require the effective exercise of sovereignty, and the United States proved up to the challenge.

How did the United States eventually succeed where other imperial powers had failed? What had changed aside from lines drawn on an imperial map? The answer to the first question is that the United States succeeded by offering white settlers a combination of physical protection, secure property rights, and white supremacy in exchange for their loyalty. The process was not a quick one, nor was it uncontested. The Illinois Country's attachment to the United States was threatened from without by rival powers and from within by ambitious men who initially were not convinced that their best interests lay with the new republic.[4] The answer to the second question is related to the first but a little trickier. We have to look beyond the lines drawn on maps by European and American officials to understand *how* the Illinois Country became Missouri and Illinois. We have to "follow the money."

In the eighteenth century the economy of the Illinois Country was based on the fur trade, although some of its inhabitants were farmers. But in the early years of the nineteenth century, commercial agriculture began replacing the fur trade as the primary economic activity in the region. This meant that the animals living on the land were no longer the region's principal commodities. The land itself was to be surveyed and sold. With this shift came the necessity to displace not only the animals, but also the Indians living on that land. To do so in turn required white settlers to embrace the idea of the United States exercising effective sovereignty over the Illinois Country in order both to receive protection from Indians resisting the loss of their lands and to secure a recognized title to the various pieces of land those settlers coveted. The transformation of the Illinois Country into the states of Missouri and Illinois was thus essentially an economic one: the story of the change from furs to farms.

This story, then, is not primarily an American story about national expansion. It is instead a story about a specific place that underwent various political, demographic, and most importantly, economic changes that created the terms and conditions by which it was incorporated by the United States. I do not address the question of whether or not this incorporation was inevitable. Instead, I begin with the assumption that for every place in what is now the United States there was a particular—and anything but inevitable—set of processes by which the shift was made from a colonial past to an American future.

In examining the history of the Illinois Country, this project builds on the recent work of several historians who have begun to rewrite the history of the trans-Appalachian West. Richard White's *Middle Ground* is the starting point for much of this work, and its importance can hardly be overstated. White shattered forever the myth of a West not empty, but essentially inert—waiting for the sweep of history to engulf it after American independence. His description of events taking place in the West while history's spotlight shined on the eastern seaboard paved the way for a generation of scholars. White's work and that of many others has done much to introduce racial and ethnic complexities to the history of the trans-Appalachian West. I will argue that the Illinois Country in this period was an international crossroads with a highly diverse population and ties in several directions to international markets and competing imperial powers.[5]

My emphasis on the economic transformation of the Mississippi valley builds also on the work of historians who have recently begun to look at the colonial-era development of the region as part of a wider Atlantic World perspective that looks at the events of these years as being driven primarily by economic actors—by entrepreneurs both white and of color—whose attachment or relationship to France, Spain, England, or the United States did not constitute the principal part of their identities (to use an anachronistic term). In other words, these people did not explicitly think of themselves as French, Spanish, English, or American. Their decisions were based primarily on their cultural backgrounds, kinship ties, religious affiliation, business relationships, and only sometimes by their loyalty or attachment to something that in the future would be called a nation.[6]

On a more basic level I am also arguing for the usefulness of the idea of an Illinois Country after 1763. In the late nineteenth and early twentieth centuries historians began producing state histories for both Illinois and Missouri that largely ignored the people and places on the opposite side of the Mississippi River.[7] By the middle of the twentieth century the historical bifurcation of the Illinois Country was entrenched. Major works and textbooks separated Illinois and Missouri and often placed them in different geographic regions due to the invariable use of the Mississippi River as an organizational and conceptual dividing line. Illinois, as part of the Northwest Territory, generally gets just a brief mention as following in the footsteps of Ohio and Indiana in its path to statehood. Missouri invariably appears later in these works, its significance based first on its place at the center of the congressional crisis that resulted in the Missouri Compromise and later as the stepping-off point for the exploration and settlement of the "West." The focus of these twentieth-century narratives was not Illinois or Missouri specifically, but rather the westward thrust of the developing nation.[8] My contention is that we can better understand the histories of both Illinois and Missouri, the histories of the diverse peoples who lived there, and the issues surrounding the early expansion of the United States by looking at this region as the people living there did—as a coherent society straddling the Mississippi River and undergoing a dramatic change from an economy based on the fur trade to one based on the sale and settlement of the land.

Recently, some historians have begun to move the fur trade closer to the center of the story of America's "first" West,[9] but for many its importance continued to be overlooked. Works that describe a late eighteenth-century West full of separatist plots and imperial intrigue largely ignore the complications for Spanish and British diplomacy that the fur trade spawned. But correspondence between Spanish officials during the 1790s shows a greater concern with British traders encroaching on Spanish territory in pursuit of trade than with the more commonly referenced fear of Americans taking up arms to challenge Spanish control of the Mississippi River. British policy makers, in turn, refused until 1795 to vacate forts located in American territory not principally to protest American violations of the 1783 Treaty of Paris or to have locations from which to incite Indian violence against American settlers, but because the fur trade lobby in London sought to maintain their dominance in the trade for as long and for over as wide an area as possible.

Histories of the War of 1812, when they include the Illinois Country at all, continue to underestimate the role of the fur trade in determining Indian loyalties and alliances. Instead, the loss of Indian lands—only part of the equation—is typically cited as the only perspective from which to analyze Indian behavior, ignoring the fact that many Indians in the region did not see white settlers as an imminent threat to their lands.[10] Of more immediate concern to those Indians was the disruption of the fur trade and their access to needed trade goods. The decision of whether or not to fight often turned on the question of which side appeared to be the more reliable trade partner, not which side had designs on the Indians' land.

The fur trade thus continued to tie together the Illinois Country in the minds of imperial policy makers and the lives of inhabitants for several decades after the political division of the area in the 1760s. For Spanish officials the trade was a source of frustration as they found themselves subsidizing a colony whose economy generated profits for traders working in the region and to the British merchants and manufacturers who supplied them. For British officials, the fur trade represented their best hope to secure valuable allies in the event of a war. Indians, meanwhile, relied on the trade to supply them with the goods they had come to depend on and with the leverage it gave them over their rivals to the north and west. For the United States, once it controlled both sides of the Mississippi River, the fur trade was an obstacle to both the elimination of European influence in the West and to the rapid distribution of land that white settlers demanded as the price of their attachment to the young nation.

The link between secure property rights and the incorporation of the Illinois Country is closely examined in this project. It may surprise some to learn that no public land sales took place in either Illinois or Missouri until 1814. This meant that until then land acquisitions in both territories involved tracts obtained via colonial grants from France, Spain, and Great Britain and military grants issued after the American Revolution. After the Louisiana Purchase, territorial land commissions investigated these holdings, which were the source of ongoing conflicts in the Illinois Country for more than a decade. Efforts to acquire secure titles to land affected Indian policy, slavery, and sovereignty in ways previously obscured by an overemphasis on the Northwest Ordinance as the template for western land distribution. The actions of the national government in taking steps to provide access to land—in the form of squatters' rights—prior to public auctions proved crucial to the ultimate success of its imperial project in the Illinois Country. Once again, the US government responded to the demands of white settlers.

In the past generation historians have produced a wealth of work altering the view we have of Indians in the colonial and early national periods.[11] Their chief accomplishment has been to acknowledge the agency of Indian peoples and to begin to describe the variety and complexity of the Indians' experiences. Again, White's *Middle Ground* is an essential text, but many other historians have advanced the view of Indians as skilled imperial players in the long struggle for control of North America. Unfortunately, the appearance of so much good work has so far done little to change the basic narrative of the opening of the Old Northwest. The problem is one of chronology and geography. Indians are part of the narrative only at certain times and in certain places, and the importance of the Mississippi River as a boundary is invariably exaggerated. The result is a West where the Indian "problem" was solved temporarily with the 1795 Treaty of Greenville. Though of obvious importance, this treaty did not, in fact, end conflict in the area until the War of 1812. Indians displaced by the treaty moved west, and many settled in Spanish Illinois (Upper Louisiana) and were still living there when the Missouri Territory was created in 1812. Others stayed on the east side of the Mississippi until they were again displaced by one of the several treaties negotiated by the territorial governor William Henry Harrison between 1803 and 1809.[12]

Formal Indian removal also took place in the Illinois Country outside of the standard narrative timeline. While the national policy of removal did not take hold until the early 1830s, in Missouri removal was a contentious issue at the time of statehood and contributed to the belligerence displayed by Missourians throughout their statehood process. Angered by the reluctance of the federal government to assist in displacing Indians, Missourians were in no mood to even consider federal restrictions on slavery. In Illinois, the white population was concentrated in the southern third of the state, an area already vacated by the local tribes. Here it was land speculators more than actual settlers who coveted Indian lands. To add further complexity to this issue, in territorial Missouri there were still many areas where whites, Indians, and métis peoples coexisted in multiracial communities. This was not the case in Illinois, for reasons having to do with the general depopulation of the area that occurred following the Seven Years War.[13]

In contrast to the developments taking place in Indian history over the past two decades, the issue of slavery in the Old Northwest had been relatively quiet—until quite recently. A new generation of historians has breathed new life into old debates about the significance and circumstances of slavery and white supremacy in the West during the early national period.[14] As a part of the Northwest Territory, Illinois (but not Missouri) was subject to Article VI of the Northwest Ordinance, which prohibited the introduction of slavery into the territory. Historians in the nineteenth century generally credited this provision with preventing slavery in the Old Northwest, particularly in Illinois where the existing slavery of the French period was allowed to continue after the passage of the Ordinance.[15] In the twentieth century, however, the consensus swung toward an assessment of the Ordinance as an ineffectual tool for the prevention of slavery. Historians argued that slavery could not have flourished in Illinois due to the climate and absence of plantation agriculture. It was also widely noted that de facto slavery did exist in the form of long-term indentures, which were legalized in the Indiana territory and then continued in Illinois after its separation from Indiana in 1809.[16] Illinois politicians sidestepped the slavery issue during the statehood process, and the slavery question was not settled until 1824, when Illinois voters defeated a referendum to hold a convention to revisit the state's constitutional treatment of slavery.[17] I contend that the Northwest Ordinance, by discouraging the immigration of slaveholders, *was* responsible for the elimination of slavery in Illinois, although the state was slow to eliminate indentures and extremely harsh in its treatment of free blacks.

While more has been written about slavery in Missouri, historians have focused mainly on the national implications of the crisis surrounding Missouri's admission to the Union.[18] This study will look more closely at the issue of slavery *within* Missouri. There is evidence that the vehement support for slavery during the admission crisis was tied closely to the general frustration that Missourians felt with the federal government. A perceived lack of support during the War of 1812 and the previously noted desire to pursue Indian removal without federal constraint (and ideally with federal support) compelled many Missourians to support slavery as a matter of principle, if not personal interest.[19]

Finally, the connection between slavery and the price of land was extremely important to settlers and speculators on both sides of the Mississippi River. While most settlers feared that slaveholders would drive up the price of land, speculators welcomed that prospect. The inherent conflict between these two positions unfolded differently in Missouri and Illinois, partly because of the Northwest Ordinance, and had much to do with pushing one state in the direction of slavery and one toward free soil.

From Furs to Farms examines the history of the Illinois Country by using secondary sources as well as newspapers, petitions, land records, other records (colonial, territorial, state, and congressional), travel narratives, journals, and public and private correspondence. Chapter One includes a brief discussion of French settlements in the Illinois Country up to the 1750s, and an examination of the Seven Years War and its effects in the area as well as the ramifications of the 1763 Treaty of Paris. The subsequent failures of the Spanish and British to establish effective sovereignty in the Illinois Country are analyzed in terms of the inability of imperial officials to address the demands of white settlers for physical protection, secure property rights, and white supremacy. The establishment of St. Louis in 1763 on the west bank of the Mississippi River was perhaps the most significant event in this period and was not at all an imperial project. In the absence of imperial authority in the immediate aftermath of the Seven Years War, entrepreneurs, including Pierre LaClède and his stepson Auguste Chouteau, began building a town to be used as a base to develop the fur trade in both the immediate surrounding area and in the lands bordering the Missouri River to the north and west. The relationship that developed between the Chouteau clan and the Osage Indians proved crucial to the growth and eventual prosperity of St. Louis.

On the east side of the Mississippi River in what was now considered British territory, the absence of authority combined with the prospect of living as putative subjects of a Protestant king to induce most of the French-speaking inhabitants to cross over to the west side of the river, with many choosing to settle in the new town of St. Louis. During the Revolutionary era and its aftermath, the eastern half of the Illinois Country struggled economically and demographically under British and then American "rule."

Chapter Two explores the period just before and after the Louisiana Purchase. The focus is on the crucial role played by the people of St. Louis and its environs in helping the United States to begin the construction of effective sovereignty on both sides of the Mississippi River. It was during this period that the economic transformation of the region began as white settlers—mostly Americans—began moving into the Illinois Country and starting farms. The demand for lands occupied by Indians merged with and accelerated the decline in the fur trade and brought with it a need for the acknowledgment of a sovereign authority that could both facilitate the appropriation of Indian lands and validate the titles of those who coveted those same lands. Land commissions established on both sides of the Mississippi River spent years sorting out the various colonial-era land grants before the sale of what were now deemed public lands could begin.

Concurrently, the United States set out to incorporate the newly acquired lands into its federal union, with mixed results. In what became Missouri, tensions between French-speaking creoles and incoming Americans mixed with the ongoing competition for Indian lands to produce a challenging and contentious environment for American officials. In Illinois, political factionalism developed around the issues of slavery and land titles. In both territories land commissioners spent years trying to cope with language barriers and spotty or fraudulent records as they sorted through colonial-era claims in order to clear the way for the survey and sale of public lands.

Chapter Three examines the effects of the "Wars" of 1812 in the Illinois Country. The complicated interplay between Indians, white traders, and white settlers, and between the United States and Great Britain, resulted in outbreaks of violence throughout the region that demand analysis from a local perspective to fully understand their import and connection to the ongoing economic transformation of the Illinois Country, its concurrent incorporation into the Union, and the conflict between the United States and Great Britain. In this region Indian loyalties were mixed, with some groups choosing to side with the British and others with the Americans. The absence of federal support for the war effort on either side of the Mississippi River both necessitated the mobilization of local militia groups and fostered a resentment of the US government that threatened the ongoing incorporation of what were now the territories of Illinois and Missouri.

By the end of the war little had been resolved militarily, and it was left to American officials to negotiate an end to the violence in the region, a process that took more than a year and was in stark contrast to Andrew Jackson's decisive victories in the lower Mississippi valley. Once peace was achieved, settlers poured into both Illinois and Missouri, accelerating the economic and demographic transformation of the region and further marginalizing the remaining Indians and their white trading partners.

Chapter Four describes the statehood processes in Illinois and Missouri and analyzes the sharp contrast between the two. Slavery, Indian policy, and land allocation were crucial in both places, but because of specific circumstances, were handled differently. Illinois had been established as a territory under the terms of the Northwest Ordinance, which banned slavery with only a few exceptions. De facto slavery in the form of long indentures was prevalent, however, and the men behind the statehood movement were split between those favoring acceptance of the slavery ban and those wishing to challenge it when they drafted their state constitution. In the meantime, with public land sales now underway, all agreed on the need to accelerate the process of surveying and selling the lands that had previously supported a thriving fur trade.

In Missouri, slavery was legal throughout the territorial period but faced an unexpected challenge by congressional lawmakers that developed into a full-blown national political crisis lasting over a year. Missourians on either side of the slavery issue united in the meddling of a federal government that had done little to support the territory during the War of 1812 and seemed to be doing little to facilitate the dispossession of Indian lands in the territory. The fur trade was declining within the territory's borders, and the Chouteau clan and others joined white settlers in the growing scramble for land. They did, however, continue to invest in the fur trade in areas farther west and would provide the opening wedge in the drive by Americans to open up the Great Plains and Rocky Mountains to trade and eventual settlement.

Chapter Five focuses on the post-statehood constitutional referendum battle in Illinois and on Indian treaties orchestrated by William Clark. Proslavery politicians in Illinois pushed for a convention to legalize slavery by amending the state's constitution, but they were defeated by antislavery forces after a protracted and socially disruptive campaign. During the same period Clark's indefatigable efforts to acquire Indian lands by negotiation rather than violence resulted in the United States' acquisition of title to nearly every acre of land in the states of Illinois and Missouri. Coupled with the settlement of the slavery issue in Illinois, the construction of effective sovereignty in the former Illinois Country was complete, as was the transformation from a fur trade to an agricultural economy.

A note on terms used in this study. I have chosen to use *incorporation* to describe the process of integrating the Illinois Country territories into the Union. *Sovereignty* as used here is to be understood as including the acknowledgment and general compliance with the rule of law, the exclusive (or near exclusive) use of organized violence, and the loyalties, or in the language of the time the attachments, of the peoples in the area under consideration. In the vernacular, sovereignty might simply be described as "authority." As I argue, treaties negotiated from afar often bestowed what I call "titular" sovereignty on a particular imperial power, to little or no effect on the frontier. Effective sovereignty was much tougher to establish; hence my repeated references to the "construction" of sovereignty.

The people who transformed the Illinois Country acted for the same reasons most of us do the things we do: a combination of aspirations—of hopes and dreams—and of necessity. We try to balance what we need or want with what we think we must do depending on circumstances. One of the tasks of the historian is to try to understand how that balance was struck by the people we study without losing sight of the fact that those people were usually not thinking of their actions from a historical perspective. But sometimes they were. In the early decades of the nineteenth century the peoples of the Illinois Country were acutely aware that they were living in a period of profound change. Some embraced these changes, some resisted, and all tried to best play the hands they had been dealt. Pierre Chouteau was one such man who will figure prominently in this story. As a member of the LaClède-Chouteau family that founded St. Louis, Chouteau had from his teens been involved in the fur trade, literally living in two worlds: one Indian and métis, and one white. After the Louisiana Purchase Chouteau understood that his particular balancing act required him to make it known to American officials that he could be of value to the United States. In a letter to President Jefferson he did so: "Be persuaded, Monsieur, that in every circumstance, whether for purchase of land or for commercial and friendly relationships with the savage nations, I will employ without reserve for the glory and interest of the United States the credit which I have among the nations, a credit which is fortified by a commercial relationship with them which has not been interrupted in more than twenty-five years."[20]

Emerging as the nexus of the various groups involved in the shift from furs to farms, men such as Choteau, in the words of historian Jay Gitlin, "went from being frontier brokers to brokers of frontiers."[21] Profit, not political ideology or racial hatred, was the central element in the transformation of the Mississippi valley. As returns from the fur trade declined at the same time that white settlers arrived looking for lands to farm, Chouteau and his fellow brokers worked to persuade Indians to relocate to lands farther west. These men participated in treaty negotiations that often served to forestall violence rather than to take place in its aftermath. And they welcomed and assisted incoming American officials in establishing the institutional infrastructure required to get the new territories of Illinois and Missouri up and running. From their ranks came surveyors, judges, Indian agents, and militia officers. Seeking profits in the midst of change, Chouteau and his cohort treated their Indian trading partners with surprising—for that era—respect and restraint, and were responsible for the relative absence of the endemic violence that accompanied the American advances into the Ohio and Tennessee valleys. In the end, however, the Indians of the Mississippi valley were gone, along with the animals that had provided the basis for their way of life, replaced by waves of white settlers looking for their American futures in the very land itself.

1 / The Colonial Eighteenth Century in the Illinois Country

The first Europeans to visit the Illinois Country were French missionaries, fur traders, and explorers—including iconic figures such as LaSalle, Joliet, and Marquette—who during the late 1600s pushed south and west from Canada to explore, trade, and proselytize in the western Great Lakes and the Mississippi valley. Their first settlements were along the Illinois River in what is now north central Illinois. By the early 1700s the French had moved farther south and established the towns of Cahokia and Kaskaskia near the Mississippi River opposite present-day St. Louis. For more than fifty years these towns were a part of the vast arc of French towns and trading posts in North America that stretched from the St. Lawrence River to the Gulf of Mexico. Because of its distance from colonial officials, the Illinois Country was left mostly to itself, free from most of the imperial regulations and institutions that dominated the lives of the French people living and working in New France (Canada) and lower Louisiana.[1]

An economy centered on the mutual benefits of the fur trade provided the foundation for relatively peaceful relations between French settlers and Indians in the Illinois Country during the first half of the eighteenth century. That peace was shattered during the 1750s when intertribal conflicts within the region coincided with imperial warfare between the French and British farther east—the Seven Years War—resulting in a dramatic reordering of the social, political, and economic arrangements in the region. In the early 1760s the treaties ending the war cost the French their North American colonies and split the Illinois Country in two, with Spain acquiring the lands on the west side of the Mississippi River and Great Britain those to the east. The region's strongest military power during this era was the Osage nation. Living on the west side of the Mississippi River, the Osage used access to European goods to dominate their Indian neighbors to the south and west and to command respect and accommodation from their European neighbors to the east.[2]

In the years between the Seven Years War and the close of the eighteenth century, Great Britain, Spain, and the United States tried and failed to establish sovereignty—supreme power or authority—in the Illinois Country. Indian opposition to British postwar policies took the form of a widespread rebellion that prevented British officials from even reaching the Illinois Country for over two years. Spain struggled also, with Indian and French opposition to its mercantilist trade policies and a general lack of resources with which to effectively govern the colony. During the Revolutionary War, Americans led by George Rogers Clark captured the British half of the Illinois Country for Virginia, but postwar austerity led Virginia to essentially abandon its efforts at civil rule, while the United States did little to fill the vacuum in the years that followed.[3]

During the 1780s and 1790s the economy of the Illinois Country began to change, as the gradual disappearance of fur-bearing animals in the region shifted the focus of the fur trade to the north and west—up the Missouri River—at the same time that white settlers eager to exploit the fabulous agricultural potential of the region began arriving.[4] These incoming settlers shared a strong desire for three things: secure property rights, physical protection from hostile Indians, and racial supremacy for whites. Also arriving, however, were eastern Indians displaced by American expansion into the Ohio valley and also eager to acquire good lands along the Mississippi River. By the end of the eighteenth century it was clear that any imperial power wishing to exercise sovereignty in the Illinois Country would have to address issues surrounding the region's changing economy and the divergent perspectives of its current occupants and those just arriving—with more to follow in their wake.

French Settlements, 1699–1762

The permanent European settlement of the Illinois Country began as a collection of French villages on both sides of the Mississippi River running from present-day St. Louis to the mouth of the Ohio River. In 1699 priests representing the Seminary of Foreign Missions founded the village of Cahokia on the east bank of the Mississippi. About a year later and about eighty miles to the south, the Jesuits founded Kaskaskia. The purpose of the two villages was to continue the missionary work that the French had begun along the Illinois River in the last decades of the seventeenth century. The fertile floodplain lying between the two villages—later named the American Bottom—ran for more than one hundred miles north to south between the Mississippi and the bluffs that started about a mile inland.[5] In the 1700s the area's great fertility and strategic location at the intersection of travel routes to both Canada and the Gulf of Mexico led many French colonials to choose the Illinois Country as a more promising location to live than Canada or lower Louisiana. Settlement there was not officially sanctioned, but distance from French officials rendered that point moot, and the Illinois Country grew and prospered. In 1717 France transferred the colony from Canada's jurisdiction to Louisiana's, and the first French officials arrived in Kaskaskia that year. Aside from the fort they built and garrisoned, their presence brought few changes. Government in the Illinois Country tended to be local and very limited. A few more villages were settled in the following decades, including Ste. Genevieve, the first French village on the west side of the Mississippi. French entrepreneurs tried lead-mining on the west side of the Mississippi but met with limited success because of the interference of local Indians, a lack of mining technology, and the absence of a reliable workforce. Agriculture was more successful, however, and by the 1740s the Illinois Country was easily feeding both itself and the rest of Louisiana.[6] It was the fur trade, however, that fostered the strongest ties among the peoples of the Illinois Country and between those peoples and an emergent Atlantic World economy.[7]

Dating back to the early 1600s when the first permanent French settlement in North America was established at Quebec, the fur trade had provided the basis for mutually beneficial relationships between Indians and Europeans. For Indians, the trade provided access to coveted European goods. For the French, the trade provided a source of potential profits and of prospective converts to Christianity. There was a downside, however. Existing rivalries among Indian groups were exacerbated by the fur trade, as the competition for furs and for the goods they bought—guns in particular—intensified quickly. The French, in turn, were drawn into these rivalries, as were the Dutch and later the English settlers, who also became involved in the North American fur trade. By the end of the 1600s French traders, often accompanied by Christian missionaries, had pushed deep into the North American interior in pursuit of trade and of souls to save. The Illinois Country, straddling the Mississippi River, was a long way from Quebec and as far inland as the French would prove capable of occupying on a sustainable basis.[8]

The demographic makeup of the Illinois Country included French creoles, métis, blacks, and Indians, not living together in a middle ground of refugee groups but in an Indian-dominated region that welcomed—and incorporated—Europeans largely on its own terms. Relations between the French and Indians were generally good. The Osage, living on the west side of the Mississippi River, were the largest Indian nation in the area, and during the eighteenth century they used their geographic position between the French settlements of the Mississippi valley and the Indian nations to the west to build a formidable empire. Access to French trade goods drove their success, and the French-Osage alliance served both parties well. There was also both black and Indian slavery in the colony. The Catholic Church played a role in promoting cohesiveness within the colony by baptizing the offspring of French fathers and Indian mothers, some of whom were later baptized themselves, thus sparing the second-generation métis the stigma of being labeled *sauvages*.[9] For close to a half century the Illinois Country enjoyed relative peace and prosperity.[10] But its position as the midpoint in France's long imperial arc of North American settlements meant it would inevitably be drawn into the great struggle between France and Great Britain for North American dominance.

Beginning in the 1740s British traders began pushing deeper into the American interior, competing with the French and Spanish for the lucrative Indian trade. This development coincided with an uptick in violence in the Mississippi valley as Indians competed among themselves for furs and game that were no longer as plentiful as they once had been.[11] By the mid-1750s war had broken out in the upper Ohio valley between the French and British and their Indian allies. The Illinois Country saw little fighting in the ensuing war, but was profoundly affected by its outcome. The treaties ending the war gave the lands on the western side of the Mississippi River to Spain and those on the eastern side to the British. The French empire in North America had vanished "with the stroke of a pen."[12] Although neither the French nor the Indian and métis peoples of the Illinois Country had been as much a part of something called the French empire as imperial officials imagined, the political reorganization of the region would contribute to the economic transformation that was about to begin.[13]

Spain and Great Britain in the Illinois Country, 1762–1776

With the Mississippi River having become an international border, sovereignty was now, for the first time, a subject of concern in the Illinois Country. Prior to the Seven Years War the colony's inhabitants had mostly ruled themselves, and local conflicts usually involved Indian rather than European rivalries. The fur trade and agricultural surpluses united the colony's peoples and provided for stability without the need for much authority. So for many of the inhabitants of the Illinois Country, the war's outcome was deeply unsettling. Most of the area's Indians had supported France and found it hard to believe their French father (Onontio) had abandoned them. The French living on the east side of the Mississippi River had become at least nominally the subjects of a Protestant king, and many chose to move across the river to what was now Spanish Louisiana. No one could profess to know what the intentions of either the Spanish or British were for their newly acquired territories. In the meantime a loose confederation of Indians in the Great Lakes and Ohio valley launched attacks on British forts throughout the region in protest against the postwar policies of the British. Generally referred to by historians as Pontiac's Rebellion, the uprising succeeded in capturing several British forts and in preventing Great Britain, for two years, from taking formal possession of its half of the Illinois Country.[14] The Indian challenge to British sovereignty in the West ultimately failed when the hoped-for return of the French never materialized. Upon receiving a message from the last remaining French official in the Illinois Country that Indians would receive no support from France, Pontiac lifted his siege of Detroit and the rebellion sputtered to an end. In October 1765 Captain Thomas Stirling finally arrived at Fort Chartres, and British rule was initiated with a proclamation declaring religious freedom and the upholding of property rights—including slavery—for the area's European inhabitants.[15]

Across the Mississippi River the Spanish also struggled to take control of their portion of the Illinois Country. Louisiana's first Spanish governor, Antonio de Ulloa, faced immediate resistance from the people of New Orleans following his arrival in 1766. Increased British trade activity in the Gulf Coast and in the Mississippi valley added to his troubles, and in response he sent Captain Francisco Ríu up the Mississippi in 1767 to construct fortifications at the junction of the Missouri and Mississippi Rivers. On his way Ríu visited Ste. Genevieve and St. Louis, where, in contrast to New Orleans, the people of both towns welcomed the incoming Spanish.¹⁶ St. Louis had been founded in 1764 by Pierre LaClède, his stepson, Auguste Chouteau, and several families relocating from the east side of the Mississippi River. LaClède moved to the Illinois Country from New Orleans in possession of what was characterized as a crown concession for the Indian trade in the colony, and although this concession was rendered moot by the switch to Spanish sovereignty, LaClède and the other founding families enjoyed immediate success in both their town-building and Indian trade endeavors. In St. Louis, Captain Louis St. Ange de Bellerive, a former French official, held both civil and military command at the request of the Spanish governor. Upon his arrival Ríu assumed military command of the territory but quickly ran afoul of the people of St. Louis when he tried to bring the Indian fur trade under more direct control in response to British trade encroachments in the upper Mississippi valley. Ríu's order banning traders from traveling to the Indian villages without a trading license issued from New Orleans accomplished little beyond eliciting immediate defiance of the orders by local traders and outrage from the Indians. Ríu was quickly recalled and replaced by Captain Pedro Piernas, appointed the first lieutenant governor of what the Spanish called Upper Louisiana. Under Piernas and his successors the Spanish regime succeeded in limiting Indian aggression but had little success in preventing British traders from operating in its territory.¹⁷

A closer look at the founding of St. Louis underscores the idea that sovereignty had counted for little in the Illinois Country until after the Seven Years War. Pierre LaClède was a French-born merchant who had come to New Orleans in 1755 to make his fortune. With the help of his mentor, the merchant Gilbert Maxent, Laclède was on his way to doing so by the early 1760s, despite the fact that France's fortunes in the ongoing Seven Years War were sinking fast.¹⁸ Even as the British navy gradually strangled French shipping and with it the military viability of France's New World colonies, merchants and officials in New Orleans prospered.

Louis Billouart, comte de Kerlérec, was the governor of Louisiana from 1753 to 1763. As the Seven Years War raged on Kerlérec complained to his superiors about the distress being caused by the dearth of French ships and goods reaching New Orleans. This much was true. But it was not the whole truth, for while the colony's military establishment was indeed suffering, smuggling, privateering, and piracy were flourishing— with the lines separating one activity from the others difficult to distinguish. Accusations involving Kerlérec's participation in those activities clouded his tenure as governor and eventually led to his recall, but not before a group of New Orleans *négociants* (traders) signed a petition in his support. The organizer of the petition was Gilbert Maxent, who presumably without irony said of Kerlérec that "we express ourselves as most gratified with the protection he has given us and the many services he has rendered us . . . in helping the furtherance of our interests in every direction."[19] One of those directions was north, and Maxent and Laclède set about to exploit the possibilities presented by the fur trade in the Illinois Country.

By the time Laclède left New Orleans in August 1763, he likely knew the French government had ceded all of Louisiana to Spain the previous year. This news would have rendered legally moot the exclusive trade agreement Maxent and Laclède had obtained from Kerlérec's successor, Jean-Jacques-Blas d'Abbadie, but would have also given the partners the confidence to move ahead with their plans, knowing they were headed to an area that would be under little, if any, imperial control for the foreseeable future. In any event, within six months of their departure LaClède and his stepson Auguste Chouteau had reached the Illinois Country and begun building the town they named St. Louis. And by the fall of 1767 when the first Spanish official, Captain Francisco Riu, arrived in St. Louis, the village was on its way to becoming a successful town. The mercantilist regulations Riu introduced, as previously noted, were flouted from the moment of their announcement.[20] The fur trade was drawing more and more people into the Atlantic World economy, but the impetus came not from imperial expansion but from the multiethnic, multiracial assortment of peoples living and working in the Mississippi valley.

East of the Mississippi River, many of the French inhabitants made plans to move to Upper Louisiana rather than live under British rule. Despite the British proclamation concerning religious freedom and property rights, becoming subjects of a Protestant king held little appeal for most. Over the next generation, some French villages were almost completely depopulated, and all suffered considerable losses.[21]

British and American merchants and land speculators, however, saw opportunity in the Illinois Country and moved quickly to take advantage of the switch in sovereignty. Most prominently, the Philadelphia-based trading company, Baynton and Wharton, sent a large flotilla of boats down the Ohio River to Illinois and began trading operations in Kaskaskia. Their aim was to develop three markets for trade: the local Indians, the French inhabitants, and the British army. George Croghan, who had considerable experience in the Indian trade, was Baynton and

Wharton's point man in the region. His efforts were largely unsuccessful, however, in the wake of Pontiac's Rebellion, which had taken a heavy toll on British and American traders in the West. The Indian trade thus remained in the hands of French merchants working on both sides of the Mississippi River. Their chief suppliers were the growing group of mostly Scottish merchants, many of whom had come to Canada to fight in the Seven Years War and stayed to pursue commercial opportunities. They teamed with the French merchants and traders of the Illinois Country to dominate the local markets, and within a few years Baynton and Wharton withdrew from the western trade.[22]

Land speculators fared little better. Encouraged by a 1757 legal decision in England known as the Camden-Yorke opinion, speculators believed they had the right to purchase land directly from the Indians. In the early 1770s the Illinois Company and the Wabash Company were formed for that purpose, and both purchased huge tracts in the Illinois Country from a number of Illinois tribes, most notably the Piankeshaws. Behind these companies were an assortment of British and American speculators who believed their purchases did not require confirmation from the British crown. They were ultimately thwarted by the onset of the American Revolution and the subsequent assertion by Virginia that it held title to most of the lands between the Appalachians and the Mississippi River.[23]

In the meantime the Quebec Act of 1774 placed the Illinois Country within the boundaries of Canada and banned all settlement west of the Appalachians. British Illinois, however, continued to languish in a kind of political no-man's land as the American revolution precluded the establishment of any British civil institutions for the administration of the region. Instead, a small British garrison was maintained amid the shrinking population of what had once been a generally peaceful and prosperous French colony.[24]

The Revolutionary Era

In the mid-1770s the American Revolution reached the Illinois Country in the form of George Rogers Clark and his small army of backwoodsmen. Clark was a Virginian who had been in the first wave of Americans to move to Kentucky, and he soon found himself caught up in the violence between white settlers and Indians. Believing that British officials at Kaskaskia and Detroit were responsible for arming and inciting the Indians (mostly Shawnees), Clark approached Virginia's governor Patrick Henry in December 1777 with a plan to capture the British half of the Illinois Country.

> The town of Kuskskies [Kaskaskia] contains about 100 families of French and English and carry on an extensive trade with the Indians.... Roseblock [Rocheblave] who acted as Governor, by large presents engaged the Waubush Indians to invade the frontiers of Kentucky; was daily treating with other Nations, giving large presents and offering them rewards for scalps ... if it [Kaskaskia] was in our possession it would distress the garrison at Detroit for provisions, it would fling the command of the two great rivers into our hands, which would enable us to get supplies of goods from the Spaniards, and to carry on trade with the Indians.... I am sensible that the case stands thus—that [we must] either take the town of Kuskuskies, or in less than a twelve month send an army against the Indians on the Wabash, which will cost ten times as much, and not be of half the service.[25]

Virginia, as noted, claimed most of the territory between the Appalachian Mountains and the Mississippi River under the terms of its original colonial charter, and Governor Henry and a number of other officials had hopes of acquiring lands in the West for themselves. Securing Illinois for Virginia was seen as a necessary step toward that goal and one that would also benefit the American cause. In January 1778 Henry and his executive council, which included Thomas Jefferson, George Mason, and George Wythe, told Clark they would move quickly to procure funds from the Virginia legislature to pay for his campaign.[26]

In the summer of 1778, Clark's small army arrived in Illinois and captured Kaskaskia without firing a shot. The local French held little affection for the British and quickly chose to take their chances with the Americans, particularly after being told by Clark that France and the United States had recently entered into treaties of trade and alliance. Within weeks Clark sent delegations to Cahokia, 80 miles to the north, and to Vincennes, about 180 miles northeast of Kaskaskia on the east bank of the Wabash River in today's Indiana. Both groups succeeded in securing the allegiance of the local inhabitants, giving the Americans at least nominal control of the three principal towns in British Illinois. Clark next moved to neutralize the area's hostile Indians and succeeded for a time in reducing the number of war parties that were ravaging the American settlements in nearby Kentucky.[27]

While Clark's conquest of Illinois had been surprisingly easy, administering the new territory proved next to impossible. In late 1778 Virginia created the county of Illinois and appointed Colonel John Todd as county lieutenant. Todd and Clark, though, had no money and few supplies and were kept afloat only through the efforts of the American merchant Oliver Pollack in New Orleans and the generosity and self-interest of the French merchants Gabriel Cerré and Charles Gratiot. Pollock worked with pro-American Spanish officials in New Orleans to forward supplies to Clark. Despite being named by the Continental Congress as an official American agent, Pollock had to use his own funds to pay for most of the goods while he waited in vain for reimbursement from Congress. Cerré and Gratiot, meanwhile, saw in the Americans a way to bid farewell to the British while furthering their own commercial aspirations. They too used a considerable amount of their own goods and credit to help Clark and Todd supply the Americans occupying Illinois.[28] Yet within a year the Americans were using force to acquire supplies after the locals began refusing to accept worthless American scrip. Pollack sank into insolvency and Cerré and Gratiot moved across the Mississippi to Upper Louisiana, though all three remained sympathetic to the American cause. Todd soon left the territory while Clark slowly lost credibility with the Americans he had brought to Illinois as well as those across the Ohio River in Kentucky whose priority was Indian-fighting—not securing Illinois lands for Clark's wealthy Virginia backers. In 1782 Virginia let Illinois' county charter lapse, and the territory again entered a political no-man's land described by one historian as the "period of the city-states."[29]

In Upper Louisiana the American Revolution did little to further Spanish interests. Spain belatedly entered the war against the British and succeeded in winning territory in the Gulf Coast region but lost ground farther north when British blockades dramatically cut the amount of goods reaching St. Louis via New Orleans. The trade relationships between St. Louis merchants and their Canadian counterparts filled the breach, and the shift in the fur trade toward Canada accelerated. The result was a further weakening of Spanish authority as attempts by Spanish officials to disrupt this illegal trade created conflict with the white, métis, and Indian inhabitants of Upper Louisiana.[30]

At the conclusion of the American Revolution diplomats placed the western border of the United States at the Mississippi River, acknowledging Clark's conquest of the British half of the Illinois Country. Most observers on both sides of the Atlantic, however, believed the final disposition of much of the West was still an open question. British diplomats cited the failure of the United States to comply with all of its treaty obligations as just cause for the retention of several western posts in the Great Lakes region. British officials in America also signaled to their Indian allies a continued commitment to defending Indian sovereignty in the western Great Lakes.[31] Amid ongoing violence between Indians and American settlers in the Ohio Valley, it seemed the United States might be headed toward the same type of "titular" but not effective sovereignty that had plagued successive imperial efforts in the region. More specifically, the United States seemed as unable as Spain to prevent British trade encroachments in their territory, while an effective method of distributing land in the West appeared to be years away and the physical security of those who might acquire those lands could not be assured. In Illinois an observer explained, "when the United States achieved independence, the Americans took possession of merely the ruins of what had been the Illinois Country." Government was nearly nonexistent, the population was declining, and in 1784 Spain closed the Mississippi River to American traders, threatening the ability of western farmers to bring their surplus crops to market. European observers routinely predicted a breakup of the United States while American leaders worried openly about the republic's ability to secure the loyalties of those settling in the West.[32]

The Americans Arrive

In the generation following the 1762–1763 splitting of the Illinois Country, the fates of its eastern and western halves diverged. By the 1780s a weakening Spanish empire west of the Mississippi River acknowledged its inability to exercise effective sovereignty by relying on French traders such as the Chouteaus to maintain peace in the territory through economic diplomacy with the Osage. And while British trade encroachments continued to threaten Spanish imperial interests, the successful flouting of mercantilist trade policies by residents of Upper Louisiana allowed the fur trade economy to flourish and was one reason more people were moving into Upper Louisiana than were leaving. East of the Mississippi those remaining in Illinois sent a steady stream of petitions and memorials to Congress, asking for civil government and an end to the chaos and oppression that had accompanied Virginia's short-lived rule.[33] Most American officials, however, saw effective sovereignty as more of a long-term goal than an immediate expectation even after the passage in 1787 of the Northwest Ordinance. For the peoples of the Illinois Country (slaves excepted), Upper Louisiana was clearly a better place to live at this time—safer for whites and Indians and with better economic prospects for anything except subsistence farming, which still provided an easy living along both banks of the Mississippi River.

While commerce had attracted the first group of Americans to Illinois in the 1760s, it was the fertility of the American Bottom that drew the second group. Clark's soldiers had noted the quality of the land during the 1778 campaign, and by the mid-1780s many had returned with their families to settle in the area that was eventually named for them. Virginia law forbade any settlements north of the Ohio River, but neither Clark nor John Todd tried to enforce the ban, believing American settlers were needed to help hold the territory for the United States.[34] As the Americans trickled in, they squatted on lands still owned by Indians, because the only land owned by Europeans and potentially available for purchase was the town lots in the scattered French villages that held no attraction for Americans who had come to the area to take advantage of the fertility of the American Bottom. These families chose to take their chances in Illinois—despite the lack of land for purchase—because they either lacked the money to actually purchase land or were frustrated by the situation in nearby Kentucky. There a complex tangle of shingled land claims was slowly sorted out, for the most part, in favor of wealthy Virginians who had the time and money to hire surveyors and lawyers to represent their interests. In Illinois squatting seemed to present better odds for success, and few could have imagined it would take as long as twenty years to gain clear title to their lands.[35]

In the meantime, the American squatters were joined by a handful of merchants and land speculators such as John Edgar, William Morrison, and Pierre Menard who came to Illinois to pursue the opportunities they believed US sovereignty would bring. A quick look at the backgrounds of these men reveals the diversity of those settling in Illinois at the time. John Edgar was born in Ireland, and while serving in America he left the British naval service in 1776 before settling in Kaskaskia in 1784, where he built a flourmill and began buying land from the French. Eventually considered the wealthiest man in Illinois, he was elected or appointed to numerous positions during the course of a long public career. William Morrison was born in Philadelphia and came to Illinois in 1790 representing his uncle, Guy Bryant, in the merchandising firm known in the West as Bryant and Morrison. He opened a store in Kaskaskia and also began buying land from the French. Pierre Menard was born in Canada, the son of a French soldier who came to America to fight in the Seven Years War. Menard moved first to Vincennes in the 1780s and then to Kaskaskia in 1790, where he also opened a store and began acquiring land.[36] Three distinct groups of Europeans—the resident French, American squatters, and merchant speculators—along with the territory's Indians, now waited to see if the United States could bring order to the eastern half of the Illinois Country.

Virginia's attempt to establish civil government in Illinois, as mentioned briefly, had failed miserably. John Todd, the county lieutenant, after appointing militia officers for the county's three districts, joined George Rogers Clark on May 12, 1779, to address the citizens of Kaskaskia and hold the county's first election. At a festive and undoubtedly emotional occasion, the people selected one of the Americans' chief supporters, Gabriel Cerré, to head the Kaskaskia district court. Similar elections were held in Cahokia and Vincennes at about the same time. Within weeks, however, the new justices issued a memorial to the Virginia legislature with a list of grievances that included the killing of livestock by soldiers, the seizure of supplies without payment, and the sale of liquor to the Indians. By the end of the year Clark, Todd, and Cerré had all left Illinois, and the courts ceased almost all functions except for the unauthorized issuance of land grants.[37]

On January 5, 1782, the county of Illinois ceased to exist, Virginia's legislature having failed to renew its charter. Describing the following years as "the period of the city-states," the historian Clarence Alvord explained: "During these years of neglect the government in the villages of the Illinois country resembled that of the ancient Greek city-state more closely than any that has elsewhere existed in the western hemisphere. Practically cut off from the rest of the world and from the only power which might legally exercise authority over it, each village was forced to become a self-governing community."[38] Varying degrees of disorder and oppression characterized life in Illinois villages and settlements for the next several years. In Kaskaskia the American John Dodge made his home in the old French fort on a bluff overlooking the town, scoffing at the remnants of civil government and, with his henchmen, bullying the town's people. A local priest, Father Gibault, wrote to his bishop describing the general situation in Illinois: "There is no distinction from the greatest to the least except that of force. . . . Everybody is in poverty, which engenders theft and rapine. . . . No commandant, no troops, no prison, no hangman, always as in such places a crowd of relatives or allies who sustain each other."[39] Learning that Virginia had ceded its western land claims to the national government in 1784, various groups sent petitions and memorials to Congress asking for immediate government. There was no response until the summer of 1787, when Colonel Josiah Harmar, commandant of the US troops in the west, arrived in Kaskaskia as part of an inspection tour to assess conditions in Illinois.[40] His visit proved a disappointment to those settlers who had received land grants from country officials. Since Congress had forbade settlements north of the Ohio River, the grants were essentially worthless. Harmar, in turn, was little enamored of the French he encountered, writing to his superior that "all these people are entirely unacquainted with what Americans call liberty. Trial by jury, etc., they are strangers to. A commandant with a few troops to give them orders is the best form of government for them."[41] These sentiments became for a generation the standard American assessment of the French living in the West.

At this low moment the French and American settlers temporarily set aside their differences and joined together in hiring Barthelemi Tardiveau to take their grievances directly to Congress. Tardiveau was a mercantile adventurer who came to America from his native France in 1777, stopping in Philadelphia before moving on to Kentucky, where he supplied flour to Virginia's western troops in return for land warrants. It was there that he met Colonel Harmar and convinced the colonel to hire him as an interpreter and adviser. Sensing an opportunity to acquire more land, the opportunistic Tardiveau stayed on in Illinois after Harmar's departure and soon persuaded 52 French and 137 American settlers to allow him to tell Congress about their ill treatment and discontent in hopes of obtaining a land grant for each, with Tardiveau to receive one-tenth of all land so acquired.[42] Armed with a mass of notes and documents detailing the losses suffered by the French at the hands of Virginia's troops, he traveled to New York in the fall of 1787, where he presented a series of memorials to Congress. A few months earlier Congress had passed the Northwest Ordinance to organize the settlement and government of the West and had also sold to speculators several million acres of land in what is now Ohio. Other groups were lobbying for similar large land purchases in Illinois, but none succeeded. Tardiveau, however, managed to interest Congress in the plight of the French living in Illinois, obtaining a four-hundred-acre grant for any inhabitants who on or before 1783 had professed themselves citizens of the United States. No provision, however, was made for the later-arriving Americans, and although it proved to be many years before the French received their land (most of the grants were sold to speculators during the long wait), the land grants and the Northwest Ordinance were the first concrete steps taken by the United States to secure the loyalties of those living in Illinois.[43]

The early results of those steps were not encouraging. In Illinois the reaction to the Northwest Ordinance, particularly by slaveholders, was negative. Article VI stated: "There shall be neither slavery nor involuntary servitude in the said territory," and despite a provision specifically exempting those in Illinois whose property rights had been guaranteed first by Great Britain and then Virginia, the exodus of French inhabitants to Upper Louisiana again resumed. In 1790 the governor of the Northwest Territory, Arthur St. Clair, visited Illinois and tried to mollify worried slaveholders by explaining that Article VI was merely prospective and not a threat to existing slavery in the territory. Some were reassured, but on balance St. Clair's explanation served mostly to confuse the situation. While in Illinois the governor created its first county, St. Clair County. The governor, his secretary, and three judges constituted the territory's first government and they established courts, a militia, a coroner's office, and civil and criminal laws along with the fines and punishments to be imposed when they were broken.[44] Illinois finally had a civil government, but Congress had failed to satisfactorily address the issues of slavery and land ownership and had shown no signs of yet being able to guarantee the physical security of Americans living in the West, where violence between whites and Indians was spreading from the Ohio valley to threaten villages and settlements in Illinois.

Now officially a part of the Union, the people of Illinois were yet to be convinced that the Union deserved their loyalty and affection. One noteworthy example was Barthelemi Tardiveau. While in the East lobbying on behalf of Illinois' residents, Tardiveau also wrote and circulated a memorial called *Mémoire sur le Mississippi*. First presented to France's minister, the Count de Moustier, the memorial explained that the future prosperity of the West depended on the free navigation of the Mississippi River and that since Spain was foolishly insisting on preventing it, "do we risk error in thinking that Louisiana may once again become an object of serious attention to France?" Describing the current conditions, he explained, "The inhabitants of the Illinois villages tread disdainfully the richest soil of the universe and it is from us [the Americans] that they receive all the necessities of life.... These people need a Protector—the first to stretch a hand to them will procure the greatest acquisition that can be hoped for in the New World. Happy my native land should she not pass by this opportunity."[45] Here was a French émigré characterizing himself as an American but placing the Illinois villagers in some indeterminate category while urging his native country to reclaim Louisiana from Spain. Tardiveau's memorial was read with interest by Moustier but also by Lord Dorchester, the governor of Canada, who obtained a copy and forwarded it to his home government, and by Diego Gardoqui, the Spanish chargé d'affaires, who sent it along to *his* government. Gardoqui quickly decided that a man such as Tardiveau was worth cultivating and so agreed to attempt to acquire for Tardiveau a six-year contract to export American tobacco through New Orleans. Tardiveau headed back west, writing along the way to his friend St. John de Crevecoeur about the risks to private property that continued to plague Illinois:

> Two men who detest me, because I have broken the hold of their despotic and arbitrary authority over the unfortunate inhabitants of Illinois, imagined that Congress would not have the leisure to concern itself with this section, and have taken advantage of my absence to take from me by means of a court and a jury of their choosing, a farm which cost me three thousand piastres and which is worth ten thousand. With the arrival of the Governor and the judges I shall, I hope, regain my rights; but the usurpers have been in possession for two years, and are making the most of my orchards, which are the finest in the place.

Without fear of the federal government, certain individuals were using the local courts to expropriate property. Tardiveau then explained to Crevecoeur the major reason so many Illinois settlers were moving to Upper Louisiana:

> Yes, most of them have gone over to the Spanish bank, but it is not, as you insinuate, because they need Priests and Churches; They have Priests and Churches; and I do not need to tell *you* that the American government would take neither from them if they remained. They have been forced to abandon their settlements in order to protect their property, their negroes that they risked losing because of an unjust act [the Northwest Ordinance] of an ignorant and heedless Congress.

Tardiveau and others in Illinois wanted a government that would protect—not threaten—their property. If the United States could not supply one, Tardiveau was ready for a move to "some place where I'll find more satisfaction than I do here."[46]

Upper Louisiana proved to be that place, and Tardiveau in the early 1790s got involved with relocating a group of destitute French immigrants from the failed town of Gallipolis, in present-day Ohio. In the midst of negotiations to move these settlers to Illinois, Tardiveau wrote to Baron Carondelet, the governor of Louisiana, who was interested in attracting immigrants to Upper Louisiana. Carondelet invited Tardiveau to New Orleans and offered him a deal to recruit one hundred French families to the territory and to build flourmills in New Madrid and Ste. Genevieve in hopes of supplying the garrison of the entire colony of Louisiana. Tardiveau accepted the offer and took an oath of allegiance to Spain in December 1793. He lived in Upper Louisiana until his death at fifty in 1801. In an ironic footnote to this story, the proposed flourmills were never built because the workmen hired for the construction were requisitioned to help build fortifications for an expected attack (that never occurred) by a French legion recruited by Edmond Genet and that involved both Tardiveau's brother and George Rogers Clark.[47]

Barthelemi Tardiveau's arrival and departure from Illinois demonstrates the fungible nature of loyalties at this time. Attracted by the prospect of securing land many considered unmatched, Tardiveau entered into a contract with Illinois settlers, lobbied Congress, and returned to serve as a judge and militia officer. He became an American. But he also hedged his bet by cultivating French and Spanish officials. In the end he chose to become a Spanish subject because the United States could not meet his perceived needs. Uncertain rights to land and slaves, combined with the lack of access to a market for agricultural surpluses and threats from hostile Indians, made Illinois a relatively risky place to settle during this period.

Spanish Louisiana after the American Revolution

In Upper Louisiana the situation in the 1780s and 1790s was different. Land was available almost for the asking, and although clear and complete titles required a trip to New Orleans for official documentation, few expected that the grants casually issued by Spanish officials would ever be challenged, and so most never bothered with the process. Slaveholders faced no threats to their property in black slaves, and the illegality of Indian slavery under Spanish rule was more a call for the slow elimination of the practice than a mandate for abolition.[48] Relations between Indians and whites were characterized by sporadic rather than endemic violence, although this was more a function of successful trade diplomacy and the lack of large numbers of settlers encroaching on Indian lands than on Spanish military power. The 1780 attack on St. Louis by a combined British-Indian force that had to be repelled by the local militia fighting behind locally financed fortifications was further proof of Spanish weakness. Many residents of Upper Louisiana longed for France's return to North America while bemoaning Spanish mercantilist policies that rewarded groups like the Chouteau family with favorable trade concessions.[49]

From the perspective of Spanish officials overseeing a vast empire in the Americas, Upper Louisiana had become a big headache. They ruled a territory whose expenses each year exceeded revenues and that faced threats from all sides. British traders were moving south and west from the Great Lakes into the Upper Mississippi valley, diverting more and more of the fur trade to Canada. The Americans to the east grew in numbers each year and also in belligerency after the Mississippi River was closed to American trade in 1784. In the 1790s, while the French Revolution raged in Europe, French radicals were at the center of at least one credible plot to invade the territory. The result was a succession of moves and countermoves aimed at shoring up Spanish power on the cheap.[50] Spanish policy makers believed the best way to bolster their strength in Upper Louisiana was to attract immigrants: whites settlers whose loyalties might be secured by meeting their needs for land and access to foreign markets via New Orleans and Indians, and who could provide a buffer between white settlements and the powerful Osage. During the 1780s a steady trickle of Peorias, Shawnees, and Delawares had begun moving on their own to Upper Louisiana in response to the violence occurring in the Ohio valley. In 1786 the métis Louis Lorimier arrived in the territory to establish a trading post at Cape Girardeau. Like Barthelemi Tardiveau, Lorimier was a complex character whose history demonstrates the shifting loyalties of those living in the West.[51]

Born in Canada around 1748 to a captain in the French army and his Canadian wife, Lorimier was a trader living in present-day Ohio when the American Revolution began. A Tory who participated in raids on American settlements in Kentucky, he was allegedly part of the group that in 1778 captured Daniel Boone. In 1782 American troops led by George Rogers Clark burned Lorimier's trading post after robbing it of $20,000 in furs and merchandise. In 1787 Lorimier moved to Upper Louisiana, where he received a land grant from Lieutenant Governor Manuel Pérez, who encouraged him to recruit other eastern Indians to join him in the territory. Among the twelve hundred Shawnee and six hundred Delaware Indians who followed Lorimier to Upper Louisiana was the mother of Tecumseh, who left most of her family behind, including the young boy who with his brother Tenskwatawa would later launch a pan-Indian movement from their base in Indiana Territory. By the 1790s Lorimier operated a successful trading post while serving as the commandant of the district of Cape Girardeau. Following the Louisiana Purchase, Lorimier served the United States as an Indian agent for many years, meaning he had spent various parts of his life as a subject of the French, British, and Spanish crowns before becoming a US citizen, all the while living in a succession of predominantly Indian and métis communities.[52]

In Upper Louisiana Lorimier found himself in the middle of a conflict between Spanish officials and the Osage nation, whose internal power struggles spawned breakaway bands that began attacking white settlers in the 1780s. In 1787 Governor Estaban Miró suspended all trade with the Osage, which only served to increase the attacks and antagonize those traders who depended on the Osage for their livelihoods. In 1792 Upper Louisiana's new lieutenant governor Zenon Trudeau lifted the trade ban, with approval from Miro's successor, Francisco Carondelet. But when Osage depredations again increased and began to be directed against friendly Indians (including those associated with Lorimier), Carondelet reinstated the trade ban and encouraged Spain's Indian allies to declare war on the Osage—which they refused to do without Spanish assistance. The sporadic attacks continued.[53]

In another attempt to bolster security in Upper Louisiana, Governor Miró got permission from the Crown in 1787 to recruit Americans to move to Spanish territory. In exchange for taking an oath of loyalty, the incoming settlers were offered free land, commercial privileges, and religious toleration. Miró secretly hired an American general, James Wilkinson, to promote the separation of Kentucky from the United States or at least help recruit Americans to move into Spanish territory. At the same time Spain's minister to the United States, Diego Gardoqui, launched a plan with the American businessman George Morgan to recruit American settlers and eastern Indians to help establish a town on the west side of the Mississippi River.[54]

The results of these moves were disappointing. Wilkinson collected money from Spain for several years without ever doing much to promote Spanish interests. Morgan established the town of New Madrid in 1789 but quickly ran afoul of Wilkinson, who saw in him a potential rival, and of Governor Miró, who objected to Morgan's plans to sell land that was to be given to him at no cost. Within a few months Morgan abandoned his new settlement (which did fine without him) and moved back to the United States. Miró's successor, Francisco Carondelet, ended the offers of free lands for Americans, expressing in a letter to his superior the general view of Americans held by Spanish officials:

> Your Excellency will see himself obliged to take ... the most active measures to oppose the introduction of those restless people, who are a sort of determined bandits, armed with carbines, who frequently cross the Mississippi in numbers, with the intention of reconnoitering, of hunting, and if they like the country, of establishing themselves in the *Provincias Internas* [Upper Louisiana].... Five or six thousand of these ferocious men who know neither law nor subjection are those who are starting the American establishments.... A little bit of corn, gunpowder and balls suffices them, a house formed from the trunks of trees serves them as shelter; their corn crop finished, they raise camp and then go further inland, always fleeing from any subordination and law.[55]

Carondelet, in the meantime, directed the lieutenant governor of Upper Louisiana, Zenon Trudeau, to recruit immigrants arriving in the United States to settle instead in Upper Louisiana and to crack down on Indians—particularly the Osage—trading with the English. In a series of letters over a nine-month period between the fall of 1793 and summer of 1794, Trudeau explained to Carondelet the state of affairs in Upper Louisiana. He started by explaining that the locals were intimidated by the Osage in that "It is only necessary for one person to be killed by the Osages in the circle of our establishments to make them all relinquish work, even the most urgent work on the land." Cutting off trade or making war on the Osage were also poor ideas: "Nothing is more easy for the Osages than to communicate with [reach] the Mississippi and to call new traders to them.... Our forces have not allowed us any resistance and our weak establishments [settlements] cannot yet support this burden." In the meantime, the English "have penetrated and traded their merchandise this year at such a low price that our traders have been robbed, maltreated, and ridiculed." Finally, "It is very difficult for me to attract here Germans, Dutch, and French royalists as you desire. None have appeared in our environs. Only a few Canadians have come.... These men all have a liking for voyaging and are definitely not cultivators." This last line points to the fact that Spanish officials realized that Upper Louisiana not only needed more settlers, but settlers committed to agriculture, since the fur trade was clearly in decline. Trudeau wrote, "your excellency will see by the report how small is the value of the commerce of Missouri, which yearly decreases more and more. The introduction of merchandise increases imperceptibly, but the amount of peltries taken out by traders grows less and less." Carondelet agreed and was equally pessimistic about the situation: "True riches lie in agriculture, and this requires a competent population and easy outlets: Louisiana is susceptible to all these advantages, but present circumstances are not favorable to our views."[56]

By the end of 1793 Spain faced other threats. War between France and Spain began that year and a French diplomat, Citizen Edmond Genet, arrived in the United States with ambitious plans to both secure US commercial support for revolutionary France and recruit and commission officers for attacks on Louisiana, Florida, and Canada (France was also about to go to war with Great Britain). One of those Genet recruited was the Revolutionary War hero George Rogers Clark, who was now living in Kentucky, broke and embittered, having never been reimbursed by Virginia or Congress for his considerable personal expenditures during the war. Clark and his brother-in-law James O'Fallon were recruiting men for an attack on Spanish Louisiana when O'Fallon learned from his friend Thomas Paine, then in France, that Genet was on the way to the United States with similar plans of his own. Clark wrote to Genet in Philadelphia, explaining that "The possession of New Orleans will secure to France the whole Fur, Tobacco and Flour trade of this western world. . . . All we immediately need is money for provisions and ammunition for the conquest," and to "first expatriate our selves, and become French citizens."[57] Genet responded by commissioning Clark as "Major General in the armies of France, and Commander in Chief of the French Revolutionary Legions on the Mississippi River." But despite the fancy title, Clark did not receive the funds needed to launch the attack. Opposed by Secretary of the Treasury Alexander Hamilton, Genet never collected any of the money owed to France by the United States, money he had counted on to finance his military adventures. Clark was left further in debt but with full recognition of the scare he had given the Spanish. "From the most moderate Calculation the Spaniards have expended on the Mississippi, within these last Six months four million of Dollars, when But a few thousands was Spent by us in keeping them in Such Continual Dread and now with a small Suply Of money and orders to persue the plan all their preparations would prove fruitless."[58] Luckily for the Spanish, Clark's prediction was never put to the test.

The cost of preparing to defend Louisiana against an American or French attack, as Clark noted, was large and forced Governor Carondelet to abandon plans to make war on the Osage. Instead, he turned to the Chouteaus, who were again ready to substitute commercial diplomacy for the use of force. In May 1794 Carondelet accepted Auguste Chouteau's proposal to build and garrison a fort in proximity to the largest Osage settlements. In return the Chouteaus received a six-year monopoly on the Osage trade and $2,000 a year to pay the men stationed at the fort. A year later Fort Carondelet was open for business, but it was more a glorified trading post than a military installation. For a short time Governor Carondelet, the Osage, and the Chouteaus were all satisfied.[59]

In the meantime, several of the traders and merchants left out of the Osage deal formed a partnership, with the backing of Lieutenant Governor Zenon Trudeau, to extend the fur trade farther up the Missouri River. Trudeau hoped the traders would return with information about the activities of the British on the Upper Missouri. The Missouri Company, however, failed in two attempts to reach the tribes of the Upper Missouri, being blocked on the way by hostile tribes. A third attempt, led by James Mackay, a Scottish trader who had recently become a Spanish subject, reached the Mandan villages of modern-day North Dakota, where they overran a British trading post before returning to St. Louis with few furs but a wealth of geographic information about the region.[60]

In the mid-1790s Governor Carondelet and other Louisiana officials continued to wrestle with the threat of attacks, both commercial and military, on their colony. In 1793 Carondelet sent a military expedition up the Mississippi River to drive British traders out of that region. A leading Canadian merchant, Andrew Todd, was captured, and like many others, including Tardiveau, Wilkinson, and Lorimier, took an oath to the Spanish crown. Todd then joined the Missouri Company, securing a monopoly for the fur trade of the upper Mississippi River region. His death in 1796, however, led to the collapse of the company and the continued British control of a large portion of the lucrative fur trade of the upper Mississippi River. Carondelet also tried to use his limited military resources to shore up Spanish control of Upper Louisiana. In 1795 he sent Manuel Gayoso up the Mississippi River with a naval squadron to impress the inhabitants of the district with a show of force and to assess the level of French sympathy for revolutionary ideology. While in Upper Louisiana Gayoso also met with James Wilkinson and others in hopes of resurrecting the plans for western Americans to break away from the United States, but news of the Treaty of San Lorenzo (Pinckney's Treaty) between the United States and Spain put an end to that initiative. On the heels of the Jay Treaty between the United States and Great Britain, the political situation in the Illinois Country entered a new phase.[61]

The Treaty of San Lorenzo included a provision opening the Mississippi River to American trade. With the river open, the threat of an American attack on Louisiana dissolved, as did the chances of western Americans acting in concert to secede from the United States. At the same time, the Jay Treaty included a provision requiring the British to surrender their western posts, which they finally did in 1796. From the imperial capitals of London, Madrid, and Philadelphia it seemed as if the question of sovereignty in the West had been settled. But in the Illinois Country little actually changed. If the opening of the Mississippi River to foreign trade helped the commercial prospects of Americans living in Illinois, the military and commercial threats posed by hostile Indians and their British trading partners continued. Loopholes in the Jay Treaty allowed British traders to continue operations in the region, even after the key posts at Detroit, Michilimackinac, and Prairie du Chien had been handed over to Americans. In Upper Louisiana, Spanish officials learned from a visiting French general, Victor Collot, of a proposed invasion of the territory by the British, with whom Spain was once again at war. Collot himself fell under suspicion of inciting plans for an insurrection, and he fled St. Louis but was captured in New Orleans and deported. Governor Carondelet responded by sending another naval squadron up the Mississippi, this one led by Lieutenant Colonel Carlos Howard, who concluded that while an insurrection was unlikely, the potential for a British attack necessitated a buildup in St. Louis's military fortifications.[62]

Governor Carondelet now reversed his policy on American immigration in hopes of securing manpower to defend Upper Louisiana from the expected British attack. This time the allure of free lands and no taxes proved more successful, and American settlers, many from Kentucky where good land was already expensive and scarce, now poured into Upper Louisiana. These included Daniel Boone and his large family as well as Moses Austin, who planned to establish a lead-mining operation near Ste. Genevieve. Although Carondelet's successor, Manuel Gayoso, tried to stop the flow of Americans by restricting immigration to Catholics, it was too late. The Americans were on their way to having the numerical majority they would enjoy by the time of the Louisiana Purchase in 1803, and Upper Louisiana—in fact, all of Louisiana—became in the final years of the decade a bargaining chip in Spain's imperial diplomacy.

In 1800 Napoleon Bonaparte and his foreign minister Talleyrand secured the retrocession of Louisiana to France, setting the stage for the next phase in the struggle for sovereignty in the Illinois Country.[63] The year 1800 also marked the beginning of a new political era on the east side of the Mississippi River. In that year the Northwest Territory was split, with Ohio becoming a state and the rest of the territory, including Illinois, becoming a part of Indiana Territory.

Race Becomes an Issue

Beginning in the late 1790s Americans moving into the Illinois Country began making race an important issue. To be more precise, the incoming Americans brought their growing racial hatred with them as they began taking up lands in the area. As has been noted, despite the long history of Indian and black slavery, mixed-raced peoples and communities flourished in the Illinois Country for much of the eighteenth century. With trade relationships serving to keep Indian-white violence to a minimum, race was, despite the existence of slavery, more a part of the social and cultural landscape than a major issue driving political or economic policy considerations. That all changed after the American Revolution. The cycle of violence and reprisals that began in the Ohio valley during the 1760s and continued into the 1790s fundamentally altered the racial views of those who lived through it. For the most part, American settlers stopped viewing Indians as individuals or small groups who might be friend or foe. Instead, they now considered all Indians as threats to be eliminated. For their part, most Indians residing in the Illinois Country continued to have a more complicated view of race. Some began moving toward a general racial hatred of whites, while many continued to distinguish between their Americans enemies and those among the French, British, and mixed-race peoples who were their friends, allies, and trading partners.[64]

In 1786 Indians attacked a small Illinois settlement, killing five Americans and taking two prisoners. James Andrews, his wife and daughter, and James White and Samuel McClure died in the attack, and two of Andrews's daughters became captives. The attack created panic in the American Bottom, and settlers began erecting forts and stations, as was the custom in the Ohio valley during the Revolutionary War. One settler explained that "The whites not only fortified to protect themselves, but were compelled to mount guard day and night for their safety. When a man was plowing in the field, one other or more were stationed outside to protect him."⁶⁵ George Rogers Clark wrote Congress on behalf of those living in Illinois. "They have it in their power to be of infinite service to us . . . but having no law or government among them, they are in great confusion, and without the authority of Congress is extended to them, they must, in all probability, fall a sacrifice to the savages." For those just arriving in Illinois, none of this was new. They were used to Indian-white violence as well as to the indifference of Congress. And that was part of the problem. The Americans that gave the American Bottom its name did not care—if they even knew—that the French towns of Cahokia and Kaskaskia had developed in immediate proximity to Indian villages. Most were like the Whitesides, "born and raised on the frontiers of North Carolina, and emigrated to Kentucky. They had been inured to Indian hostilities . . . from their early years to manhood." In 1785 their patriarch, William Whiteside, learned that a group of Indians was camped nearby, supposedly planning to either kill or rob him and his family. Before daylight Whiteside, his brothers, and a few others surrounded the camp and proceeded to kill all but one of the Indians.⁶⁶

The racial violence of the Ohio valley had now spread to Illinois and soon crossed the Mississippi River with the Americans who responded to Governor Carondelet's call for immigrants in 1795. This is not to say there had been no Indian-white violence in Upper Louisiana prior to the arrival of American settlers. Osage violence against white settlers, however, had been sporadic, and the white response typically restrained and based on commercial diplomacy. The perceived military superiority of the Osage precluded any other policy, as did the fur trade economy that had as its basis cooperation and kinship ties among whites, Indians, and métis peoples in the region. But as the shift from furs to farms accelerated, the compelling basis for cooperation across racial lines was replaced by an equally compelling basis for hostility and violence, as white settlers with no interest in doing business with Indians sought instead to dispossess Indians of their lands.

The years between 1763 and 1800 were a time of great upheaval in the Illinois Country. The former French colony was split in two by the treaties ending the Seven Years War, and in the decades that followed the focus of the region's economy began to shift from the fur trade to agriculture while a succession of imperial regimes struggled and failed to establish effective sovereignty. The principal reasons for the fur trade's decline were the dwindling numbers of fur-bearing animals in the region, competition from British traders based in the Canadian Great Lakes, and the influx from the east of Americans and Indians whose principal aim was to grow crops on the fertile lands of the Mississippi valley. Effective sovereignty, meanwhile, was going to require the loyalty and attachments of at least a substantial majority of the white inhabitants of the Illinois Country. This is not to discount the military or even the cultural potency of the Indian and métis peoples living in the region, but at this time there existed no pan-Indian movement with an eye to anything more than local autonomy and access to European goods. Most Europeans and Americans, meanwhile, acknowledged the military superiority of Indians in the Illinois Country, which served to help keep the focus on trade and diplomacy rather than violence and dispossession—at least for the time being.[67]

The means by which an imperial power in the Illinois Country might win the loyalty and attachments of the white population involved three issues: secure property rights, physical security, and racial supremacy. Each of these issues was also connected to the economic shift that was taking place. The first to emerge was the demand for secure property rights. In Upper Louisiana this issue manifested itself most consistently in the conduct of the fur trade. Although Spanish officials wanted more farmers and fewer fur traders in their colony, the inhabitants of Upper Louisiana considered the livelihoods provided by the fur trade—even as it began to decline—to be an essential property right. Spanish mercantilist policies were opposed from the start as inherently corrupt, as licenses were sold to "those who could afford to pay," allowing a few families to dominate the trade. Within a few years even those favored by Spanish officials began to flout the restrictions on trade with foreigners, as the Mississippi River proved to be a very porous international boundary. The competition posed by British-Canadian traders, who also ignored the Mississippi boundary, likewise undermined Spanish sovereignty. The threat posed by the Osage Indians when their supply of trade goods was interrupted added to the pressures on Spanish officials to make the most money they could from the licensing system while ignoring the endemic violations of trade policy that occurred.[68]

On the American side of the Illinois Country the demand for secure property rights involved trade, slavery, and land. As more and more settlers took up lands along the fertile American Bottom, they demanded access to the Mississippi River to facilitate the export of agricultural surpluses. The options for Americans affected by Spain's closing of the river to foreign trade were to relocate to Upper Louisiana, organize an invasion of Spanish territory, or threaten to break away from the United

States. The antislavery provision of the Northwest Ordinance was another threat to property in Illinois. Governor Arthur St. Clair's letter to President George Washington was one of many warnings sent from the frontier to the capital warning of the consequences of the slavery ban. "St. Louis . . . has been greatly advanced by the people who abandoned the American side. To that they were induced . . . partly by the fear of losing their slaves, which they had been taught to believe would all be set free on the establishment of the American Government. . . . Could they be allowed to bring them back with them, all those who retired from that cause would return to a man."[69] There is little doubt that these sentiments had an effect on subsequent US policy in the territory, as Illinois settlers were allowed to establish de facto slavery in the form of indentures (some for as long as ninety-nine years) during the years leading to statehood.

Land was perhaps the thorniest issue involving property rights in Illinois. The US government had every intention of making land available for those wishing to settle in Illinois but simply lacked the resources to implement a system for administering that land in any coherent manner during the 1780s and 1790s. This was a major problem, as there were many people who had received land grants from France, Great Britain, or Virginia prior to the United States' acquisition of the territory. The Canadian historian John Weaver explains that "An absolute property right to land would mean a right to use it; to transfer it to another by gift or bequest; to capture the capital value of the land by sale; to claim immunity against expropriation of the property; and to operate without a term limiting the possession of these rights." In Illinois, as in other frontier or borderland areas, people such as Barthelemi Tardiveau "clutched just a few sticks from this bundle of rights."[70] Figuring out how to make the various land grants, warrants, and claims into a secure title to land was a problem that took many years to solve in Illinois. But it was clear from the 1780s that any power able to do so would have a major claim to the affections and loyalty of the many settlers whose desire for land was paramount.

Physical security was the second issue involving effective sovereignty in the Illinois Country, as both Indians and whites sought places to live that were as free as possible from the threat of attack. During the post-Revolutionary period, large numbers of Indians moved west from the Ohio valley to Upper Louisiana to escape the endemic violence. Once there they found a measure of security but still faced a tricky diplomatic situation involving white settlers and Indians whose claims to the region's lands predated theirs. White settlers in Upper Louisiana not only experienced sporadic attacks from local Indians but also the 1780 attack engineered by the British, and the ongoing threats of invasion posed by the French and the Americans in the 1790s. Whatever physical security they enjoyed during this period resulted more from their own diplomacy and Indian alliances than from the actions of the Spanish empire. In Illinois, meanwhile, an influx of Americans brought with it the violence and growing racial hatred that had developed in the Ohio valley. Prior to 1800 there was little or no help on this front from the US federal government, and settlers were forced to balance their desire for good land with assessments of their ability to defend themselves from potential attack.

Finally, rising racial tensions were another impediment to effective sovereignty in the Illinois Country during the last years of the eighteenth century. For nearly a century, whites, Indians, and métis peoples lived in relative peace in the region, even amid widespread black and Indian slavery, and it was not until the 1790s that race itself became important. During the next thirty years it became a bigger and bigger issue, as white Americans moving into the Illinois Country expressed a desire to remove all Indians from the region and to prevent free blacks from settling there. Métis peoples, meanwhile, like other people of color, faced pressure to move out of the way of white settlers, but preferably not too far away, to serve as intermediaries between Indians and whites.[71] Slavery also became a point of contention on both sides of the Mississippi River, with Missouri ultimately choosing slavery and Illinois no slavery in the years surrounding statehood. At the root of racial tensions was the shift from furs to farms. The vast majority of white settlers moving into the region had little interest in the Indian fur trade and an all-consuming interest in acquiring lands to farm. As the focus of the fur trade moved up the Missouri River, the economy of the Illinois Country became centered around the land itself—not the animals living on the land.

As a new century began, the peoples of the Illinois Country found themselves in the midst of political, economic, and demographic changes. Although officials in far-off capitals continued to treat the Mississippi valley as if it were a pawn in an imperial chess game, those living there had repeatedly demonstrated the ability to thwart external attempts to convert the titular sovereignty acquired by treaty into effective sovereignty. Against this backdrop, the gradual shift in the region's economy from furs to farms was already both literally and figuratively remaking the landscape of the Illinois Country, as the transformation of the Mississippi valley began in earnest.

2 / The Louisiana Purchase, Territorial Government, and Contested Lands

In the first years of the nineteenth century a series of dramatic political changes redrew the map of the Mississippi valley, reuniting the two halves of the Illinois Country and ending the Mississippi River's tumultuous forty-year career as an international boundary. Congress, in the spring of 1800, divided the Northwest Territory into Ohio—soon to reach statehood—and Indiana Territory, which included present-day Illinois. Later that year Spain returned Louisiana to France in a secret treaty followed less than three years later by Napoleon Bonaparte's decision to sell Louisiana to the United States. During the next several years Congress separated Illinois from Indiana Territory and Missouri from the future state of Louisiana. By 1812 Illinois Territory and Missouri Territory, with their respective capitals at Kaskaskia and St. Louis, were on their way to statehood.

Amid these changes, issues involving land, slavery, political representation, and Indian removal tested the willingness of the Illinois Country's white inhabitants to attach themselves to the United States and its claims of sovereignty. Indian groups, meanwhile, pursued a number of specific objectives, depending on their location. To the east of the Mississippi River the goal for most was to slow or stop the spread of white settlers onto Indian lands. To the west the Osage tried to prevent encroachments by incoming Americans and by displaced eastern Indians seeking new lands to settle.

The reunification of the Illinois Country did not significantly alter the trajectory of the ongoing economic transformation of the Mississippi valley, but it did accelerate the process. Lewis and Clark's expedition up the Missouri River helped validate the belief that the fur trade's future was to the north and west, and that the British remained a formidable competitor for the trade—even within the borders of the United States. Congress had passed a bill in 1796 for the establishment of federally run trading factories to be operated in the West as one means to counter British threats to the region while gaining greater control over Indian peoples. After the Louisiana Purchase the factory system would be extended across the Mississippi River for the purposes of marginalizing British traders while appeasing white settlers and speculators by using the factories to enmesh Indians in debt as a step toward dispossessing them of more lands.

The limited capacity of the federal government during this period, however, was clear. Put simply, the imperial reach of the United States—like that of many empires—exceeded its grasp. Among the first to discover this fact were Meriwether Lewis and William Clark. Wintering in the St. Louis area prior to their ascent of the Missouri River, they found themselves short of money, manpower, and expertise. Necessity was in this case a virtue, as the relationships developed by Lewis and Clark during those months advanced the larger US projects of attachment and incorporation. The explorers' reliance on a handful of influential French and métis merchants who had overnight become their fellow citizens foreshadowed federal efforts to appoint many of the same men to fill administrative posts. Meanwhile, federal land commissions in both territories struggled with a colonial hangover of contested and fraudulent land claims at the same time that officials worked to get the federal system of surveys and public land sales up and running. Finally, slavery and indentured servitude as political and economic issues mixed with the push to dispossess Indians of their lands to create a climate where white supremacy—as an avowed goal of many new arrivals in Illinois and Missouri—threatened to trigger both political chaos and general violence in the region.

The Illinois Country on the Eve of the Louisiana Purchase

At the close of the eighteenth century the effects of the Illinois Country's dwindling fur trade were being felt on both sides of the Mississippi River. In Illinois settlers petitioned Congress, complaining, "But that from the decay of the Indian Trade which they chiefly depended on for support and from the Depredations committed on them by the Indians . . . they are much reduced and feel themselves unable to pay the Duty imposed . . . on patents issued for lands or the Expences attending the obtaining of such patents." Their wish was for Congress to exempt them from the costs involved with surveying and issuing titles to the fertile lands the petitioners hoped to farm themselves or sell to new arrivals.[1] Across the river, Spanish officials disagreed about how to best regulate the trade in Upper Louisiana. Some thought that exclusive concessions provided a better chance to control the Indians by hindering their ability to renounce debts owed to one trader while establishing credit with another. Others argued that the presence of British traders in the area made this advantage moot and so favored an open licensing system.

Underlying both positions was the reality of corruption within the colony, where bribes were expected in exchange for trade concessions. In 1800 the Chouteaus' concession for the Osage trade was renewed over the protests of Manuel Lisa and other traders calling for free trade along the Missouri River. In 1802 Manuel Lisa went over the head of Lieutenant Governor Carlos Delassus, traveling to New Orleans where he persuaded Intendant Juan Morales to reassign the Osage concession to him and his partners. In St. Louis, the Chouteaus complained that they would suffer greatly from the abrupt loss of business, while the Osage, already in the midst of an unrelated succession crisis, splintered into two groups under the added pressure of choosing whether or not to honor the mandated change in trade partners. To complicate matters further, rumors of the Spanish retrocession of Louisiana provided a backdrop to the fur trade competition as well as to a major controversy involving the Mississippi River itself.[2]

On October 18, 1802, Morales, under secret orders from Spain, closed the port of New Orleans to deposit by foreign traders. This meant that American goods coming down the river could no longer be stored in New Orleans's warehouses prior to being loaded onto ships leaving the port. In the United States the closure elicited a belligerent outcry, as France was quickly blamed for the closure because news of the "secret" retrocession of Louisiana in October 1800 had reached the United States by December 1801. Though facing political pressure to take military action against Spain, President Jefferson remained calm, believing war with any European power was foolish, particularly since Europe was temporarily at peace.[3]

Although Jefferson knew the stakes were high, procrastination along with quiet diplomacy seemed a wiser course. In April 1802 he wrote his French friend DuPont de Nemours, predicting "this little event, of France's possessing herself of Louisiana, which is thrown in as nothing, as a mere make-weight, in the general settlement of accounts, this speck which now appears as an almost invisible point in the horizon, is the embryo of a tornado which will burst on the countries on both sides of the Atlantic and involve in its effects their highest destinies." That same month Jefferson wrote to Robert Livingston, the US ambassador to France, a famous letter speculating about acquiring New Orleans, describing it as "on the globe one single spot, the possessor of which is our natural and habitual enemy." Nemours, however, advised the president that threats would only irritate the Emperor Napoleon and that the purchase of not just New Orleans, but possibly all of Louisiana would prove less expensive, by far, than belligerence.[4]

Taking this advice to heart, Jefferson eschewed bellicosity and instead moved ahead on several diplomatic fronts. Jefferson's diplomacy in this period showed a grasp of the North American imperial situation possessed by few, if any, others. He had long been interested in sending an expedition to seek a water route to the Pacific and was aware of the importance of the Missouri River itself, once writing, "the Missouri is, in fact, the principal river, contributing more to the common stream than does the Mississippi."[5] In January 1803, the president informed Congress that Indians living near the Missouri River "furnish great supplies of furs & peltry to the trade of another nation" via "an infinite number of portages and lakes." Jefferson thought "an intelligent officer with ten or twelve chosen men" might succeed in "extending the external commerce of the U.S." if such an expedition was posed to the Spanish as a "literary pursuit."[6] Cabinet member Albert Gallatin hoped that the planned expedition might help prevent the "occupying of any part of the Missouri country by G.B . . . [since] the future destinies of the Missouri country are of vast importance to the United States."[7] A weak Spain could be tolerated by the United States as, essentially, a trustee for Louisiana, but British trade encroachments and the imminent return of the French were unacceptable. The president promptly dispatched James Monroe to Paris to assist Livingston in negotiations to acquire New Orleans and possibly the Floridas. In this light the Louisiana Purchase and the Lewis and Clark Expedition can be seen not as unrelated, but as complementary diplomatic initiatives. At the same time, the eastern half of the Illinois Country—now part of Indiana Territory—became a crucial part of Jefferson's complex imperial strategy.

The governor of Indiana Territory was William Henry Harrison, who since his arrival in the territory had been involved primarily in Indian relations, land claims, and local agitation over the antislavery provision of the Northwest Ordinance. In early 1803 Harrison became the linchpin of the administration's Indian policy as well as part of its larger imperial machinations when Jefferson appointed him a commissioner of the United States with full power to make treaties with Indians anywhere north of the Ohio River. Jefferson also wrote Harrison with a detailed explanation of his Indian policy and the urgent need to move expeditiously:

> we shall push our trading houses and be glad to see the good and influential individuals among them run in debt, because we observe that when these debts get beyond what the individuals can pay, they become willing to lop off by a cession of lands. At our trading houses we mean to sell so low as merely to repay our cost... this is what private traders cannot do, for they must gain... we shall thus get clear of this pest without giving offence or umbrage to the Indians... [who] will in time either incorporate with us as citizens of the United States or remove beyond the Mississippi... we bend our whole views to the purchase and settlement of the country on the Missisipi from it's mouth to it's Northern regions, that we may be able to present as strong a front on our western as on our Eastern border.... Whatever can now be obtained, must be obtained quickly. The occupation of New Orleans, hourly expected, by the French, is already felt like a light breeze by the Indians.... Under the hope of their protection, they will immediately stiffen against cessions of land to us.

Harrison proved to be an effective agent of the federal government, eventually executing thirteen different land treaties that netted the United States millions of acres. He shared Jefferson's belief that the best way to control Indians was by trade. He was at odds, however, with Jefferson's belief that "our strength and their weakness is now so visible that they must see we have only to shut our hand to crush them."[8] Harrison had earlier called for federal garrisons at Kaskaskia and on the Illinois River to project US power into the Illinois Country because he knew that the relative strength and weakness of the contending parties, including British and Spanish traders as well as the Indians, was a matter of question, with American superiority anything but "visible."[9] The question was deferred, however, when on April 30, 1803, the Louisiana Purchase was signed, bringing all of Louisiana into the expanding American empire.

Lewis and Clark and the Transfer of Upper Louisiana

The acquisition of Louisiana presented President Jefferson with new domestic and imperial challenges. In November 1803 he wrote de Nemours about his plans: "Our policy will be to form New Orleans, and the country on both sides of it on the Gulf of Mexico, into a state, and as to all above that, to transplant our Indians into it, constituting them a mounted constabulary to prevent emigrants from crossing the river, until we shall have filled up the vacant country on this side."[10] This statement would prove to be among the most naïve ever made by Jefferson, as the terms of the Louisiana Purchase called for Louisiana's inhabitants to be protected in their liberty, property, and religion. This presumably included their homes, farms, and businesses, which few would likely consent to abandon to take up residence east of the Mississippi. Domestic political opposition to the Purchase from Federalists was another challenge, as were Jefferson's own scruples about the constitutionality of the acquisition. But the momentum was all on the side of expansion, and on October 20, 1803, Congress ratified the purchase treaty.

On March 9 and 10, 1804, ceremonies took place in St. Louis to mark the transfer of Upper Louisiana from Spain to France and then from France to the United States. Historians tend to overlook these ceremonies because the official transfer of all of Louisiana had occurred in New Orleans the previous December.[11] Some do, however, note the coincidental presence of Lewis and Clark in St. Louis that winter, sometimes mentioning that Meriwether Lewis was an official witness to the ceremonies. Their presence *was* on one level coincidental, as plans for the expedition had been made before President Jefferson knew of the Louisiana Purchase; but it has been shown that the two events were not unrelated. In the months following the establishment of their winter camp on the Mississippi River, Lewis and Clark developed relationships with many of St. Louis's leading men and women that proved invaluable. The explorers received crucial assistance in preparing for their expedition while demonstrating to the peoples of Upper Louisiana a preview of US sovereignty that initially seemed in line with the Louisianans' own political and economic aspirations. The correspondence of Lewis and other Americans in the area, meanwhile, provided Jefferson with further evidence that his vision of the West as an Indian preserve, cleared of white settlers, was deeply flawed.

The immediate value of the vast territories that accompanied the acquisition of New Orleans, described both then and now as unrecognized by most Americans, was certainly obvious to the inhabitants of Upper Louisiana and to the businessmen of London, Montreal, and New York involved in the international fur trade.[12] Lewis and Clark also quickly learned that a large part of Jefferson's prospective Indian preserve was, in fact, dominated by the Osage nation. The explorers realized that the leading white men of the territory would not and should not relocate east of the Mississippi, since their ties to the Osage and to the Missouri River fur trade were assets that the United States needed to secure. In fact, the titular sovereignty acquired by the United States in the Louisiana Purchase would count for little if the attachments of the inhabitants of Louisiana could not be secured. Clark had visited St. Louis six years earlier as part of his efforts to settle the tangled financial affairs of his older brother George Rogers Clark, the Revolutionary War's "hero of the West." At that time he met most of the "gentlemen of character" in the towns on both sides of the Mississippi and came away with a favorable impression.[13] These same men and women were now waiting for the American takeover, wondering whether their fortunes would rise or fall with the change. An Indiana judge wrote the president that "the People are wealthy & the Land rich. Most of them are averse to the Cession of Louisiana to the U.S. but I think by a little attention & moderation they may be easily won over." Another judge recommended Upper Louisiana's surveyor general Antoine Soulard for a similar post in the new territory, explaining that employing foreigners in the new government would help attach them to the United States.[14]

Lewis and Clark's arrival in Upper Louisiana had an immediate effect on the dynamics of the transfer. Here were two men who could be said to represent the best the young nation had to offer. Both were born to prominent eastern families, yet had served the military in the West. These men were not Indian haters and saw themselves, correctly, as ambassadors to the newly acquired territory, where they hoped to promote attachment and forestall discontent. For much of the winter one or both of the explorers stayed at the St. Louis home of Pierre Chouteau. Few knew more about conditions on the Missouri River than the Chouteau clan, and the explorers were eager for any information that might benefit the expedition. Pierre and his brother Auguste helped the explorers determine what supplies were necessary for travel and trade on the river and provided up-to-date maps. Auguste also arranged for seven experienced boatmen to accompany the expedition on the first leg of their journey. After preparing an inventory of Spain's Upper Louisiana properties for outgoing officials, Pierre gave a copy to Lewis to forward to the president.[15] A year earlier Lewis had been living in the White House, serving as Jefferson's personal secretary. Now, on the frontier, but sleeping in a fine home that would not have been out of place in tidewater Virginia, Lewis saw that Jefferson's plans for the new territory were unrealistic. He wrote the president, explaining that St. Louis and its leading families were clearly not obstacles to be removed, but rather, assets to be carefully cultivated by the incoming Americans.[16]

In late February Captain Amos Stoddard arrived to execute the ceremonial transfer and was, like Lewis and Clark, surprised by his first impressions of Louisiana. At the March 10 ceremony he told the assembled crowd, "you are divested of the character of Subjects, and clothed with that of citizens...."[17] He later wrote his mother from St. Louis, "The country is beautiful beyond description. The lands contain marrow and fatness, and produce all the conveniences, and even many of the luxuries of life.... They live in a style equal to those in the large sea-port towns, and I find no want of education among them." Describing the warm welcome given him by the people of St. Louis, he wrote to his mother that "These acts of civility I was obliged to return, and my station required it. Accordingly, I also gave a public Dinner and Ball at my own house, and the expense amounted to 622 Dollars, and 75 cents. I am in hopes, however, that the Government will remunerate me for this expense."[18]

Stoddard's instructions were to perform "all the Functions both civil and military, which have been heretofore exercised by the Spanish Commandants.... With this Difference however, that whereas, under the Spanish Government, the civil & military Functions were confounded & blended together, by you they must be kept, carefully separated & distinct." It was no easy task, and within days he was complaining to his superiors. "It is an endless task to find out the laws and steady maxims of the late Spanish Government. The fact appears to be, that the laws, rules of justice, and the forms of proceeding, were almost wholly arbitrary, for each successive Lieut. Governor has totally changed or abrogated those established by his predecessor." Stoddard also lacked the funds to meet his most basic responsibilities without relying on the generosity, however potentially self-serving, of the Chouteaus and other wealthy merchants. Records show that the Chouteaus advanced funds to the Americans to pay wages to workmen and soldiers as well as for basic supplies. By late spring Stoddard was deeply in debt to the people he had come to rule, as, for that matter, were Lewis and Clark.[19]

Another problem for the incoming Americans was the local Indians and their expectations.. By expanding beyond the Mississippi River, the

United States had in one sense moved backward in time, bringing itself again into contact with Indian groups that had little fear or respect for the young nation. Even Jefferson presumably knew that these Indians could not be easily "crushed." As hundreds came "to see their new father, and to hear his words," Stoddard worried that "if the customary presents be denied or suspended, they will commit depredations or murders on the Inhabitants." He later noted that the Osage "certainly do not pay that respect to the United States that is entertained by other Indians—and in some instances they have assumed a pretty elevated tone."[20] Secretary of War Henry Dearborn responded to Stoddard's plight by arranging for a shipment of tobacco and whiskey to be sent from Kentucky, warning that he should be sparing in its distribution "not so much from principles of occonomy on the part of the United States as from motives of friendship and humanity as it respects the Indians."[21] The irony was presumably not lost on Stoddard.

Congress, meanwhile, worked to pass a bill establishing a system of government for the new territory. The president kept alive his wish to remove whites from the district by having a bill introduced to continue military rule indefinitely. During a vigorous debate many members expressed the view that the new Americans were not ready for self-government. In the end, Congress passed a bill dividing Louisiana into two districts. New Orleans and its environs were designated as Orleans Territory while Upper Louisiana became the District of Louisiana and was placed under the control of Indiana's territorial officials, who were to take power on October 1, 1804. Spanish laws would be retained until altered or repealed by the governor and territorial judges. Subdistricts were to be created and commandants with civilian and military authority assigned for each. Land grants made after the October 1, 1800, retrocession were nullified and force was sanctioned to remove squatters. In effect, the governance act as passed was to serve as a substitute for naturalization, delaying full citizenship until the Louisianans were ready for even the limited self-government prescribed by the Northwest Ordinance.[22]

Opposition to the new bill developed immediately. In St. Louis, local leaders, led by the Chouteaus and Charles Gratiot, formed a committee to convey their objections to Stoddard. A general convention was planned and a circular sent to the outlying districts, inviting them to send representatives. The chief objection to the bill was the provision to nullify land grants made after the Spanish retrocession. Land titles had been issued in a haphazard manner during the years of Spanish rule, and many families felt threatened by the provisions of the new statute.[23]

On May 19, two days before the Corps of Discovery pointed its boats west to begin the journey up the Missouri River, Pierre Chouteau, accompanied by several Osage leaders, headed east to meet President Jefferson. Lewis and Clark had, with Pierre, planned the important diplomatic initiative. In the party were five young men, sons of leading Upper Louisiana families: Chouteau, Gratiot, Brouis, Lorimier, and Vallé. Lewis had arranged for the young men to enroll in the US military academy at West Point. Also on the way to the president was a large collection of scientific specimens gathered by Lewis over the winter and copies of several maps compiled by Auguste Chouteau, Antoine Soulard, and James Mackay showing the latest geographic information available for the Missouri River watershed.[24]

This delegation arrived in Washington on July 11, 1804. At their meeting President Jefferson spoke to the Osage representatives about the prospects for stability and coexistence. "Never more will you have occasion to change your fathers. . . . Our dwellings indeed are very far apart; but not to far to carry on commerce & useful intercourse. You have furs and peltries which we want, and we have clothes and other useful things which you want. Let us employ ourselves then in mutually accommodating each other."[25] The president was demonstrating a better understanding of conditions in Louisiana, perhaps due to the letters he had received from Lewis. Missing from Jefferson's speech was any mention of the sale of Indian lands or the relocation of eastern tribes. The primary goal of the United States along the Missouri River, at least for the present, was safe navigation in order to expand the fur trade—at the expense of British traders currently operating in the region.

Within a week of his arrival in the capital, Jefferson named Pierre the agent of Indian affairs for the District of Upper Louisiana, although Treasury Secretary Albert Gallatin, for one, was suspicious of Chouteau. "He seems well disposed, but what he wants is power and money. He proposed that he should have a negative on all the Indian trading licenses and the direction & all the profits of the trade carried on by Government with all the Indians of Louisiana. . . . As he may be either useful or dangerous I gave no flat denial."[26] In fact, it made perfect sense for the United States to employ men such as Chouteau because he was the American best qualified to pursue the federal government's goals in the West: peaceful relations with Indian nations and an expansion of trade up the Missouri River toward the Pacific Ocean. Could the administration afford to disqualify him because he and his friends shared those goals and would surely profit from them? And what of the Osage, with the most potent military in the District of Louisiana? They also sought peace and expanded trade, as long as that trade ran through their villages. As the delegation headed back toward St. Louis, all parties were, for the most part, satisfied. Pierre Chouteau, born into one European empire and living for most of his life in another, would now, in the new territory, represent the US government.

Back in St. Louis, Stoddard struggled with growing unrest. A town committee warned him that "to preserve the New territory of the united States from the horrours which differente American Colonies have lately experienced; by giving you notice that there exist amongst the Blacks a fermentation—which may Become dangerous and which seems to be increased by the report spread by some whites, that they will be free Before Long." This new fear was a direct result of the connection of the district to Indiana Territory, where slavery was prohibited.[27] Beneath the unrest, however, there was a growing sense that many Louisianans were ready for attachment to the United States but intended to claim political and commercial rights in exchange. From Ste. Genevieve, Jean-Baptiste Vallé proclaimed, "We are now all Americans, and as such I will devote myself to my country's service and to the welfare of my fellow citizens as I have done under all other governments." Native Virginian William C. Carr was a lawyer who moved to the District in April. In a letter to Senator Breckinridge he admitted that

> truth compells me to inform you that the French here are much better citizens, than the Americans . . . (who) I believe to been villains and fugitives from the justice of their country. . . . Some time since the people of St. Louis had a convention which truly in a republican manner elected a committee of 7 persons, to . . . draw up & adopt such resolutions as might be conducive to the interest of this district. . . . After having witnessed this Republican conduct & the peaceable quiet demeanor of the French in this country, how can it be argued that the Louisianans, are not prepared for the reception of a Republican government?[28]

The general convention called for in April finally took place in September. Auguste Chouteau opened the meeting, declaring, "we for the first time are exercising the rights of freemen, to petition to the government for the redress of grievances. Wish to God our first communication with congress instead of being an application for redress, had been an expression of thanks?" The delegates voted to draft a petition to be delivered to Congress by Auguste Chouteau and Eligius Fromentin, detailing their specific objections to the governance bill. The petition protested the unfairness of being annexed to Indiana, citing the District's distance from the governor and the fact that slavery was proscribed in Indiana, and thus might be abolished in Louisiana at some future date. Also protested was Congress's right to invalidate land grants that took place before the onset of US sovereignty. Finally, the Louisianans denounced the authorization given to the president to move eastern Indians across the Mississippi. "Great God! a colony of Indians to maintain and protect us in our liberties and properties! . . . Would your honorable Houses acknowledge in all the powers of Europe the right to collect in one body all their convicts, amounting in number to twice or perhaps three times your own population, and to vomit them on your shores?"[29] In closing, they acknowledged that the petition was perhaps a bit too strongly worded, but only because they wished to show their zeal and worthiness to be called Americans.

By casting their protest as an exercise in republican citizenship the petitioners demonstrated both a grasp of republican rhetoric and a genuine desire to have their grievances addressed before unrest became sedition. Their fundamental objection was to rule from afar by authorities who did not understand their problems and whom they could not directly influence. Not everyone agreed, however. A petition from Ste. Genevieve charged that the St. Louis convention was little more than an attempt by a small group to maintain the favored position they had enjoyed under Spanish rule.[30] The evidence, however, points to the conclusion that the grievances expressed in the petition were shared by most of those living in the District.

On October 1, 1804, Governor Harrison of Indiana and the territorial judges met in Vincennes and enacted statutes for the District concerning local government, criminal punishment, territorial courts, and slavery. Harrison then traveled to St. Louis, where he was warmly greeted. He took up residence for two weeks in the home of Auguste Chouteau and proceeded to appoint many of the District's leading men to government posts. Charles Gratiot was named the presiding judge and Auguste Chouteau, Jacques Clamorgan, David Delaunay, and James Mackay became justices of the Court of Quarter Sessions. Auguste Chouteau was also named justice of the peace and Antoine Soulard was reappointed as surveyor.[31] After his visit Harrison reported to Jefferson that "It gives me great satisfaction to be able to inform you that nine tenths of the people of this Country are warmly attached to the Government of the United States." Harrison was also happy to report that the Chouteaus had furnished over $2,000 in gifts that facilitated the signing of a treaty with five Sauk and Fox chiefs who were in St. Louis to ransom a Sauk prisoner in a murder case. The treaty netted the United States a fifty-million-acre cession (the first to include lands west of the Mississippi) in northern Illinois, southern Wisconsin, and part of Missouri, including the "Spanish Mines" lead district in eastern Iowa. Auguste Chouteau had earlier acquired half of the mines claim from Julien Dubuque (61,500 acres) and had had other large claims in the area, as did Pierre and others in their circle. A provision in the treaty specifically protected these claims.[32]

After returning to St. Louis, Pierre Chouteau pushed aggressively for complete control of the Osage trade as necessary to his effectiveness as agent. He wrote to Congress, claiming "These reflections are dictated to me by the purest zeal for the interest of the United States . . . and by my fear of seeing the good will, the efforts I have put forth, and my credit and standing among the savage nations become, so to speak, useless, because of the false steps and the imprudent and even seditious proposals of the whites who traffic with them."[33] Chouteau's private interest in the Osage trade was at this point indistinguishable from the public interest of the United States to see the Osage happy, peaceful, and amenable to American traffic up and down the Missouri River, allowing the fur trade and American sovereignty to develop. When considering the fact that Chouteau had an Osage wife and children and had been formally initiated into the tribe, it becomes even harder to categorize him or his activities in a way that fits the dichotomies typically seen in American history. Moving freely between his St. Louis mansion, the halls of Congress, and the wilderness lodges of the Osage, he is a quintessentially ambiguous figure, yet somehow emblematic of his times and of the United States' incorporation of the Illinois Country.[34]

Early Territorial Politics and Attachments

William Henry Harrison's popularity in Upper Louisiana as the all-powerful representative of the federal government contrasted with his sinking popularity in Indiana. From western St. Clair and Randolph counties (later part of Illinois), petitions were sent to Congress asking again for the suspension of Article VI (proscribing slavery), but also for expanded suffrage, new roads and mail routes, approval of old land grants, preemption rights for squatters, and even for annexation to the District of Louisiana. They complained of being on the western fringe of Indiana and saw an opportunity to be formally reunited with their friends and families across the Mississippi River. Congress demonstrated its ignorance of the Illinois Country by rejecting the annexation appeal, saying, "the Laws and local attachments of the People of Louisiana being different from those in said Western Counties, and the former being separated from the latter by the large and, sometimes, impassable River Mississippi."[35] For people used to crossing the river on an almost daily basis these words could have only increased their determination to be represented in Washington by someone who, at a minimum, had some knowledge of the region's geography. To this end people living in Indiana's western counties pushed to advance Indiana to the second stage of territorial government, which would enable the territory to send a representative to Congress. After delaying, Harrison finally scheduled a referendum on the issue in late 1804. This was too late to salvage any political support for the governor in Indiana's western counties, where an anti-Harrison faction characterized him as power-hungry and not committed to legalizing slavery or expediting land claims.[36] Harrison, in the meantime, faced an Indian backlash against his earlier land treaties even as he continued to pursue new ones. Urged on by the administration, he acquired the salt springs area on the Ohio River (in present-day Illinois) and issued leases to private individuals to produce salt for sale in Indiana and Kentucky.[37]

In July 1804 the administration appointed land commissioners for Vincennes and Kaskaskia to adjudicate claims for land grants made by Congress in the 1780s and 1790s and by French and British officials prior to the Revolution. At the same time, federal surveyors began arriving in present-day Illinois to begin surveying the lands acquired in Harrison's treaties.[38] What in theory was a coordinated effort by government officials, treaty negotiators, land commissioners, and surveyors was in practice a difficult and contentious set of processes hindered by Indian hostility, fraud at several levels, and a lack of manpower that exacerbated the other problems. At stake was the ability of the United States to respond to the changing economic and political landscape of the Illinois Country in order to successfully secure to the Union the attachments of people living on both sides of the Mississippi.

Attachments were a source of constant speculation and calculation during these years. One memorial to Congress asked for preemption rights to land, citing the petitioners' "attachment to their country and to the constitution of the united states," while another, addressed to the president, was sent to "convince him that the inhabitants of Louisiana, new citizens of the United States, are deeply attached to their new country." At a St. Louis town meeting, oaths of allegiance were taken to "afford the members an opportunity of gratifying their impatience to give to the United States an unquestionable pledge of their affection and entire devotion." An American official explained that political factionalism did not "proceed from a Want of attachment to Our Government," while another warned of Canadian fur traders trying to influence "the temper, dispositions, and attachments of the Indians."[39] Behind these statements is the recognition that the incorporation of the Illinois Country was more than a matter of titular sovereignty. Pieces of paper signed by the United States and its European rivals *did* matter, but so did the voluntary choices of the thousands of people inhabiting the lands in question. People were aware that borders—lines drawn on paper—had been and could again be redrawn. In one sense, discussions of attachments were akin to informal votes or referendums on the question of whether and when effective sovereignty could be established without the will and ability to use overwhelming coercive force.

But questions surrounding land ownership and attachments were also indications of the region's economic shift from furs to farms. In the eighteenth century, land in the Illinois Country had been less important than the animals living on it. Indians and whites had often clashed, but when they did the cause was more often than not related to the fur trade. Attachments to an empire had been less important, less relevant, than kinship ties—real or fictive—between individuals or small groups. Now the animals were disappearing and the land becoming a commodity, and an attachment to someone or something that could validate one's claim to a specific piece of land was becoming increasingly relevant.

In the meantime the United States moved ahead in March 1805 with an act to establish the Louisiana Territory. General James Wilkinson was appointed governor and Congress established for Louisiana a political system akin to the Northwest Ordinance's first-stage government: a governor, a secretary, and three judges, with legislative powers—all appointed by the president. The act made no reference to land grants, but in May three commissioners (in Indiana there were two-man commissions) were appointed to adjudicate the numerous pending claims.[40] Word had already reached Washington that widespread fraud was occurring in Louisiana, partly due to the liberality of outgoing Spanish officials who had reportedly left stacks of signed grants to their favorites, to be filled in as needed.[41]

In late June Wilkinson arrived in St. Louis and moved quickly to assert American sovereignty over the territory. Wilkinson was a peculiar choice for this role, as President Jefferson was undoubtedly aware that the general had once been and likely still was employed by Spain as a spy.[42] In August the new governor sent Lieutenant Zebulon Pike up the Mississippi River to select locations for prospective US garrisons while at the same time showing the American flag to the Indians and to British traders on the upper Mississippi River. In the same month Wilkinson declared the Missouri River closed to British subjects, requiring an oath of loyalty to all seeking trading licenses. He had quickly sized up the situation, explaining to Secretary of War Henry Dearborn:

> the Indian trade, From Hudson's Bay and the St. Lawrence, to the remotest streams of the lakes, the Mississippi and Missouri is nearly monopolized by British Traders, their factors Agents and Engageés, and their goods are imported and their furrs exported through British posts; the privation We Suffer from this diversion of our rightful commerce, is a trifling ill, when compared to the transcendent influence, which is thus acquired and perpetuated by a foreign power, over the aborigines within our national limits.[43]

Wilkinson knew, however, that there was no easy fix to the problem of British poaching. Cutting off British traders' access to Louisiana's Indians, if it could be done, would quickly alienate the Indians, who were still a potent force in the region. He wrote again to Dearborn with his concerns:

> When I estimate the number and force of the Indian nations, who inhabit the Country watered by the Missouri and Mississippi, and who if not made our friends become our enemies.... When I cast my eyes over the expanse of territory to be occupied or controuled, and glance at futurity, I hope you will pardon me Sir for observing... that we are not in sufficient strength, of men or means, to meet the occasion and profit by the favourable circumstances of the moment.[44]

Wilkinson was not alone in questioning the ability of the United States to impose its will in Louisiana. The president learned from Rufus Easton that his plan to "retard the settlement on the west side of the Mississippi" would fail because the government had no means by which to prevent squatting—on either side of the Mississippi—and because any disputes with local Indians would result in the river being closed and the loss of both private commerce and public revenue from local lead mines and salt springs. Easton recommended that the administration move instead to take control of the lead-mining district as one step in generating the revenues needed to effectively administer the territory. Congress had recently passed a bill authorizing the president to employ an agent to collect information on the lead mines, already a trouble spot where rival factions led by Moses Austin and the notorious John Smith T were fighting—sometimes literally—to engross the choicest tracts.[45]

Wilkinson's entanglement in the private disputes between rival entrepreneurs in the Ste. Genevieve mining district provides a good window into the rapid disintegration of his administration. The general's long history of mixing public and private business had continued in Louisiana, as he arranged before even arriving for eastern trade goods to be shipped to St. Louis—at government expense—and sold at a profit.[46] Yet within weeks he accused the commandant of Ste. Genevieve, Major Seth Hunt, of abusing his office by partnering with Moses Austin in a mining venture on what Wilkinson considered public lands. He eventually had Hunt arrested, and all prominent parties in the territory quickly took sides in the dispute, thus initiating the intense factionalism that contributed to Wilkinson's removal the following year. His backing of John Smith T also exacerbated the ruthless competition over floating land claims and ancient French titles that frequently involved violence between the principals and their backers. In the fall of 1805, Aaron Burr's arrival added another dimension to the intrigue and factionalism developing in the territory.[47]

Although he is more widely known as a former vice president and the killer of Alexander Hamilton (in a duel), Burr's adventures in the West during this period have also been the subject of a great deal of historical analysis. Burr was a friend of Wilkinson and the brother-in-law of the territory's secretary, Joseph Browne, and as such his arrival seems fraught with implications, but in truth he did little to directly affect events in the territory. A number of people, including Smith T, were tainted by their association with his alleged filibustering expedition, but Wilkinson and Browne deftly distanced themselves from Burr, as did Harrison, prior to Burr's arrest and prosecution for treason (he was acquitted). In one sense, however, Burr *was* an important figure in the history of the Illinois Country because the failure of his allegedly traitorous plan was seen by Thomas Jefferson and other easterners as a welcome demonstration of westerners' loyalty—or attachment—to the United States.[48]

Returning from his brief sojourn in Louisiana, Governor Harrison in 1805 guided Indiana into the second stage of territorial government, which included a nonvoting representative in Congress, a five-man legislative council, and an elected assembly. Under the provisions of the Northwest Ordinance, the president was supposed to appoint the council from a list of ten men nominated by the territory's assembly, but Jefferson sent the list back to Harrison with instructions to select the five men himself, avoiding all Federalists and "land jobbers."[49] In a welcoming statement to his hand-picked council, Harrison praised the Louisiana Purchase as making possible an Indian policy that would increase Indian dependency on the federal government and would, in turn, hopefully lead to a friendlier attitude toward the United States. He also contrasted US Indian policy with that of other civilized nations whose policies seemed calculated to "produce[d] the entire extirpation of the unhappy people whose country they have usurped." To the already "humane and benevolent intentions of the government" he hoped to add the banning of liquor sales to the Indians.[50] Harrison had by now convinced himself that what was good for the United States was good for the Indians. Specifically, he sought control over the fur trade as a means to preserve the peace, limit the baneful effects of alcohol—and facilitate the steady transfer of land from Indians to the United States.

Trade Factories, Land Claims, and Political Instability

In addition to land purchase treaties he negotiated in these years, Harrison worked with Wilkinson in 1805 to negotiate a treaty preventing a war between the Osage and several rival groups allied against them. As the largest and strongest tribe in the Illinois Country, the Osage faced many enemies and so worked to maintain good relations with the Americans, as they had done with the French and Spanish, as a means by which to perpetuate their power. Good relations ensured reliable access to trade goods (particularly guns), but by the end of 1805 Osage and American interests were heading in opposite directions.

In 1796 Congress passed a law for the establishment of federal trading factories to be built in the West. Supporters of the bill aimed to eliminate alcohol from the trade, protect Indians from exploitive traders, and undersell British and Spanish trading companies whose representatives were thought to be working systematically to undermine American-Indian relations. In a January 1803 confidential message to Congress that included a request to fund an expedition to ascend the Missouri River, President Jefferson explained, "At these trading houses. . . . We consequently undersell private traders, foreign & domestic, drive them from the competition, & thus, with the good will of the Indians, rid ourselves of a description of men who are constantly endeavoring to excite in the Indian mind suspicions, fears, & irritations towards us." Whether wishful thinking or deliberate obfuscation, Jefferson's description of the early results from the trade factory policy did not line up with the situation in Louisiana. Efforts to block British traders from entering the territory were turning one-time Indian friends into enemies: precisely the effect predicted by Governor Wilkinson in his letter to Secretary of War Dearborn. When John Treat arrived in the territory to establish a federal trading factory on the Arkansas River, he was met by traders in a panic over the debts owed them by the Osage. Fearing for their lives if they tried to collect without bringing new goods, they warned that the Osage had many enemies who wished to take advantage of what was quickly becoming an arms shortage.[51]

If the Americans could somehow keep British traders out of the territory but not be able themselves to provide the necessary goods, they faced the potential for widespread violence. Spain had kept the Osage happy by turning a blind eye to the Chouteaus' (and others') smuggling of British goods into Louisiana. Pierre Chouteau was now a US Indian agent and expected to enforce the prohibition not against British goods but against British traders. But Chouteau was an Osage himself by marriage and ceremony, expected to look out for his people at a time of great peril. East of the Mississippi River Harrison faced less immediate pressure on this front than did Wilkinson and his successors because it was impossible to prevent the Indians from crossing over into Canada to trade with the British. But it was clear that the replacement of roving traders with US trading factories was a tricky business and one where timing was essential. Whenever and wherever goods became scarce, trouble would follow.

Another source of unrest in the territories was the inability of the federal government to move expeditiously to solve the growing land claims problem. The commissions on both sides of the Mississippi River quickly bogged down in the face of missing and forged documents, congressional entreaties to respect legitimate colonial claims, language problems, and the factionalism that surrounded both territorial administrations. In Indiana, settlers were again calling for the western counties (today's Illinois) to be separated from Indiana. This time the calls were not for annexation to Louisiana, but for a new territory. Petitioners again invoked their loyalty to the Union, this time harkening back to the 1790s when "unalterably attached to their Country, they rejected with Indignation and Contempt the insidious offers which were made to them. . . . Liberty and Poverty were preferable to all the Advantages which a Despotic Government could bestow." Now they claimed their friends across the river in Louisiana were each being promised 640 acres and wondered why they could not get a similar offer. In Louisiana Territory the argument was inverted, as petitioners complained that they could not get their Spanish concessions confirmed, nor were they being offered access to the public lands that sat empty.[52]

These petitions, sent less than a month apart, were intended to pressure Congress to take steps to facilitate the land claims process. They had some success, as Congress eased some of the rules used to adjudicate the claims and even included an early version of preemption rights. But as the fears of widespread fraud became a reality, the commissioners moved ever slower, trusting almost no one. Harrison, meanwhile, stonewalled complaints in his territory while Wilkinson, across the river, pandered to the French, promising to expedite their claims, particularly those of his wealthy new friends whom he saw, with some justification, as crucial to the American project in Louisiana. A big problem in both territories, however, was the lack of resources. More commissioners and more surveyors (as the magnitude of their task became apparent) were needed. But the federal government did not provide them. Was it Republican frugality? Or was it perhaps political foot-dragging by easterners uninterested in seeing more western lands on the market? The evidence is contradictory but the result is clear: no public lands were sold until 1814 in Illinois and 1818 in Missouri.[53]

Wilkinson's pandering to the French points to his role as a polarizing figure in Louisiana as well as to the particular dynamics of the territory itself. In addition to arresting Seth Hunt he was early on involved in a shaky indictment of Rufus Easton for land fraud. Neither case resulted in a conviction but the pattern seemed clear. Most Americans in the territory considered Wilkinson an autocrat and quite possibly corrupt. William Carr, a young lawyer in the territory, described the general's presence as a "triumph of aristocracy over virtue and republicanism. . . . Mr. Jefferson appears to desire the conciliation of a minority of French demagogues even at the expense of a majority of the citizens of the United States."[54] To Americans Wilkinson seemed unctuous and overbearing; to the French charming and reassuringly paternalistic. He reminded them of the type of governors and the type of system they were used to. The French found the Americans' way of doing things slow and cumbersome and felt the newcomers were obsessed with litigation. Amos Stoddard noted a general slowdown in trade and credit among merchants who "murmured at a system calculated to produce delays, and in many instances to create expenses equal in amounts to the sums demanded."[55] There had been no lawyers in the colonial Illinois Country on either side of the river, because there were no roles for them in either the French or Spanish systems. Justice had been arbitrary, but swift, and usually subject to persuasion, if the right approach was taken.

Appearances notwithstanding, Wilkinson's powers were not those of a colonial governor and his administration ultimately proved as much a disappointment to his French supporters as an affront to everyone else, particularly those anxious to see the French become Americans in more than name. John B. C. Lucas was a friend of Albert Gallatin and an ex-congressman from Pennsylvania who had served in Louisiana Territory as a judge and land commissioner. He wrote Gallatin, explaining that "far from inviting the french inhabitants at st. louis to come to our manners he steps foreward and goes to theirs." By the spring of 1806 a flood of correspondence moved east with reports of Wilkinson's favoritism and the resulting factionalism that was engulfing the territory. For men like Rufus Easton, William Carr, John B. C. Lucas, and Samuel Hammond, the issue was not Wilkinson himself, but the damage he was doing to the incorporation process. They recognized that land claims were the biggest cause of dissension in the territory and that Wilkinson's actions were exacerbating an already contentious issue. Hammond wanted the administration to know that most people "Cannot be Considered as partakeing any thing of party spirit, or to proceed from a Want of attachment to Our Government, but from a conviction that the nature of their Claims has not been understood by those who had framed the Law."[56] To his detractors it was clear that Wilkinson had chosen to side with the biggest frauds and speculators and they were therefore compelled to resist. These Americans also made a distinction between the French with small claims, and those who were members of the wealthy "Junto" that enjoyed Wilkinson's support. To their eyes a few bad actors among the French were ruining things for everyone. French solidarity postponed the general recognition of that fact, however, for several years.

In the summer of 1806 Thomas Jefferson decided the general's talents were needed elsewhere and dispatched Wilkinson to New Orleans, although he did not formally remove him from office. Jefferson was learning, however slowly, that Louisiana was not an empty wilderness, admitting that his initial combining of civil and military authority had been a mistake and that Wilkinson's appointment had been partly due to Jefferson's viewing Louisiana "not as a civil government, but merely a military station." The president also took a closer look that summer at the land commission, deciding finally that while mistakes were being made, there was no evidence of corruption on the part of the commissioners and their work should continue. He also tried to expedite the claims process by assigning Louisiana Territory to the surveyor general's office, which sent surveyor Silas Bent to replace Antoine Soulard, a holdover from the Spanish era.[57]

Bent's arrival failed to expedite the claims process, in fact retarding it when he discovered widespread fraud involving missing or backdated surveys. Soulard defended himself by characterizing Bent's findings not as evidence of fraud but of the vagaries of a colonial system that had not been designed to conform to the rigors of the new regime. Both men were partly correct. While many surveys were in fact backdated and therefore technically fraudulent, the explanation had more to do with the perverseness of the Spanish system than it did with attempts to mislead the commission. In truth there were hundreds of claimants who had received land from Spain but had never gone through the complex and costly process of obtaining a complete title. Spanish officials, aware that a complete title involved a trip to New Orleans to obtain signatures that would likely require bribes, had given most landowners a pass, letting them claim lands with only rudimentary documentation. Now the American commissioners wanted proof that the lands had been properly surveyed, obtained before the retrocession, and occupied and cultivated in the intervening years. At this point the commission itself fell prey to faction as Clement Penrose and James Donaldson pushed for greater leniency, while John B. C. Lucas continued to take a harder line. Bent, meanwhile, was without work and therefore without income, as the commissioners refused to order any surveys while they waited for Congress and/or the administration to clarify their instructions.[58] To the relief and joy of everyone in the territory, on September 23, 1806, Meriwether Lewis and William Clark returned to St. Louis with the Corps of Discovery. Perhaps the two could pick up where they had left off two years earlier.

New Leaders Face Old Problems

During their expedition to the Pacific Ocean and back, Lewis and Clark had continued their general diplomatic efforts. They met and spoke with dozens of Indian groups, usually delivering at some point a standard speech explaining that they represented a new "father" who wished for the peace and prosperity that reliable trade would bring. They also sent a group of Arikara Indians to St. Louis, where James Wilkinson arranged for them to travel to Washington to meet the president. Wilkinson wrote ahead to justify the cost of the delegation by explaining that the Arikara chief Shahaka had "great influence over the Nations of the Upper Missouri," and might, if sufficiently awed by his trip, become an "important Instrument of Humanity & of policy." Wilkinson also lobbied for the payment of a $1,100 bill for a Sioux interpreter used by the explorers, arguing that the expense was justified because British traders were trying to hire the man on the basis of his relationship with Sioux tribes.[59]

Lewis and Clark were determined to undermine British trade relationships in Louisiana, employing a variety of strategies to do so. Their overtures to British traders included offers of temporary employment with the potential for full-time positions as US Indian agents. To one they explained, "We believe that the surest guarantee of savage fidelity to any nation is a thorough conviction on their minds that their government possesses the power of punishing promptly every act of aggression committed on their part against the person or property of their citizens." Here was the harder side of Jefferson's Indian policy: the threat of punishment rather than seduction into debt. Of course, the preference was to avoid violence by awing the Indians with trips east where they would have an "ample view of our population and resources," after which they would return west to "convince their nations of the futility of an attempt to oppose the will of our government." This strategy had, of course, been used by European colonial powers for nearly two centuries, but Lewis and Clark were ostensibly explorers, not imperial emissaries. The Louisiana Purchase, however, added a diplomatic imperative to their expedition, and they joined with Wilkinson, Pike, and others to promote the construction of US sovereignty west of the Mississippi River by building trade relationships with the Indians while working to undermine British interests.[60]

Upon their return to St. Louis, the explorers received a heroes' welcome before setting off for Washington, where within months Lewis was named the new governor of Louisiana Territory and Clark the head of the militia and chief US Indian agent for all groups excepting the Osage, who remained the responsibility of Pierre Chouteau. Frederic Bates took over as acting governor pending Lewis's return to Louisiana and began the task of straightening out the mess left by Wilkinson. Bates moved to organize the militia to restore law and order in the violent mining district, where the United States was missing out on significant revenue due to its inability to prevent squatters from mining its lead. Bates also ended Wilkinson's practice of selling trading licenses, believing that it was inappropriate for American officials to profit from the licensing process.

To the east William Henry Harrison also stepped up his efforts to organize a reliable militia, a task that took on greater urgency after the *Chesapeake* affair in June 1807, in which three Americans were killed when their ship, in American waters, was fired upon by a British navy vessel searching for deserters. Anti-British sentiments swept through the United States subsequent to the incident, and the evidence shows that a change in British policy in the West also followed. In the decade following the Jay Treaty, British officials had been instructed to distance themselves from their former Indian allies even as Canadian traders continued to work hard to maintain their relationships in the region. In Britain a tug-of-war was taking place between manufacturing interests favoring a policy of friendship with the United States, and fur trade interests wanting to move aggressively against the Americans from the Great Lakes to the Pacific Ocean. While both groups were to a large extent hostage to the imperatives of the Napoleonic Wars, after the *Chesapeake* incident Canadian officials were instructed to begin repairing their frayed relationships with Indians living in the Great Lakes area.[61]

Harrison saw what he thought were signs of this policy in the rise of the Prophet, a Shawnee medicine man and the younger brother of Tecumseh. Large groups of Indians were flocking to the Prophet's village in Greenville, Ohio and Harrison reported to Secretary of War Henry Dearborn that "traders who are attached to our Government are unanimously alarmed and agree on the opinion that a general combination of Indians for a war against the United States is the object of all these messages and councils." The evidence, however, shows that the Prophet and his brother Tecumseh were at this time acting independently of the British. Tecumseh's goal was a pan-Indian alliance to block the advance of white Americans into Indian lands, while his brother was the latest in a line of nativist religious leaders who built followings based on a rejection of white culture. Over the next few years Harrison met with both brothers (never together) on several occasions and developed something of a tragic relationship with each of them. After the Prophet moved his community to Indiana, Harrison warned him to steer clear of involvement with the British. The Prophet responded with professions of independence from all white influences and for a time convinced Harrison that his intentions were to remain at peace with the United States.[62]

Harrison's land purchases from "treaty chiefs" and the concurrent efforts of the Jefferson and Madison administrations to replace British traders with federal trading factories essentially drove the Indians east of the Mississippi River into the arms of the British. Neither private traders nor trade factories were able to reliably supply the Indians with necessary trade goods, and so the Indians became increasingly receptive to the idea that the Americans cared mostly about taking their lands. During face-to-face meetings Tecumseh, the Prophet, and Harrison developed considerable respect for each other even as they began to see themselves as inevitable enemies. As the United States pursued an increasingly belligerent trade policy with Great Britain, the Indians sought support from the only available source. This dynamic culminated in Harrison's 1811 attack on the Prophet's settlement at Tippecanoe and contributed to the drive for war in 1812.[63]

After returning to Louisiana to assume his duties as governor, Meriwether Lewis faced Indian problems of a different nature, though still related to trade competition. In 1808 the Osage responded to the blocking of British trade in the territory by conducting a raid on St. Louis. They burned buildings and stole horses, stopping short of actual violence but sending a clear message that they would not accept the status quo. Later that year a US delegation moving up the Missouri River to return the Arikara chief Shahaka to his nation was turned back by Sioux warriors determined to prevent the Americans from using the river unless suitable trade policies were guaranteed. Again the weakness of the United States was exposed, forcing the new governor to adjust his Indian policy. Lewis sent William Clark to negotiate with the Osage, and Clark returned with a treaty that promised a trading factory in proximity to a large Osage village in exchange for a huge land cession. When a delegation of Osage who had not participated in the negotiations with Clark arrived in St. Louis a few weeks later to protest the terms agreed to, Lewis called upon Pierre Chouteau to renegotiate the treaty. It was later revealed that Chouteau himself might have instigated the Osage protests because Clark's treaty did not include provisions to protect lands Chouteau had earlier received as a gift from the Osage.[64]

By the end of 1808 both territories were in turmoil. In Indiana the repeated failure of petitions to suspend or revoke the Northwest Ordinance's slavery ban led to the passing of an indenture law that created a de facto form of slavery. This did little to calm the political waters because a growing antislavery movement was developing in the territory's eastern counties, fueled by an influx of settlers from New England. An unlikely alliance between proslavery representatives of the western counties and antislavery representatives of the eastern counties resulted in the 1808 election of Jesse Thomas as the territory's delegate to Congress. In early 1809 Thomas's efforts to promote a bill to divide Indiana succeeded, and Congress created Illinois Territory, naming as its first governor Ninian Edwards.[65]

Lewis and Edwards took office as the shift in the Mississippi valley economy from furs to farms accelerated. While the focus of the fur trade moved away from the Illinois Country and up the Missouri River, Indians in Illinois and Louisiana (soon to be renamed Missouri) faced hostility from land-hungry Americans. At the same time, British traders, with encouragement from their government, worked to increase trade with those same Indians—within the borders of the United States. Concurrently, the land commissions in both territories struggled with a backlog of claims and a lack of resources by which to process them amid the growing clamor by white settlers for lands to farm and by speculators for lands to sell to others to farm. White inhabitants of both territories, meanwhile, exhibited a growing solidarity in their hostility to the policies of a federal government perceived as weak. They wanted title to the lands they felt, in many cases, they already owned. And they wanted political rights to be used to secure slavery and the development of a society based on white supremacy. The federal government was as yet unable to make those things happen, but it was being pushed to do so by some of the very people it employed as its representatives in the territories. Those representatives, in turn, were driven in varying degrees by self-interest and by pressure from the people they ruled, who themselves were slowly developing a sense of nationhood, of attachment to the *idea* of the United States as the best vehicle by which to pursue the boundless futures they envisioned. In the short run, however, things would get worse in Illinois and Louisiana before they got better.

Meriwether Lewis was the most prominent political casualty of this tumultuous period. Lewis believed he had answers for the host of problems he had inherited, but lacked the authority, time, or personality to achieve any tangible results. His Indian policy was based on his belief that "there are but two effectual chords by which the savage arm can be bound, the one is the love of merchandize, and the other the fear of punishment." This much mirrored Jefferson's views, but Lewis differed with the administration on the value of trading factories, believing agents should be assigned to specific tribes because the Indians moved around so much.[66] Within months Lewis had alienated both his superiors in Washington and the citizenry of the territory. He was chastised for giving orders to US military officers and reviled for court-martialing citizens who failed to respond to a militia summons. He moved aggressively to prevent squatters from settling on federal lands without finding a way to expedite the processing of land claims. Worst of all, for the usual reasons, his Indian policy showed no signs of success. British traders continued to find ways to supply Indians with arms and other goods, meaning many tribes remained dangerous and hostile to Americans, many of whom faced either economic ruin by being shut out of the Indian trade or physical peril by being exposed to Indian depredations.[67]

Lewis's problems in the territory reached the breaking point in 1809 when he gave a private fur-trading company a contract to make another attempt to return Shahaka to his people. The company's owners included the Chouteaus and many other prominent St. Louis traders, as well as Lewis's brother Reuben and William Clark. Though successful, the expedition was met with extreme disapproval by William Eustis, the new secretary of war. Eustis complained to Lewis:

> In the instance of accepting the volunteer services of 140 men for a military expedition to a point and purpose not designated, which expedition is stated to combine commercial as well as military objects, and when an Agent of the Government [Pierre Chouteau] appointed for other purposes is selected for the command, it is thought the Government might, without injury to the public interests, have been consulted.

Eustis went on to explain that several drafts drawn by Lewis on the federal government would not be honored. The reason given in each case was the lack of prior approval. In closing, Eustis stated that President Madison had been consulted and "the observations herein contained have his approval."[68] Within days of receiving this letter Lewis, his finances now in ruins and his reputation threatened, left the territory and headed to Washington to defend himself from both the political embarrassment and financial devastation that Eustis had inflicted upon him. In a letter to his brother, William Carr explained, "Our governor left us a few days since with his personal affairs altogether deranged. . . . I apprehend he will not return. He has drawn on the general government for various & considerable sums of money which have not been paid; of course his bills have been protested." Lewis, in fact, did not return to the territory, instead taking his life on the way to Washington.[69]

William Clark and Pierre Chouteau also came under fire from the Madison administration for perceived mistakes of their own. Eustis wrote Clark rejecting several appointments of agents and interpreters, saying, "It does not appear necessary that the expense attending our Relations with the Indians in the Territory of Louisiana, should be four times as much as the whole expense of supporting its civil government." Chouteau was, in turn, criticized for accepting the assignment to lead the Shahaka expedition while still serving as agent to the Osage. The new administration seemed determined to cut costs in the territory while also reining in the behavior of appointed officials. But unlike Meriwether Lewis, Clark and Chouteau enjoyed wide support in Louisiana, where their actions were better understood. In the absence of overwhelming force or the ability to prevent British traders from supplying arms, successful Indian relations required interpreters and métis agents with ties to hostile groups. Similarly, using Chouteau's diplomatic abilities to ensure the safe return of Shahaka was more good policy than conflict of interest. From distant Washington, however, the appearance was of extravagant expenditures involving men whose public and private initiatives were too closely intertwined. This perception gap, not an uncommon occurrence in core-periphery relations, was exacerbated by the employment of men such as Pierre Chouteau, Antoine Soulard, Charles Gratiot, Louis Lorimier, and others who were now Americans, but whose loyalty—or attachment—to the United States was still suspect, and whose influence on Lewis, Clark, and Wilkinson, to name a few, was considered potentially problematic.[70]

No such concerns had accompanied Ninian Edwards's appointment as governor of Illinois Territory. A Kentucky politician and judge born in Maryland, Edwards had close ties to influential easterners and presided over a territory whose prominent "foreigners" had for the most part already moved across the Mississippi River. The French who remained, with few exceptions, were clustered in a few villages along the river and wished only for their small land claims to be approved. There were larger claims, however, belonging to a handful of mostly American speculators whose intense partisan politics had culminated in Illinois' separation from Indiana and in a famous murder involving the rival of land commissioner Michael Jones. Edwards arrived, determined to eliminate the "considerable degree of party spirit [that] divided the people of this Territory."[71] He replaced many officeholders with men he considered nonpartisan and was largely successful in calming the territory's political waters, at least for a time. Indian relations were not an immediate problem. Harrison's treaties and the fact that few Indians lived near the settled areas of Illinois meant that during Edwards's first year in office, Illinois was spared the costly expenditures that plagued its neighbor across the Mississippi River.

Land Commission Quagmires and the Approach of War

The ongoing struggles of the federal land commissions in Illinois and Louisiana were both helping and hindering the construction of US sovereignty in the territories. The protracted claims process made it clear to all involved that the federal government would, for better or worse, determine the legitimacy of everyone's land holdings. Gone were any notions of purchasing land directly from Indians or of buying or selling colonial land grants without their having first been validated by the commissions. But the lengthy delays and lack of men and materials with which to take depositions, survey old claims, and survey public lands for purchase undermined confidence in both the integrity and the competence of the federal government.

Several problems contributed to the maddening slowness of the commissions' work. The first involved the clear evidence of fraud in both territories. In Illinois many, if not most, of the congressional grants of the 1780s and 1790s wound up in the hands of a few prominent speculators. While they likely purchased most of these grants in good faith, they were unable to provide acceptable documentation and so in many cases resorted to forged titles or backdated surveys in presenting their claims. In Louisiana, the lax practices of Spanish officials left many with no titles to substantiate their claims, creating another class of potentially fraudulent claims. Also problematic were numerous "floating" grants in both territories. These grants could be located wherever the holders wished and were often used to engross lands thought to contain marketable quantities of lead. Many had changed hands several times and clearly involved fraud.[72]

Another problem was the language barrier. Most of the French-speaking inhabitants, particularly those in remote locations, knew little about the claims process. When the commissioners traveled to these areas, most landholders were unable to present valid claims. To these people the government seemed to be acting in a capricious or even corrupt manner as they informed many that their homes and farms might be lost. Interpreters were crucial but costly, and the records are filled with correspondence between the territories and Washington arguing over the necessity of such outlays.[73]

A third problem was the cost of surveying existing land claims. Unlike surveying unoccupied lands, where contiguous tracts could be surveyed in a systematic manner, the commissioners were forced by the nature of the claims process to order surveys of lands spaced widely apart. Who was to pay for these inefficient surveys? Should the claimants pay for surveys on tracts they had occupied for years and might wait years more to gain clear title to? Many had no money to do so anyway, and it seemed to many that the United States stood to benefit by any surveys completed because lands—private and public—adjacent to those surveyed invariably rose in value, as proven in Ohio and Indiana, where public sales were already taking place. Again, the records are filled with correspondence over the problems connected with the surveys. Threats to quit by surveyors because they had not been paid, crossed in the mail with warnings of possible termination due to excessive costs and missed deadlines.[74]

Struggling to solve these problems were the commissioners themselves. Faced with an almost overwhelming responsibility, they were often at odds with each other due to the considerable discretion they were forced to exercise. Irrespective of congressional and executive efforts to closely prescribe the claims process, in the field subjective judgments were routinely called for. In Louisiana, the hard line taken toward claimants by John B. C. Lucas placed him at odds with his fellow commissioners, Clement Penrose and James Donaldson. In Illinois, Michael Jones and Elijah Backus operated in a smaller community and faced tremendous pressure from the men who stood to gain or lose the most from the rulings. From Washington, Secretary of the Treasury Albert Gallatin tried his best to rationalize the claims process, but to no avail. Reports were submitted years after they were due, and upon arrival they still had to be submitted to Congress for examination and approval.[75]

However, along with frustration, the land claims process by 1810 had begun to produce a subtle shift in perspective within the territories. As it became clear that fraud was a major reason for the delayed reports, French solidarity began to break down, particularly in Louisiana. During the Wilkinson administration the large claimants were often referred to collectively as the Junto. But whereas in 1805 the Junto was perceived as working for all French claimants in a French-American split in interests, it eventually came to be viewed as a group working only to promote its own economic and political interests. The fault line was now between large and small claimants. John B. C. Lucas explained the change to Gallatin:

> it appears that the Bonafide Land Claimants who are without exception Claimants for small quantities of Land are fully sensible that their interest is perfectly distinct from that of those persons who have large claims indeed they appear to believe that the Laws of congress would have been less Nice and particular had it not been for the large and suspicious Claims ... therefore they have separated, and have adopted different means to obtain relief from congress.[76]

Petitions from small claimants no longer displayed the belligerence of those sent in the immediate post–Louisiana Purchase period. Asked for were "laws to sanction their Just right; but also wish those rights sanctioned while they live to enjoy them, and before they come to suffer, or become insolvent for want of [the lands'] use." The commissioners attested to the validity of these fears by explaining that "at present the uncertainty of landed property renders it of little or no value." And from Illinois came the observation that "At present the titles of Land is so uncertain that emigrants are unwilling to purchase Consequently the Country remains unsettled."[77]

This evidence compels a revision of the standard story of land-hungry settlers pushing their way onto Indian lands *ahead* of the federal government's efforts to acquire title from the Indians. While it is true that some squatters did settle on Indian lands, there were concurrently millions of acres in the Illinois Country, already acquired by Harrison for the United States, that would not feel a white man's plough for another generation. One reason for this was that for the federal government, acquiring Indian lands required fewer resources than surveying and selling it did. Another was that Jefferson and Gallatin understood that under the provisions of the Jay Treaty, British traders were allowed to trade in US territory in areas still owned by the Indians. The Treaty of 1783 had given the Northwest to the United States, but the British did not give up their forts in the region until the Jay Treaty was signed in 1795. The Jay Treaty, however, included provisions that allowed British traders to continue to do business in American territory well into the new century.[78] Thus, the Indian troubles that grew during these years were not primarily due to white settlers encroaching on Indian lands. More inflammatory was the aggressive federal policy—faithfully implemented by Harrison—to purchase Indian lands well ahead of survey, sales, and settlement.

A more immediate problem for most Indians was trade, or rather, the lack of it. There were multiple causes. The declining populations of fur-bearing animals in the region was one. Another was the international embargoes attempted by the Jefferson and Madison administrations, which resulted in shortages of British-made goods in the West. Finally, attempts to block British traders west of the Mississippi (where the United States asserted that the Jay Treaty did not apply), amid the ongoing transition from roving traders to trading factories, appeared to many young Indian hunters and warriors as parts of a general effort by Americans to prevent them from providing for their families. In response, Indian efforts to secure arms and allies increased in 1810–1811, as did depredations against whites in remote areas. Territorial officials in Louisiana and Illinois repeatedly warned Washington of impending warfare and the need for regular troops to be sent west.[79]

The first years of the nineteenth century had been eventful ones in the Illinois Country. Thanks to the Louisiana Purchase, the original French colony was reunited, though under a new flag. For the United States, the diplomatic efforts of Lewis and Clark began the process of constructing sovereignty in the region. In St. Louis, prior to heading into the uncharted West, the two men—of necessity—worked to attach prominent Louisianans to the United States with ties of self-interest and a shared vision of future prosperity. In the months that followed, as the Corps of Discovery ascended the Missouri River the explorers tried to do the same with Louisiana's Indians, with some success. But diplomacy does not take place in a vacuum, and the Mississippi valley's changing economy meant that the Illinois Country the explorers returned to as heroes in 1806 and as administrators in 1808 was an altered landscape, both literally and figuratively. As fur-bearing animals grew fewer, as swamps were drained and trees were felled, farms proliferated, peopled mostly by white settlers for whom the land was less a habitat than an engine of production: a commodity. And the commodification of land rendered both the animals and the Indians living on the land, expendable. For the peoples of Illinois and Louisiana, future prosperity would not be the result of a shared vision but of contrasting visions that would have to be negotiated—or fought over.

East of the Mississippi River, federal Indian policy was based on the idea of enticing the Indians into debt and then accepting their lands in lieu of cash when the debts could not be paid. In practice, however, the Americans were unable to prevent British traders from continuing to dominate what was left of Illinois' fur trade, and the basis for most of William Henry Harrison's treaties was not Indian indebtedness but bribery and power struggles among Indian leaders. Although Harrison acquired millions of acres for nominal sums, the treaties he negotiated spawned organized resistance to the federal government and drove a wedge into Indian society, pitting treaty chiefs and their followers against the mostly younger, militant hunters and warriors who opposed the sale of lands beyond the Greenville Treaty line.

West of the river, newly minted Americans such as the Chouteau clan adjusted to the altered landscape by redirecting their fur-trading efforts north and west while simultaneously plunging into new roles as land speculators, and as territorial and federal officials. Indian groups on both sides of the river, meanwhile, were compelled not by the strength of the United States, but by the declining fur trade, to operate from a position of relative weakness, forced to choose between moving farther west in search of furs and uncontested lands, joining the switch from furs to farms, or uniting in resistance with the help of the British, who had their own agenda to pursue.

As the second decade of the nineteenth century began, the *idea* of the United States—of the Union—was evolving in Illinois and Louisiana under the pressures of a changing economy. Institutions in the territories would remain shaky for years. Opposition to federal policies would in some important ways grow. But the incorporation of the Illinois Country was under way. Land would be the reason given, then and now, for the growing violence in the West, but trade would be every bit as important a factor as the shift from furs to farms erupted into warfare.

3 /   From Tippecanoe to Portage Des Sioux:
      The Wars of 1812

On July 3, 1812, Touissant Pothier, an employee of John Jacob Astor's South West Company, arrived at St. Joseph's Island in Lake Huron with the news of Congress's June 18 declaration of war against Great Britain. Two weeks later the British commander at St. Joseph's, Captain Charles Roberts, landed on the north side of the nearby island of Michilimackinac with a force consisting of forty regulars and several hundred voyageurs and Indians. The American commander on the island, Lieutenant Porter Hanks, still unaware that the United States and Great Britain were at war, surrendered Fort Mackinac without firing a shot. The fact that an employee of Astor's fur-trading company had reached the Upper Great Lakes with news of the war ahead of any British or American military personnel was both significant and symbolic. It was significant because the loss of Mackinac led directly to the losses of Fort Dearborn—the future site of Chicago—and of Detroit, which were both important military and trading posts. It was symbolic because Astor's South West Company and its rival, the North West Company, commanded more resources in men and materials in the region than did either the United States or Great Britain, and because the competition for the fur trade in the West was largely responsible for bringing widespread violence to the region well ahead of the formal declaration of war in June 1812.[1]

The gradual decline of the fur trade was a crucial part of the complex political and economic dynamics in the West during the war years. Although land is generally cited as the principal source of friction between Indians and whites at this time, the fur trade remained—for

Indians—the most important economic activity in the region, and the centrality of British interests to the conduct of the fur trade was the main reason that the war spread far beyond the areas where land ownership was under dispute. As the number of tribes directly and indirectly involved in the war increased, so did the efforts of territorial officials to use diplomacy—with both friendly and hostile Indians—to blunt the violence. These efforts culminated in the dramatic Portage des Sioux treaty council held in Missouri in the summer of 1815. Here and in a number of smaller councils in the months that followed, the United States for the first time acknowledged the need to involve the Indians in formal negotiations to end a major war.[2] The treaties, however, along with the relative scarcity of federal resources sent to the Illinois Country during the war, created resentments among white settlers that threatened their attachments to the US government, even as the completion of the land commissions and subsequent commencement of public land sales in Illinois and Missouri strengthened those ties.[3]

During the years immediately following the war, a flood of immigrants poured into the Illinois Country in testimony to their belief that the United States could now guarantee the physical security of its settlers and provide them with the property they most eagerly sought—land. But the loyalty and attachments of the Americans living in the Illinois Country were not yet fully with the Union. They were angry about the lack of federal support during the war as well as postwar policies that seemed to coddle the Indians at the expense of white settlers. As a result, many US laws and policies were not yet respected or obeyed, and peoples' loyalties remained more with their families and neighbors than with the nation they were helping to build. At the same time, the shift in the fur trade to areas north and west of the territories of Illinois and Missouri further undermined the economic viability of Indian communities in the region at the very moment when white settlers were beginning to push politically for a federal policy of Indian removal from lands the settlers viewed as the future sites of family farms.

The Context for War

In the early months of 1812, against a backdrop of rising hostilities between Indians and whites and between the United States and Great Britain, Illinois and Louisiana (now renamed Missouri) both advanced to the second stage of territorial government. Voters would now elect a legislature, and each territory would now send an elected delegate to

Congress.⁴ Citizens and territorial officials frustrated with the federal government's handling of the land commissions, frontier defense, mining rights, and postal and transportation systems, believed a congressional delegate would help keep those in Washington better apprised of conditions in the territories. Second-stage government, however, could do little to reflect the will of the people unless the right to vote was extended to the many settlers who did not hold legal title to land. From Illinois a memorial to Congress asked for expanded suffrage, pointing out that "Many of us are now freeholders & others would long Since have become so if the Sale of public lands had not been unexpectedly delayed; All are attached to the country and interested in its support." Governor Edwards supported the request, explaining, "The population of this territory as appears by the late census amounts to 12,282 in the whole of which there does not exceed between. two & three hundred freeholders . . . this is owing to the sale of public lands having been postponed much beyond any period that was anticipated." Congress responded by passing a law in May 1812 granting suffrage to "every free white male person who shall have attained the age of twenty-one years, and who shall have paid a county or territorial tax, and who shall have resided one year in said Territory previous to any general election."⁵ With the right to vote now extended to include men not owning land, those living in the territories gained confidence in their ability to influence the federal government to take the steps necessary to protect their lives and property in the war between the United States and Great Britain that officially began in June 1812, long after violence between Indians and whites had broken out in numerous places throughout the region.⁶

Most historians have described the War of 1812 as an inconclusive conflict between the United States and Great Britain that was driven more by political agendas *within* both countries than by irreconcilable differences *between* the two. Many cite the fact that the British Parliament took steps to reduce tensions with the United States just days before President Madison's declaration of war, and that if the news had somehow been able to reach Washington in time, the war might have been avoided. But these accounts largely ignore the organized violence already occurring in the West that reached a tipping point with the November 1811 battle of Tippecanoe in Indiana Territory. At Tippecanoe an assortment of distinct but related problems involving the United States, various Indian groups, and Great Britain burst into violence involving hundreds of participants. The result was a hardening of positions on all sides and a sense of inevitability as to the likelihood of a general war in the region.

The formal declaration of war between Great Britain and the United States came as something of a relief to those Americans in the West who saw themselves as living in a state of war but without the support in men and materials that they expected the federal government to provide. It came as a relief, too, for the Indians and British subjects and officials who had been preparing for war for more than a year and who feared a repeat of 1795, when the Jay Treaty had led to the sudden abandonment by the British officials of their Indian allies.[7]

The war in the West that officially began in 1812 had its roots in the competition for the North American fur trade, despite the fact that land was and is perceived to be at the source of the conflict between Indians and the United States. For half a century, British Canadian traders and merchants dominated the fur trade by ignoring international boundaries in their push to secure the trade in the Upper Great Lakes and Missouri and Mississippi River valleys. A series of events including the 1807 *Chesapeake* controversy and the trade embargoes initiated by the Jefferson and Madison administrations provided the impetus for a reestablishment of the alliance between the British and the Indians of the region. From the British perspective, aside from the profits still to be gained from the fur trade, hostilities between themselves and the United States posed a potential threat to Canada that could be neutralized by a strong alliance with the Indians. From the Indian perspective the embargoes, which resulted in a steep decline in trade goods reaching the region, gave rise to an immediate crisis that imperiled their ability to secure the goods they had come to depend on and an additional reason to resent the Americans who were concurrently acquiring Indian lands in a series of treaties seen by many as illegitimate.[8] In Missouri the situation was further complicated by the ongoing efforts of various tribes to overturn the regional dominance of the Osage, making access to trade goods, particularly arms and ammunition, even more essential.[9] Throughout the Illinois Country in the years leading up to 1812, white settlers endured sporadic Indian attacks while Indian communities struggled to adjust to the disruption of the fur trade, changes taking place in their cultures, leadership structures, and relationships with white settlers, and the migration of eastern Indians into their homelands.

The disruption of the fur trade and its far-reaching effects began with the trade embargo initiated by the Jefferson administration in December 1807. Earlier that year the *Chesapeake* incident, in which British sailors fired upon and boarded an American vessel, inflamed anti-British feelings throughout the United States and convinced President Jefferson of the need for some action to curb British aggression on the high seas. The effect of the embargo in the West, though not easily foreseen, was significant. Both British and American traders required a ready supply of British trade goods to exchange with the Indians, and by the spring of 1808 traders and Indians throughout the region were feeling the pinch. British Canadian officials Andrew McKee, Matthew Elliot, and Robert Dickson were all married to Indian women and attuned to the issues that concerned Indians. They used the situation to strengthen their ties to the tribes by calling a conference at Amherstburg that spring, where they distributed a large amount of gifts and advised Indians to oppose further land sales to the Americans.[10]

The Amherstburg conference came after more than a decade of relative neglect by British officials toward their former Indian allies and signaled a significant change in British policy. After the signing of the Jay Treaty between the United States and Great Britain early in 1794, and following the Battle of Fallen Timbers later that year, the British commander at Fort Miami closed the gates to Indians fleeing American soldiers. To the Indians this was a stunning betrayal and a reminder of the close of the American War of Independence, when the British-Indian alliance had suffered a rupture similar to that when the British failed to provide for their Indian allies in the 1783 Treaty of Paris. Now in 1808 British officials in London and Canada agreed that the Indians should be sought as allies lest they somehow become allied instead with the Americans in a potential invasion of Canada. The strategy of bad-mouthing the Americans while providing the Indians with gifts of much-needed goods proved successful over time, although for the Indian leader Tecumseh and others in the region, the memory of past British treachery had not faded and the resumption of a military alliance did not occur until 1811.[11] If land was ultimately at the heart of the growing conflict for Tecumseh and his confederation, it was the fur trade and the alliances and relationships that grew from it that determined the ability of all Indians to provide for their families and to challenge, if they chose, the advance of white settlement in the West.

US officials in the West did their best to forestall the Indian-British alliance but faced a number of obstacles. During the years after the 1795 Treaty of Greenville, long-practiced Indian traditions of consensus and decentralized leadership were under pressure. as American officials chose to recognize certain men as chiefs empowered to make decisions presumed to be binding on all members of a tribe. Many pro-American chiefs, in fact, had little or no control over young men opposed to land cessions or interested in gaining prestige and honor by attacking white settlers or enemy tribes. The implementation of treaty provisions also got in the way of good relations. Annuities for treaty obligations were often distributed in inconvenient locations, resulting in some bands of a particular tribe receiving the majority of the annuity goods while others got little or nothing. And when US agents reneged on a promise made by President Madison to Indian leaders visiting Washington to extend credit at the American trading factory at Fort Madison, the influential Sac leader Blackhawk switched his allegiance to the British.[12]

The trade factory system itself seemed designed to drive a wedge between the United States and the Indians. For more than a century fur traders in the Illinois Country traveled to Indian villages to exchange goods for furs. Credit had long been a key element in the trade, as traders supplied goods to the Indians in the fall that were paid for with furs during the winter or the following spring. The trading factories, established to bring order to the competitive fur trade and to limit the amount of alcohol reaching the Indians, were a failure almost from the start. Indians preferred British goods to American goods and also expected to conduct trade in their own villages and to receive gifts when visiting US or British outposts. The idea of trading at a fort left many Indians with the impression that the United States was selling them goods that should have been given to them as gifts. And it got worse. As the embargo blocked access to British goods, a British official noted that the Americans would have to violate the trade restrictions to acquire the British blankets needed to fulfill specific treaty obligations. As for alcohol, the official ban on its trade only increased its value and provided a competitive advantage to traders willing to supply it.[13] In the case of the Osage the trade factory built to serve them proved especially counterproductive. Its location on the Missouri River was not only far from the majority of the Osage bands who wished to trade with the Americans, but also a magnet for hostile tribes whose proximity to Fort Osage allowed them to attack the Osage on the edge of Osage lands and closer to the hostiles' villages.

The beneficiaries of the factory system's weaknesses were large firms such as John Jacob Astor's that employed veteran boatmen and traders to penetrate deep into American territory to capture large shares of the vital trade.[14] Combined with the change in British policy, the factory system, however well intentioned, and the growth of the large trading firms, served to seriously undermine US interests in the West. Almost lost in the acrimony surrounding these developments was the fact that the overall volume of the fur trade in the region continued to decline.

Its future was farther west, and so even as many Indians in Illinois and Missouri again turned to the British as trade partners and military allies, growing numbers of Americans in both territories saw the fur trade itself not only as economically irrelevant, but as a source of instability and even danger.

The Wars of 1812

The results of these developments were apparent in the steady deterioration of relations between the Indians and Americans within the Illinois Country. Citizens in Illinois and Missouri sent petitions to Congress calling for federal help in defending the frontier against Indian aggression, and Governor Howard and Governor Edwards added their own requests for help while taking steps on their own to mobilize territorial militias and build fortifications. Edwards explained to the secretary of war that "The Indians have for some time past been in real want of powder" and "are induced to believe that they will receive all their supplies at the british Fort of St Joseph . . . this territory is now & has been for some time in a more perilous situation in regard to the Indians than any other one belonging to the United States . . . nothwithstanding all this, we have no assistance from any other quarter—not a man being engaged in service in the territory who is not a citizen of it." After the fall of Mackinac and subsequent surrender of Detroit by General William Hull, Indians ambushed American troops as they withdrew from Fort Dearborn in August 1812. In September Governor Howard joined Ninian Edwards in demanding outside help to defend his territory. "The americans here appear, warmly patriotic, and have yielded support . . . in defence of the frontier, but from the poverty of the people this cannot last . . . I believe we have British spies, among us, now in this place, and suspect a plan is forming to overrun this country."[15]

Edwards and Howard had no choice but to attempt on their own the daunting task of defending their territories while continuing diplomatic efforts to secure the support or at least the neutrality of as many of the Illinois Country's Indians as possible. In the fall of 1812 Howard deployed his militia in small mounted units that protected outlying settlements and kept hostile Indians in doubt as to the Americans' strength. Edwards tried to forestall an attack on white settlements in his territory by personally leading an expedition to Peoria, where his troops fired on a few scattered Indians and burned several villages before returning south. The territorial legislature praised the governor's effort, saying it "commands our attachment to the present administration." But the Potawatomi chiefs Gomo and Black Partridge, whose villages were among those burned, responded by renouncing their neutrality and joining the British cause.[16] For Edwards, Howard, and the US Indian agents working in the Illinois Country, the loyalties of the various tribes and bands of Indians were virtually impossible to determine. Tecumseh and the Prophet continued their efforts to build a pan-Indian anti-American alliance, and the British agent Robert Dickson enjoyed great success in his recruiting efforts due to his ability to smuggle British goods into the region for distribution to the Indians, many of whom were on the verge of starvation due to a lack of arms and ammunition for hunting. As a result pro-British, pro-American, and neutral factions competed in many Indian communities, with the balance of power shifting from one day to the next, depending on the latest developments.[17]

In contrast, whites in the Illinois Country were fully united during the winter of 1812–1813 in their anger toward the Indians, the British, *and* the federal government. General Hull, who was eventually court-martialed for his decision to surrender Detroit, was burned in effigy in the streets of St. Louis. *Missouri Gazette* editor Joseph Charless confided to Secretary of War James Monroe that "Prudential motives have induced me to withhold giving publicity to indian movements, as the country is threatened with desertion, a great number of families are preparing to remove . . . as soon as the weather will permit." Both territories' new congressional delegates wrote Monroe about the need for a common defense against the expected British-Indian attack and "the great necessity of asking from the Government effectual protection . . . unless early and efficient aid is afforded to those most exposed frontiers—Famine or the Tomahawk will most inevitably depopulate a great portion if not the whole of it." Most of those called to serve in the summer and fall of 1812 had been able to fit their service around their harvest duties, but if called upon to serve again in the spring, "no crops will be raised and distress and famine will complete the sad list of calamities."[18] Some even believed the Illinois Country would have been overrun the previous fall had British agent Robert Dickson's Indian force not been sent east to help with the fighting around Detroit. John Reynolds, a member of the militia and future governor of Illinois, wrote, "[Dickson] had prepared three or four thousand warriors ready to attack the frontiers of Illinois and Missouri. But these warriors were more needed in Canada. They were sent there and thereby we were saved. The war in Canada was our defence." As the spring of 1813 approached, the overwhelming expectation in the Illinois

Country was that the general attack avoided in 1812 would take place soon unless strong steps were taken.[19]

Governors Edwards and Howard both believed an aggressive strategy provided more chance for success than a defensive one. Each bombarded Washington with requests for men and materials needed to go on the offensive against the British and Indian forces. They argued that the territories they were responsible for were too vast, with too many scattered settlements to be effectively defended. They also wished to provide pro-American Indians with a reason to resist the pressure to switch sides, which was being reported by US Indian agents. In April Edwards wrote Monroe to explain "that the Sauks Foxes and Ioways were divided. part being for war with the U.S. and part for peace," and that those tribes had been assured "that the British were ready to supply them with ammunition clothing & provisions. that if they would not unite in the war they would be considered as Americans and that other Indians & the British would commence war upon them." In the same letter Edwards got to the heart of the dilemma facing the United States and its remaining Indian allies in the Illinois Country: "We cannot expect them to remain firm in our interest while we neither assume a warlike attitude to inspire them with fear, nor carry on intercourse and trade with them to conciliate their affections—In fact we are doing no one thing calculated to counteract the exertions of the British and therefore I conclude those exertions cannot fail of eventual success." Now a year into the war and several years into a period of open hostility between whites and most Indians in the region, the federal government faced its greatest challenge to date to its construction of sovereignty in the Illinois Country.[20]

In May 1813 the federal government finally took some action to shore up its western defenses. After organizing the entire United States into nine military districts, the War Department created a subdistrict for Illinois and Missouri under the command of Governor (now Brigadier General) Howard. A regiment of US infantry was sent to St. Louis to help relieve the burden on the territorial militias. Howard assembled a force consisting of more than 1,300 regulars and militia and in September moved up the Mississippi River into the Illinois River and on to Peoria. Like Ninian Edwards, Howard encountered few Indians during the expedition and had to be satisfied with building and garrisoning Fort Clark at this key site. The hostile Potawatomis and Kickapoos who lived in the area had spent the later winter and spring on raids into southern Illinois but were now again with the British, fighting William Henry Harrison's army as it drove into Canada. The ability to build and garrison Fort Clark was an important step. It showed that the Americans were taking the offensive and would no longer sit in their settlements awaiting Indian raiding parties.[21]

Howard's expedition, combined with victories by Captain Oliver Perry and Harrison, reversed the momentum of the war in the West. Harrison's victory in early October 1813 at the Battle of the Thames broke the power of the British and Indian alliance as British forces withdrew early in the battle, leaving Tecumseh's warriors to absorb the brunt of the American attack. The Indian defeat and Tecumseh's death during the fighting left the Indians reeling. Within weeks most of the tribes involved in the campaign accepted the temporary armistice extended by the American commander at Detroit. Both sides were to refrain from hostilities, and the Indians agreed to return all prisoners and provide hostages to be held until the war ended. Some of the Indians who signed sincerely wanted peace but others were interested only in the winter food rations Harrison provided, fully expecting to renew the war in the spring. The Potawatomis, Sacs, Foxes, Winnebagoes, and Kickapoos returning to the Illinois Country that fall were again divided between peace and war factions, while in St. Louis, Kaskaskia, and other white settlements, the knowledge of the British withdrawal from the Detroit area brought new fears that Robert Dickson was now free to direct a large-scale attack in their direction.[22]

Those fears turned to renewed anger at the federal government when in January 1814 the War Department ordered General Howard and a portion of his regular troops to report to Cincinnati. Disgruntled citizens met in St. Louis to protest the action, and territorial officials on both sides of the Mississippi bombarded Washington with protests and new calls for men and materials. In April the decision was reversed and Howard returned to St. Louis. In the meantime Governor William Clark (Howard's successor) had led an expedition up the Mississippi River to Prairie du Chien (in present-day Wisconsin), where he established another post in the heart of Indian country. Clark believed that the new fort, along with Fort Clark on the Illinois River, would prevent the Indians of the Illinois Country from being supplied from Canada. Howard agreed and upon his return sent two expeditions, one under the command of future president Zachary Taylor, up the Mississippi River to reinforce the post at Prairie du Chien. Blackhawk and his Sac and Fox forces turned back the first, and the arrival of British artillery helped defeat the second. The post itself was overrun in July.[23]

Neither of the relief expeditions included more than a hundred or so regular troops, and the enlistments of most of the militia and volunteer rangers that made up the majority of the forces fighting in the Illinois Country were either expired or close to expiring. Nor had the War Department sent any funds to pay the men who were serving. These facts, combined with the news of General Andrew Jackson's crushing defeat of the Indians at Horseshoe Bend, drove the people of St. Louis into a lather of antigovernment sentiment. They demanded a large well-run army to do the job Jackson had done for their southern neighbors. Letters and petitions sent to Washington called for a war of extermination against the hostile Indians. Territorial officials, following General Howard's death from illness, again sought the means and the strategy by which to successfully prosecute the war in the Illinois Country.[24]

Governors Clark and Edwards, realizing they lacked the manpower to replicate Jackson's success, increased diplomatic efforts to quell the fighting in the Illinois Country. Their reliance on diplomacy was an acknowledgment of a crucial difference between conditions in the Southwest and the Illinois Country. In the Southwest the Indians fighting the United States did not receive direct support from British troops, while the American forces were strengthened by the presence of warriors from friendly tribes and bands. In the Illinois Country there was not only a greater British presence but also, particularly west of the Mississippi River, tribes such as the Osage and the Sioux that could field more fighting men than the Americans. In the case of the Osage, these men were paradoxically willing to fight *for* the United States, but were prevented from doing so because of public sentiment.

In 1813 Pierre Chouteau had traveled to the Osage country, where he successfully recruited a force of Osage warriors to fight alongside their American allies. Many of the Illinois Country tribes hostile to the United States were the same British-leaning groups that were trying to push the Osage out of central Missouri. But as Chouteau headed to St. Louis with the Osage, he received a message from General Howard stating that it was considered too dangerous to bring a large party of Indians—even if presumably friendly—into the vicinity of St. Louis. Chouteau wrote the secretary of war explaining the consequences of this decision. "I cannot give you a Just idea of the disappointment and dissatisfaction of the party . . . after so long and hard a journey, deprived in a moment and without any Just cause of the hopes entertained by them to defend their allies and at the same time to avenge themselves of their long sworn enemies; I experienced the greatest difficulty in persuading them to return."[25] In fact the "just cause" Chouteau did not yet comprehend was the growing racial hatred in the Illinois Country. For nearly two centuries Europeans had competed for Indian allies to help fight their enemies. In the Illinois Country of the 1810s, however, the generalized racial hatred of the incoming American settlers precluded that possibility. To be sure, there was still some desire to distinguish Indian friends from foes. But that was a waning sentiment practiced mostly by leaders such as Pierre Menard and the Chouteaus, who continued to employ friendly Indians as guides and scouts. The opposition to employing Indians as fighting allies further complicated the diplomatic efforts undertaken by territorial leaders in 1814 and undermined the popularity of those officials in the coming years.[26]

For the Osage the rebuff only added to the increasingly isolated geopolitical position they now occupied. They faced threats from the south, east, and north by Indian groups displaced by white settlers or looking for new hunting grounds that were not yet depleted. During the war years the Osage continued to suffer from internal divisions, but were generally in agreement as to the necessity of allying themselves with the United States despite the obvious long-term threat posed by American expansion.[27]

The racial hatred that prevented territorial officials from enlisting the Osage to fight alongside American forces did not prevent Governor Clark from eventually deciding to supply arms to friendly tribes. "I have sent out the Showones & Delaways on the Northern frontiers, and policy obliges me to incourage the Osage and the Tribes on the Missouri to wage War on the Mississippi Indians & Those Missouri Tribes must either be engaged for us; or they will be opposed to us without doubt." Clark also appointed Auguste Chouteau and the prominent fur trader Manuel Lisa to carry several thousand dollars of goods, including arms, up the Missouri River "for the purpose of engaging those Tribes in Offensive operations against the Enemies of the United States." Lisa was crucial to Clark's initiatives as he was the trader with the closest ties to the tribes of the upper Missouri valley. In the fall of 1814 Lisa married the daughter of an influential Omaha chief, and by the spring of 1815 large numbers of previously neutral tribes moved east to attack their enemies on the Mississippi River—most of whom were the pro-British tribes that continued to terrorize the scattered American settlements.[28]

The diplomatic offensive succeeded in preventing any large-scale attacks on white settlements but did not mend the growing rift between the federal government and American settlers in the Illinois Country. The Americans did not want to arm Indians to fight other Indians or to secure their neutrality with gifts. They wanted the federal government to provide the territories with the men and materials that would "Jacksonize" the Indians, as one Missouri newspaper described General Andrew Jackson's actions at the Battle of Horseshoe Bend. The territorial assembly asked for "an adequate force of regular troops" to "afford us the opportunity of showing to the world our zeal & attachment to the government of the United States." Without such support, they warned, "The Spirit of the militia will become harrassed & broken by too frequent calls on their patriotism & ultimately but few we fear will be found willing to shoulder a musket in defense of a country of such immense value to the United States." A petition from a group of volunteer rangers complained about the lack of pay, saying it was "in violation of one of the Maxims of a just Government, that compensation shall be made for all services the public require and receive from individuals." The implied threat was clear. The federal government needed to do more than keep the hostile Indians at bay, or it would risk losing the support of the Illinois Country settlers.[29]

Caught in the middle were officials like William Clark, Ninian Edwards, and Howard's military replacement, Colonel William Russell. These men were no less interested in ending the war than were the citizens who berated them and their Washington superiors. Russell's tone in a letter to Secretary of War James Monroe left no doubt as to his frustration with federal efforts: "I shall detach two of our largest boats... to watch the motion of the enemy untill your pleasure respecting the future Military operations in this country shall be known for on this subject I am completely in the dark."[30] Of course, watching the enemy until Washington acted was out of the question for Russell, Clark, and Edwards. Turning instead to trade diplomacy, they relied heavily on the French citizens of the two territories, whose relationships to Illinois Country Indians provided a counterweight to the influence of British traders such as Robert Dickson. This, however, exacerbated the existing differences between the old French establishment and the recently arrived Americans.

In short, the French wanted to salvage what was left of the trade with the Illinois Country's Indians, weaning them from British influence while gradually pushing them west to make room for white settlements. The Americans wanted to crush the Indians militarily and cared more about acquiring Indian lands than salvaging the region's Indian trade. Ninian Edwards saw more merit in the former strategy and even envisioned the federal government taking over the fur trade, though not via the failing trade factories. In a letter to Illinois' congressional delegate and future governor Shadrach Bond, he laid out his case.

> If the govt. would permit the raising of a force of two hundred men furnish the necessary boats for transportation, be bound eventually to pay them as infantry—& permit them and their officers to carry on the trade—with Indians—they could be raised in ten days without any trouble to the govt. and would be entirely sufficient— This surely wd. be better than keeping men stationary in forts for purposes not as important.... It would prevent evils from growing which otherwise we shall have to exterpate with difficulty—and therefore whether considered as a measure of defence or offence is strongly recommended by both policy & interest.... In fact the plan would enable us to drive off our enemies at the same time that by our trade we would be prepared to make the indians our friends—& to secure to ourselves the undisturbed possission of their trade.[31]

Edwards's vision of a commercial infantry of federally sponsored fur traders may seem far-fetched, but it is an indication of the extent to which those responsible for administering the territories on behalf of the United States understood the strategic importance of the fur trade—even if dwindling—in this region. Unfortunately for them, neither the federal government nor a majority of their fellow citizens seemed to share these views, and so both Edwards and William Clark found their popularity at the end of the war—despite heroic efforts to defend their territories—less than it was at the beginning.

Portage des Sioux and the End of the Wars

In January 1815 news of Andrew Jackson's victory over the British at New Orleans arrived just ahead of the announcement that the Treaty of Ghent had ended formal hostilities between the United States and Great Britain. While word of Jackson's victory led to wild celebrations in Illinois and Missouri, the news of the treaty generated intense criticism. The terms negotiated at Ghent called for an immediate cessation of hostilities and for the United States "to restore to such Tribes all the rights and privileges to which they were entitled previous to the war," providing the Indians also refrained from further violence. The treaty pleased no one in the Illinois Country. White settlers argued that there could be no peace with the Indians "until we drub them soundly into it." British agents and traders were dumbfounded that their government had made peace with the United States without warning them and without acquiring any territorial concessions in the Upper Great Lakes. The pro-British Indians were disappointed, if not surprised, to be abandoned by their British allies. Many chose to continue fighting and during the spring of 1815 resumed scattered raids on white settlements.[32]

Illinois Country officials were again caught in the middle. Colonel Russell wrote to Secretary of War James Monroe from St. Louis, explaining his plight. "I have been much abused at this place for not taking stronger measures as to the Indians, not with standing the peace. My object has been since the peace merely to act, in such a way as to protect the frontier Settlements, without being too oppressive to the government but Sir, to do my duty to my Country, and grattify the whims of the people is difficult to reconsile." Russell believed the Indians "must be humbled, for their own good, and that of this country," but knew the United States was "bound down by the existing treaty, and cannot act offensively." Monroe's instructions included the admonition that "It is incumbent on the United States to execute every Article of this Treaty with perfect good faith, and the "wish to be particularly exact in the execution of the Article . . . relating to the Indian Tribes." To this end President Madison called for a large treaty council to be held during the summer of 1815 with the object being the negotiation of a series of treaties with as many of the tribes of the Illinois Country—and beyond—as could be induced to attend.[33]

The Madison administration's decision to negotiate an end to the War of 1812 in the Illinois Country marked a radical departure from previous federal policy. In the past, the United States had negotiated with the Indians either in the aftermath of an American military victory, such as Anthony Wayne's Treaty of Greenville (1795) and Andrew Jackson's Treaty of Fort Jackson (1814), or in an effort to acquire Indian lands. At Portage des Sioux, the tiny village at the confluence of the Mississippi and Missouri Rivers chosen for the gathering, the United States set about the business of negotiating peace with thirty-seven different tribal bands that it had not defeated in battle and whose members continued to attack white soldiers and settlers up to almost the start of the council in July 1815.[34]

President Madison appointed William Clark, Ninian Edwards, and Auguste Chouteau to serve as the US treaty commissioners charged with securing peace in the Illinois Country. On May 11 the three met in St. Louis to outline plans for the council. There were problems from the outset. Hostile Sacs and Foxes murdered one of the runners dispatched to invite Indian representatives to attend the council, while the *Missouri*

Gazette asked, "Shall we allow so sacred a thing as a treaty to be a passport to conduct the murderers into our houses and towns?" To provide security, the Madison administration sent 275 regular troops and two gunboats that were anchored in the Missouri River opposite Portage des Sioux. In addition, Illinois and Missouri each sent a company of militia. The administration's instructions to the commissioners were clear. "It is proper to confine this treaty to the sole object of peace." The negotiators were not to seek land cessions at this council. Instead, the federal government provided over $20,000 in trade goods to be distributed as gifts to the tribal bands that agreed to terms. In late June Indians began arriving in the St. Louis area, and by July 1 the prairie surrounding Portage des Sioux was filled with the lodges of more than two thousand Indians in close proximity to the rows of tents set up to house the American troops.[35]

On July 10 William Clark opened the proceedings with a stern speech reviewing the conduct of the various tribes during the war before stating that the British were now gone from the Illinois Country, signaling that the time had come to "bury the tomahawk and forget past transactions." Behind the scenes, tensions remained high. Clark noted the absence of the key Sac and Fox leaders Keokuk and Blackhawk. Instead, these hostile tribes had sent "a Considerable number of the most insignificant & contemptible persons." To the absent Ioways, Kickapoos, and Winnebagoes, Clark sent ultimatums giving them thirty days to either send representatives or face renewed war with the United States. Once negotiations began, however, the atmosphere at the council improved if only because neither side appeared to have much choice. The Indians could not sustain their war against the Americans without a steady supply of British arms and trade goods—an unlikely prospect since the announcement by the British commander at Prairie du Chien that "their Great Father, the King of England," was now at peace with the Americans.[36] The Americans, despite their rhetoric, lacked the manpower to sustain a war across a five-hundred-mile frontier even if they decided to ignore the provisions of the Treaty of Ghent.

On the eve of the Portage des Sioux council A. J. Dallas, the new secretary of war, wrote to Andrew Jackson, who was now, after a reorganization of the US military districts, responsible for the defense of Illinois and Missouri. Dallas informed Jackson of the upcoming council but expressed doubt as to the prospects for success, telling the general, "in the case of an obstinate persistence in hostilities, you will, as heretofore, manifest the competency of our arms to repel and punish aggression."

The letter, however, amounted to little more than bluster, as evidenced by another letter sent to Jackson just a few weeks later by the US commander at St. Louis, Daniel Bissell. Bissell, who had "no means under my controle of offering Protection but militia," told Jackson of "the great anxiety, which is felt for the defenceless frontier of Illinois & Missouri Territories." Nor was there money to pay anyone currently serving. In any event, not counting the troops posted to the treaty council, Bissell had "not more than 80 Regulars which belongs to the District."[37] All hopes, it seemed, rested with the peace negotiations.

As the summer progressed, the Portage des Sioux council yielded thirteen separate treaties attesting to a commitment to "perpetual peace and friendship" between the United States and the majority of the Illinois Country's Indians. In August several of the more recalcitrant tribes finally sent representatives, and delegations were still arriving even after the formal conclusion of the council in late September. On December 21 the Senate ratified the treaties, and five days later President Madison signed them into law. In St. Louis, negotiations continued with some of the late-arriving tribes, and on May 13, 1816, the Rock River Sacs signed the last of the peace treaties ending the war.[38]

The Postwar Landscape

The success achieved at the Portage des Sioux treaty council initially did little to mollify the citizens of the Illinois Country. The commissioners, particularly William Clark, were publicly criticized and referred to derisively as "Indian treaty-men."[39] In the short run the racial hatred of Indians, desire for retribution, and anger at the federal government's perceived lack of support combined to obscure the fact that Portage des Sioux spelled the end of meaningful opposition to white settlement in the Illinois Country. From that point the physical security of Americans in Illinois and Missouri ceased to be a source of general concern. What remained was the desire to remove all Indians from the territories, but that was now more a matter of economic opportunism and racial hatred than one of safety. The implications for the construction of American sovereignty in the Illinois Country were mixed. The attachments of the people were temporarily weakened by the federal government's actions during the war. But by taking such a large step toward guaranteeing the physical security of those same people, the United States created the conditions by which they could more effectively pursue their demands for secure property rights in land and slaves, and their vision of a society of free white male democracy, with métis and Indian peoples either physically removed, or politically, economically, and socially marginalized.

As the war wound down, the long, contentious work of the land commissions was finally completed and public land sales began in Illinois in 1814 and in Missouri in 1818. Just as important, peace along the Illinois Country frontier allowed teams of US surveyors to spread across the territories to draw the lines that transformed millions of acres of land into a marketable commodity. The result was an explosion of immigration into Illinois and Missouri by settlers enticed by glowing descriptions of the incredible fertility of the Mississippi and Missouri valleys.[40] As the pace of white settlement increased, however, old problems involving Indians, the British, and the fur trade returned.

Although the Portage des Sioux treaties marked the end of organized Indian aggression against white settlers in the Illinois Country, the ongoing struggle for control of the remaining fur trade left open the potential for renewed violence. Since the Treaty of Ghent contained no provision to prevent British traders from doing business in American territory, the anti-Americanism propagated by the British continued, as did their hold on the majority of the Indian trade. In early 1816 the American Indian agent at Prairie du Chien warned his superior that "In a few Months I shall see about 10,000 Indians. . . . I have not a Morcel to give them which depresses the influence of the United States with Indians—When a Number of them will proceed to *Fort Drummon* on *Lake Huron* to receive a Quantity of goods from the *British Government*." Governor Edwards voiced similar concerns a few months later after receiving reports from Green Bay (then still a part of Illinois) of Indians under the influence of British traders demonstrating "great discontent, and disaffection towards our govt." Edwards complained about "the imperfection of the system for the management of Indian affairs" that failed to give him any authority over the Indian agents in his territory and that prevented "good American Citizens" from displacing "a set of unprincipled British spies" as the suppliers of Indian trade goods. He concluded by again warning Washington "that nothing less, than an adequate display of Military power, or great liberality on the part of our Government, can command their obedience; or conciliate their friendship." Congress responded to this and other similar complaints from Illinois and Missouri by passing a law in 1816 banning all foreigners from the Indian trade within the borders of the United States. Although this law proved difficult to enforce and was circumvented by many traders who simply crossed the border and became American citizens in name if not by genuine attachment, it served to further strengthen US sovereignty in the Illinois Country by insuring that all goods received by Indians within US borders now came from either a federal trading factory or a trader who was at least in name—if not spirit—an American. Perhaps most important, the new law undermined the anti-Americanism being propagated in the territories by British traders whose superiors were now more concerned with maintaining market share than with political mischief.[41]

The peace treaties ending the war and the commencement of public land sales were giant steps in the transformation of the Illinois Country, but did not fully satisfy the demands of American settlers whose mistrust of the federal government still left in question their attachment to the Union. In the years between the end of the war and statehood, the citizens of Illinois and Missouri pushed hard for preemption rights to land and for the systematic removal of the Indians still remaining in the territories. Historians have generally cast these two issues as gaining national prominence in the 1820s and 1830s while ignoring their earlier importance in the Illinois Country. In fact, in 1813 Illinois squatters were the first to receive preemption rights from Congress. A similar law was passed for Missouri in 1814, but in both cases the laws applied only to lands already purchased from the Indians. The flood of settlers arriving in the two territories showed little patience for such distinctions. By the end of 1815 the number of settlers squatting on lands still owned by Indians began to pose another threat to the peace brought about by the Portage des Sioux treaties. President Madison responded by issuing a proclamation in December 1815 threatening all squatters—on federal or Indian lands—with forcible removal.[42]

Opposition to Madison's proclamation was swift and came from both settlers and territorial officials. Colonel Alexander McNair, charged with enforcing the proclamation in Missouri, pointed out that the 1814 preemption law protected squatters on federal lands who registered their claims, but that "the law has made no provision for any office to be opened, where the preemption claims are to be established and allowed." Clearly frustrated, he complained, "I cannot determine, who are, or who are not intruders on the Public lands in this territory." Notwithstanding the fairness of the proclamation, McNair was attuned to the political realities of the situation. "Much feeling has been excited on this subject, as those who may be found on public lands are the persons who have borne the storm of the Indian War . . . it is my opinion, justified by many, that five Militia men of this territory would not march against the intruders on public land." In Illinois the legislature petitioned Congress on behalf of veterans of the war who had purchased land "believing that their pay from the United States would enable them to redeem their mortgages." Now, because "the resources of the government under the pressure of the times could not meet the demands of their veterans," many were "destitute of the means of freeing their property from the incumbrances of those mortgages and contracts." Congress and the president responded to this firestorm by rushing back pay to the war veterans and by rescinding the proclamation.[43]

The mood of the people was barely improved by these measures, however. From the point of view of the majority of Americans in the Illinois Country, the federal government and its appointed officials had compiled a poor record since the Louisiana Purchase. Grievances included the slow pace of the land commissions, the lack of support during the war, the appeasement rather than defeat of the Indians, and now—worst of all—the threat by the territorial governors, backed by the president, to remove settlers rather than Indians from highly desirable lands. Had those lands been sold years earlier to the first wave of American settlers they might now be generating handsome profits either from commercial farming or through resale to the postwar immigrants. Instead, it seemed the only ones able to secure large tracts for speculation were the French, whose Spanish-era claims were widely perceived to be fraudulent even after many were confirmed by the land commissions. As for the French, they had complaints of their own, mostly having to do with the threat posed by the federal trading factories to what was left of the fur trade.[44]

Federal policies did seem to be at odds with the wishes of the people, though certainly not by design. The Madison administration's wish to live within its financial means compelled it to make peace instead of war with the Indians, which included continuing with the factory system as its only hope of limiting the flow of alcohol to the frontier. Few doubted the potential of alcohol to devastate the many Indian communities that during the postwar years were attempting to expand their agricultural and lead-mining pursuits.[45] With British influence waning and with higher-quality British goods again available at the federal factories, the fur trade became for a short time a stabilizing influence instead of a source of Indian-white conflict. The administration also saw that the aggressiveness of Jefferson and Harrison's land grab policy offered few benefits on the postwar frontier. Secretary of War William Crawford spelled out a revised land policy in 1816:

It is deemed by the President inexpedient to obtain cessions of land from the Indians which are not required for settlement. Experience has proved the extreme difficulty of preventing persons from making settlements upon the most remote points of every Cession, before the land if offered for Sale, by which the whole frontier is rendered utterly inadequate to its protection, against Indian warfare.[46]

The federal government was, in effect, offering the peoples of the Illinois Country a deal. To the Indians the offer included a slower, more orderly expansion of white settlements and reliable access to all desired trade goods except alcohol, in exchange for peace. To the Americans, physical security and property rights in cheap land were offered in exchange for attachment to the Union and acquiescence to its laws and policies, which included waiting for land to be purchased and surveyed ahead of settlement. In short, the switch from furs to farms would continue, but hopefully at a slower pace.

The postwar surge of immigration into the Illinois Country and the profits available in a fur trade operating under new rules precluded the acceptance of the administration's implicit deal. In Missouri Cherokee bands chased out of their old homes in the Southwest Territory were arriving in large numbers and clashing with the Osage and white settlers on several fronts. Groups of Delawares and Shawnees that had arrived in the 1790s looked to move farther west as they again tried to stay out of the path of white settlement. They too looked to Osage lands and expected territorial officials to cooperate in their resettlement in exchange for the support they had provided the United States in the late war. In Illinois, Sacs and Foxes who began crossing the Mississippi River for their winter hunts ran afoul of Ioways and Sioux bands uninterested in the problems facing their eastern neighbors.[47] Meanwhile, American settlers in large numbers poured into both territories and invariably ran afoul of the new federal land policies. Governor Clark tried to explain to his superiors that it was almost "impossible to Control the Traders and Bands of Indians . . . and the extention of the Settlements of White emigrants above the boundary line." Clark enclosed a petition from a group of settlers angered by an order to remove themselves even after taking "every means to obtain correct information relative to the nature of Indian claims to this country," and after being told "that we were a considerable distance within the boundaries of the United States." Another group petitioned Congress, asking for land after suffering "innumerable hardships and a loss of property to a vast amount," while they, "at the request and advice of Governor Howard erect[ed] forts along an extensive frontier . . . and did occupy said forts & furnish the same with arms and ammunition at their own expence . . . and without any pay or reward from government performed garrison duty." These petitioners felt "a confidence that the general government, altho' they could not afford prompt and complete protection to our frontier Inhabitants will remunerate them in part for the services they have rendered and the losses they have sustained."[48] From this perspective Madison's desire for the orderly transfer of lands within the Illinois Country represented nothing less than a practical impossibility for territorial officials and gross injustice for settlers who had risked their lives to secure for the United States lands that they were now told were not ready to be settled.

New developments in the fur trade also undermined the Madison administration's policies. Following the banning of British traders and the resupply of the American factories, a brief period of calm ensued before John Jacob Astor's American Fur Company began its ultimately successful drive to replace British domination of the trade with its own. Astor and his chief lieutenant Ramsay Crooks began using their political connections and intimate knowledge of the trade and its practitioners to circumvent the laws against foreign traders and against the sale of alcohol, while undercutting the federal factories and buying up most of their private competitors. One US Indian agent referred to Astor and his company as "deeply self-interested mercenary enemies" and said, "I wish to God the President knew this man Astor as well as he is known here." In fact Astor knew James Monroe, the new president, very well and had even lent money to both Monroe and to the Speaker of the US House of Representatives Henry Clay. Astor and Crooks also used their political connections to renew the drive to eliminate the federal trading factories, an effort that would finally reach fruition with the abolishment of the factory system in 1822. In the meantime the flow of alcohol and the anti-American sentiment of British traders, now working with politically secured licenses, served again to "alienate the Indians from the American government & people."[49] The task of soothing the roiling waters of the Illinois Country now fell to the incoming Monroe administration.

The federal government's growing ability to protect American settlers from physical attack was the most important legacy of the War of 1812. It had been a long time coming. The threat posed by Indians armed by British officials and fur traders made the Illinois Country a dangerous place for white settlers until 1815. Diplomatic problems between the United States and Great Britain in the run-up to the war had provided an opening for British fur traders and agents with ties to Indian communities to persuade the British government to reconstruct their alliance with Indians throughout the West. This alliance had long been recommended by British officials and businessmen in North America, but did not gain traction within England until the 1807 *Chesapeake* incident and the subsequent series of trade sanctions adopted by the United States. Federal trading factories suddenly faced shortages of goods that had been mostly of British origin, as did American officials responsible for supplying goods owed to Indians as annuities according to the terms of several treaties. Indian consumers thus had more than land grabs to provoke their anger and were willing to turn again to the British for a military alliance. In this light, the fur trade can be seen as not only of declining economic value to whites living in the Illinois Country, but as the source of Indian hostility and a dangerous Indian-British alliance.

During the war the federal government proved unable or unwilling to provide white settlers in the Illinois Country with the men and materials needed to defeat the enemy alliance. Territorial officials, however, made the most of their available resources and prevented any major attacks on white settlements. The anger felt by many citizens at the lack of federal support was exacerbated when federal and territorial officials eventually adopted a strategy of trade diplomacy as a substitute for an effective offensive campaign. The success achieved by Andrew Jackson in the Southwest served to further anger Americans in Illinois and Missouri, who longed to see a similar campaign conducted against the Indians of the Illinois Country.

In 1815 a series of treaties between the United States and dozens of Indian tribes and bands ended the War of 1812 in Illinois and Missouri. The success of the diplomatic strategy in ending widespread violence between Indians and white settlers did not, however, bring credit to the officials responsible. Men such as William Clark were derisively called Indian treaty-men and suffered politically for their actions during and after the war. The federal government had, however, begun to make the Illinois Country safe for American settlement, and the subsequent flood of immigrants was testimony to the fact that one of the chief impediments to economic change and US sovereignty had been removed.

The long-delayed sale of public lands and laws providing preemption rights for some squatters also served to advance these dual processes during this period, although citizens also proved less than appreciative of federal efforts on this front. Preemption laws in Illinois in 1813 and Missouri in 1814 helped assuage settlers angered by the long delay in public land sales that resulted from the work of the land claims commissions and the daunting task of surveying the vast public domain. Public sales finally began in Illinois and Missouri, and thousands of immigrants responded to the opportunity to acquire title to the fertile lands in the valleys of the Mississippi, Missouri, Ohio, Illinois, and Wabash Rivers. But federal efforts to keep squatters off Indian lands, and out of the more remote public lands, resulted in a backlash. Citizens already angry at the perceived lack of federal support during the war were now told that they would either have to settle in approved areas or wait a while longer to acquire land. Most chose to ignore the law and settled where they pleased.

The attachments of the people living in the Illinois Country were still not firmly with the United States, but the economic transformation of the region was in full swing. During the war both Indians and whites found themselves, for different reasons, fighting more for themselves—for their immediate family and neighbors—than for a nation, a tribe, or a trusted ally. While to some extent this is true of any conflict, it was particularly so in the Wars of 1812. For Indians the fragmentation of their communities and the history of repeated betrayals by the British accounted for the phenomenon. For whites, the lack of federal support and sense of geographic isolation were the causes. For Indians, attachment would never come. Friendly tribes and bands saw their American allies forsake them over time as racial hatred and the pace of white expansion precluded Indian assimilation or neighborly coexistence. For white settlers, however, as their demands for physical security, property rights, and racial exclusivity came closer to being met by the federal government, the sense of attachment, of loyalty to the Union, would grow. In the meantime more and more of the fertile lands of Illinois and Missouri were being brought under cultivation while cows, pigs, chickens, and horses replaced the once plentiful fur-bearing animals in a landscape that also featured fewer and fewer Native Americans

4 / Statehood for Illinois and Missouri

On November 23, 1818, an obscure, one-term congressman from New York, James Tallmadge, rose to speak against a resolution to grant statehood to one of the western territories. He had no desire "to invade the rights of the slaveholding states, or to assail their prerogatives," but believed that "the principle of slavery, if not adopted in the constitution, was at least not sufficiently prohibited." The constitution in question was Illinois', and Tallmadge's objection was swept aside—though not until after a short, but vigorous debate—as the House passed the statehood resolution by a vote of 117 to 34. On December 3 President Monroe signed the bill and Illinois became a state. The entire process took ten days.[1] Less than three months later Tallmadge more famously introduced an amendment to a bill to enable the Territory of Missouri to write a constitution in preparation for statehood. The amendment asked "that the further introduction of slavery or involuntary servitude be prohibited ... and that all children of slaves, born within the said state, after the admission thereof into the Union, shall be free at the age of twenty-five years." This time Tallmadge found a good deal of congressional support for his amendment, and the resulting national controversy lasted for over two years, postponing Missouri's statehood until the summer of 1821.[2] The contrast between the events surrounding statehood for Missouri and Illinois could not have been greater.

This chapter will examine the statehood processes for Illinois and Missouri from the perspective of the two territories while not losing sight of the larger national context within which they took place. In Illinois the Northwest Ordinance's provision banning slavery in the territories forced the future state's leaders to write a constitution that could be accepted both by Congress and by the people of Illinois, many of whom were slaveholders. Their ability to do so involved banning slavery while leaving the de facto system of indentures intact and the door open for a later move to legalize slavery. In Missouri, congressional attempts to restrict slavery further inflamed a territory already fed up with the "coddling" of Indians, slow public land sales, unresolved land claims, poor mail service, and a residue of bitterness over the perceived lack of federal support during the War of 1812. If Congress was looking for a fight over the issue of slavery in Missouri, Missourians were ready to give it one.[3]

The contrasting statehood processes for the two territories formed from the Illinois Country demonstrate both the ongoing transformation of the region's economy and the continuing difficulties experienced by the United States in constructing effective sovereignty. The federal government by the late 1810s had largely met the territory's demands for physical security and property rights but had yet to guarantee the racial dominance desired by the white settlers pouring into the two territories. Aside from the issue of slavery, support in both territories for Indian removal flew in the face of federal policies to gradually push eastern Indians across the Mississippi River if they could not be induced to assimilate. Few whites in Illinois or Missouri wished to live among Indians—assimilated or not—and fewer still had any intention of welcoming Indians from eastern states to settle on lands finally being surveyed and sold as the future homesteads of generations of white settlers to come. As the sale of public lands accelerated and the citizens of both territories looked ahead to statehood, the overwhelming majority saw a future built around farming—not the fur trade.

Land and Trade on the Eve of Statehood

In the years immediately following the War of 1812, the federal government's success in providing for the physical security and property rights of its citizens in Illinois and Missouri failed to stop the flow of complaints to Washington by citizens and by the territories' legislatures and appointed officials. Even as the desire for racial domination emerged as the main source of conflict between the settlers and the federal government, property rights issues involving land and trade lingered. From one perspective, the federal government's very success generated dissatisfaction. Settlers forced to abandon homesteads or gather in makeshift forts for protection during the War of 1812 showed little appreciation for their newfound safety in calling for federal efforts to exact revenge on hostile Indians. When those calls were not answered, settlers began lobbying for the extinguishing of Indian titles to all lands within the territories. Here antipathy toward Indians mixed with the ravenous land hunger of both yeoman farmers seeking homesteads and speculators seeking lands for resale. The passage of preemption laws and the commencement of public land sales only seemed to stimulate the demand for more land on easier terms and without regard for Indian ownership—even if the Indians whose lands were sought were allies of the United States. A similar dynamic was at work in regard to the fur trade. The successful efforts by American diplomats and Congress to prevent British traders from continuing to operate on US soil resulted not in increased profits for Illinois Country traders but in the rapid growth of John Jacob Astor's American Fur Company. This development combined with the opening of new federal trading factories to provide another source of resentment for the citizens of Illinois and Missouri.

The rush of settlers into Illinois and Missouri after the War of 1812 created a land boom that quickly spelled trouble for Indians still residing in the two territories. In early 1817 Missouri's assembly lobbied Washington on behalf of settlers ordered to vacate Quapaw lands. The resolution questioned the Quapaws' claim to the land and called for an investigation. The assembly sent a similar resolution concerning lands claimed by the Shawnees and Delawares of the Cape Girardeau area. In both cases the goal was for steps to "be taken to obtain the aforesaid title from those indians by an exchange of other lands in some more remote part of the Territory which is better suited to indian pursuits." In Illinois it was the territory's congressional delegate and its governor who were after land occupied by the Kickapoos but owned by the Illinois, a tribe that was already nearly decimated.[4]

The desire to displace Indians to make way for incoming settlers was hardly new, but in the Illinois Country the process ran up against the federal government's wish to relocate eastern tribes in both Illinois and Missouri. Secretary of War John Calhoun wrote Governor Clark with instructions regarding the "contested" lands belonging to the Cape Girardeau Shawnees and Delawares, who were longtime allies of the United States. "You will, as far as practicable, and consistent with justice, make the arrangement favorable to the Cherokees; as the President is anxious to hold out every inducement to the Cherokees, and the other Southern nations of Indians, to emigrate to the West of the Mississippi."[5]

Illinois faced similar pressure from federal officials to accommodate eastern tribes who "wish[ed] to be farther removed from the whites." To further complicate matters, Governor Edwards of Illinois hoped to acquire land from Indians in his territory by swapping it for land in Missouri, where "In the Osage purchase the Govt have enough land to spare for that purpose that would suit the Indians very well, and it is good for little else."[6]

The biggest losers in the postwar land grabs were the Osage, who were now beset by both their Indian enemies led by the Cherokees, and by their ostensible friend, the US government. The old balance of power had shifted and the Osage were now forced to move west. The more politically astute Cherokees acquired much of the Osage land to the south in what is now Arkansas while the Americans got the lands to the north, in Missouri. For the Americans, however, the ultimate disposition of those lands was not settled. Would they be occupied by eastern Indians relocating in the West or by white settlers?[7]

The Land Office officials responsible for administering public sales found themselves in the middle of that question. Public land sales finally began in Missouri in the fall of 1818, and sales were brisk but beset by a number of problems. Preemption laws had been passed for Illinois and Missouri in 1813 and 1814 respectively, but did not cover most of the lands under dispute in the late 1810s. Settlers needed an expansion of preemption rights if they hoped to gain title to those lands. In the meantime there were still many Spanish-era land claims that had been approved but awaited new titles or had been rejected but were under appeal, and lands where the date when the United States had gained title from the Indians was still under dispute. In the latter case the precise date of acquisition could mean the difference between a legal claim to preemption rights or characterization as a trespasser to be evicted.[8]

By early 1819 the Missouri assembly was actively lobbying Congress to address these issues. One memorial explained that "this uncertainty has a most injurious operation on the value and cultivation of the lands and on the public revenue derived from the sale of them." Another questioned the competence and integrity of the federal and territorial officials involved in a process "*not only arbitrary and unauthorised by law, but most unjust, cruel, and oppressive,* towards a people who have fought and bled for the Soil they cultivate." They hoped Congress would not allow "a numerous and meritorious portion of these constituents to be frustrated by the ignorance or neglect of *Territorial Authorities*, nor the illegal, arbitrary, and officious intermeddling of *Speculative land jobbing*

Executive officers." The petitioners had a point, as most of the territorial officials in both Missouri and Illinois were, in fact, involved in land speculation, including the governors, Clark and Edwards, who went as far as to try to learn in advance the areas where government surveyors were to be deployed.[9]

Congress and the Monroe administration responded to demands coming from the Illinois Country by liberalizing the preemption laws and taking another look at some previously rejected land claims. But they also kept pressure on territorial officials to keep settlers off some of the newly acquired Osage and Quapaw lands in Missouri in order to settle eastern Indians on them. These steps served to mollify Illinois' settlers but not those in Missouri, who carried their grievances against the federal government into the statehood process itself.[10]

Missouri settlers were also more at odds with the federal government than were their Illinois neighbors over the disposition of the fur trade in the late 1810s. In Illinois white settlements were mostly found in the southern portion of the territory while the areas where fur-bearing animals were still found in numbers were far to the north. In Missouri, however, St. Louis traders carried on trade far up the Mississippi and Missouri Rivers and were therefore far more agitated by government policies that seemed to wink at the continued presence of foreign traders while trying to steer most of the local fur trade to government trading factories.

Although greatly diminished in number, British traders continued to operate on American soil during this period. To be more precise, British traders assisted by French and métis boatmen and interpreters continued to operate, often with licenses obtained at Mackinac Island from American officials. Illinois Country officials wrote regularly to their superiors in Washington, citing the increase in Indian hostility to Americans wherever British traders were found to be operating. Governor Edwards pointed out that the British now "residing within our limits and Claiming the protection of our laws" were "the most infamous & wicked scoundrels" and had "actually engaged in the late war against us." Under their direction Indians were "stealing horses, robbing and abusing the Public Surveyors." Worst of all, the British were using whiskey to gain a competitive advantage over the American traders. Even more problematic was the fact that most of the British still operating on American soil now worked for John Jacob Astor's American Fur Company.[11]

Following the War of 1812, Astor's political connections and capital base combined to make the American Fur Company the dominant force in the domestic fur trade, as by 1817 the firm's shipments constituted the largest single flow of goods to the West. Astor's success underscores the challenge posed by the fur trade to American policy makers. Presidents Madison and Monroe both wanted to wean Indians from British influence without killing the fur trade. But they also wanted to push the Indians to become more agricultural. The law passed by Congress in 1816 banning foreign traders from operating in the United States served as a signal to the large Canadian firms that their days were numbered. Astor responded by buying out his Canadian partners in the Southwest Company and focusing his efforts on the domestic American Fur Company. But American officials knew that foreign traders and boatmen were needed to keep the fur trade functioning, so they allowed licenses to be issued to certain traders as exceptions to the law. As noted earlier, Indian agents in the West complained that most of those licenses were given to Astor's employees, many known to be hostile to American interests. Their protests led to a reversal of policy in 1817 by President Monroe, who now banned all foreign traders. But within months Monroe again reversed himself and decided to permit the licensing of boatmen and interpreters—but not traders. This policy was easily circumvented by the use of false job descriptions for those deemed necessary to Astor's interests. The result was that many perceived the American Fur Company to be a front for British interests.[12]

Astor was actually quite happy to be rid of his British partners and now set his sights on the other part of American fur trade policy: the US government trading factories. On this issue Illinois Country fur traders, merchants, and Indians joined Astor in opposing the federal government's policy. In St. Louis, future senator Thomas Hart Benton's *St. Louis Enquirer* spoke for local interests, citing the inferiority of government goods, the alienation of Indians forced to travel to the factories to trade, and the laziness and corruption of the government traders. An officer at Fort Armstrong on the Mississippi River echoed Benton's complaints and also summed up the Indians' case against the factories:

> the Indians, are by no means satisfied with the institution of Factories, nor can they be made to understand the object for which they were established, as it with them a secured, general, opinion, That everything emanating from a government, must be in the Shape of presents, otherwise the object is to defraud; an impression most industriously instilled into their credulous minds by the British, until it has become indelible—nor do I believe they would ever

visit a Factory—were they not taught to believe, that it is the only mode by which they can evince an attachment to the American government.

Monroe administration officials defended the factories, as had their predecessors since the 1790s. Superintendent of Indian Trade Thomas McKenney wrote to his superior, Secretary of War John Calhoun, that the Fort Armstrong officer's characterization was "totally incorrect," and that in regard to the factories, the Indians, in fact, "beg[ged] for them, and have expressed themselves highly gratified from North to South." Some Indians did support the factories because they did not sell liquor, but they were in the minority.[13]

Thomas McKenney, along with other officials who took positions opposed to Astor and his company, found themselves on the losing side. Calhoun signaled his intentions by firing the US agent at Mackinac, who had once characterized Astor as a "mercenary enemy," and instructing Missouri's governor William Clark that he wanted American Fur Company employees to be shown "proper respect . . . whilst in the lawful prosecution of their business." Thomas McKenney tried to salvage the factory system by allowing government traders to compete in the field with private traders, but realized Astor was likely to get his way. Writing to one of his agents in 1821, McKenney explained that while only a handful in Congress opposed the factory system, they could influence many despite the hypocrisy of their position. "If the design to civilize the Indians be sincere, an abandonment of them to the artifice of private traders can never be received as evidence of that necessity." A year later Astor and his antifactory allies finally got their way as Congress abolished the government trade factories. In the words of a memorial to Congress by the Missouri Baptist convention, this left the fur trade in the hands of those who would "defraud the Indians of their property, corrupt their morals, debauch their manners," and "prejudice their minds against our government, our citizens, and our manners."[14]

The net effect of these developments in the fur trade was to provide Missouri citizens with another grievance against the federal government. With the exception of a few merchants who became involved with John Jacob Astor, most local fur traders, merchants, boatmen, and interpreters suffered a loss in business following the War of 1812. Although a decline in fur-bearing animals in the Illinois Country had much to do with this, there was still resentment against federal policies that included (until 1822) the operation of government trading factories and the licensing of foreign traders in the employ of the voracious American Fur Company.

The disposition of land and the decline of the fur trade thus perpetuated the climate of resentment and mistrust between settlers in Missouri and the federal government that had begun during the War of 1812. This was in contrast to the situation in Illinois, where settlers had also been unhappy with the performance of the federal government during the war, but where there were fewer Indians in the path of white settlement and less dependence on the fur trade. These differences should not be exaggerated, but rather understood as providing the context within which the leaders of the two territories began their respective movements for statehood in 1817. Although the two movements started almost concurrently, Illinois achieved statehood sooner than Missouri, and so its statehood process will be examined ahead of Missouri's.

Illinois Statehood

An item in the September 2, 1818, edition of the *Illinois Intelligencer* described the recent signing of the state's constitution in Kaskaskia, stating, "On this important occasion, the citizens of the town assembled to fire a federal salute to perpetuate the remembrance of the day when our constitution was signed and sealed."[15] A few months later Illinois was formally admitted to the Union. Historians have generally described the process leading to Illinois statehood as routine and not contentious. As the third state carved from the Northwest Territory, Illinois followed a path already marked by Ohio and Indiana. This characterization is, however, misleading. Unlike its neighbors, Illinois did not enter the Union with an unambiguous ban on slavery. The constitution celebrated in 1818 failed to eliminate either the de jure slavery remaining from the era of French sovereignty, or the de facto slavery created later by a series of indenture laws. Illinois lawmakers had instead crafted a compromise between acceptance and defiance of the Northwest Ordinance's antislavery provision. The compromise was not intended to be permanent, however. Men on both sides of the issue knew a showdown could not be long avoided.

Slavery in Illinois was first contained and later eliminated in the face of legal and demographic obstacles that the rest of the Northwest Territory did not have to contend with. The major differences were the preexistence of slavery in Illinois, and the slow arrival of settlers from nonslaveholding areas. Immediately following passage of the Ordinance, slaveholders and land speculators began efforts to either overturn or circumvent the Ordinance's antislavery provision. Congress, meanwhile, did its best to avoid the issue. While it never responded favorably to efforts to amend or overturn Article VI of the Ordinance—the article banning slavery—Congress provided no enforcement mechanisms for the slavery ban and turned a blind eye to the territorial legislation that created an elaborate indenture system. This crucial issue was, therefore, ultimately decided in Illinois.

The Northwest Ordinance of 1787, specifically Article VI, played a decisive role in that decision. Serving as a filter on immigration, the Ordinance over the years helped shape the mix of voters who in 1824 defeated a proslavery initiative to amend the state constitution. Slaveholders were discouraged from settling in Illinois, while those opposed to slavery were encouraged, confident that the institution would eventually be eliminated. That the constitution of 1818 would have required amending to permit full-fledged slavery is testimony to the influence of the Ordinance on the delegates who drafted it. Not willing to risk congressional disapproval, the delegates compromised, and in so doing, fatally weakened slavery in Illinois.

During the War of 1812, the Illinois legislature passed two acts concerning blacks in the territory. The first, in 1813, said "that it shall not be lawful for any free Negro or Mulatto to migrate in this territory" and that if apprehended he or she would have "fifteen days to depart from the territory" or be subject "to be whipped on his or her bare back, not exceeding thirty nine stripes nor less than twenty-five stripes." The act also required free blacks already living in Illinois to register with the county clerk, providing proof of their freedom.[16] A bill passed the following year allowed slaves to be brought into the territory and hired out for up to a year "provided however, that in all such cases such slave or slaves shall be examined privately, separately & apart from his or her owner. . . . as to his or her voluntary consent." Slavery, in whatever form possible, was clearly the way Illinois hoped to address the "want of labourers" that necessitated the latter act.[17]

Illinois benefited from the tremendous westward migration that accompanied the end of the war. The preemption law of 1813 and the long-delayed sale of public domain lands encouraged settlement throughout the southern part of the territory. Many of the new settlers were southern yeomen who saw no place for themselves in the expanding southern plantation economy. Most objected to living in proximity to either free or enslaved blacks (or to Indians), whose presence seemed to devalue their yeoman values and culture. Although opposed to racial equality, many came to Illinois to escape slave society.[18]

On the other hand, most of Illinois' leaders during the territorial stage favored slavery. Ninian Edwards, Jesse Thomas, Shadrach Bond, and Pierre Menard were all slaveholders who took full advantage of the indenture system. Despite full knowledge of the laws, Edwards, for instance, registered indentures for periods of up to forty-five years. Throughout the territory blacks were bought and sold with no attempt at concealment. The appearance of blacks in wills indicates that some viewed indenture as no different from ownership. Both Missouri and Illinois newspapers contained notices for runaways, for blacks "wanted" and blacks "for sale."[19]

This was a period of accommodation between pro- and antislavery proponents. French slaveholders and Americans holding indentures coexisted with the stream of largely antislavery settlers pouring in from the southern uplands. Migration from northern states was still light, and the territory's leaders were primarily concerned with removing the remaining Indians and bringing new lands to market. Land speculation was as common as slaveholding for most of Illinois' elites. Besides the early speculators like John Edgar and William Morrison, leaders including Ninian Edwards, Jesse Thomas, and Pierre Menard purchased thousands of acres in the years just prior to statehood.[20] They were ambitious men who with few exceptions supported black servitude, yet realized the Northwest Ordinance could not be ignored during the territorial stage. In growing yet still silent opposition were not only poor whites who had fled southern slave society, but also a growing number of more substantial men who saw the end of slavery, in all forms, as the key to Illinois' future. The two sides sparred during the statehood movement of 1817–1818 before meeting in a final showdown in the convention battle of 1822–1824.

Statehood came sooner than expected for Illinois, due largely to the ambitions of a young lawyer, Daniel Cook. Born in Kentucky in 1794, Cook came to Illinois in 1815 after studying law with John Pope, a former US senator from Kentucky, who was a distant relative. In 1816 Governor Edwards appointed him auditor of public accounts. Later that year he and a friend purchased the territory's only newspaper, the *Illinois Herald*, changing its name to the *Western Intelligencer*. In 1817 the ambitious Cook decided to pursue a career in Washington, and upon his arrival secured a job delivering state papers to John Quincy Adams, who was serving as the US ambassador to Britain. The papers instructed

Adams to return home to become the secretary of state in the Monroe administration. Sailing together from London, Cook and Adams became friends, and back in Washington Cook asked Adams to help him find a job. When Adams could only offer him a clerkship, Cook wrote to Ninian Edwards that "it would not satisfy my ambition to be buried in an office.... where the world, perhaps, would never hear of such a being.... I am advised by my own judgment, as well as by his [Adams's], to return to the West, and remain there until an opportunity presents itself for my advancement." Frail and sickly since childhood, Cook was anxious to advance his career as quickly as possible (he died at 33).[21]

Before leaving Washington, Cook published two letters to President Monroe in the *National Register*, urging Monroe to develop a plan for the gradual abolition of all slavery in the United States. In the letters he raised several arguments that he repeated upon his return to Illinois. Slaves were potential insurrectionists, whose desire for freedom could easily "induce them to rally around a foreign standard and literally become vipers in the bowels of our body politic." In states without slavery "you find their political horizon calm and serene," but in "states where slavery breathes the same air with freedom, you find a clouded horizon and a troubled political atmosphere." After explaining that slaveholders were prone to idleness and that guilt over slavery would eventually spread to all Americans, Cook concluded that Monroe must promote a "gradual abolition, that, no very serious injury need to be done to the fortune of any individual." He hoped that through Monroe's influence, "the general government will take some measures preparatory to the completion of this work, and that individuals and the state governments will ultimately complete it."[22] Cook then returned to Illinois to hopefully create one of the state governments that might help end slavery in the United States, and in the process advance his own career.

But before Illinois could do anything for the nation, first it had to become a state. Most residents in 1817 assumed statehood was still a few years away since Illinois' population was known to be far short of the 60,000 required by the Northwest Ordinance. Cook knew, however, that Ohio had been admitted with less, and he began his statehood push with an editorial in the November 27 *Intelligencer*. Beginning with the audacious claim that "Our number may be safely estimated at between 40 and 45 thousand inhabitants," he argued that the territory had labored for too long under "the arm of an omnipotent executive," and the people were ready for democracy. For the sake of Illinois' future, Cook believed the question of slavery had to be decided. "At present it is doubtful whether slavery will be tolerated when a state government is formed. And many on both sides of the question are remaining in the anxiety of suspense, to know how it will be settled. It is therefore desirable to settle the question at as early a period as possible, for the purpose of giving relief to those who are wanting to emigrate to the territory."[23] Cook was both asserting the right of a state to choose its slavery policy after admission, and acknowledging that the ambiguity of the Northwest Ordinance was preventing some potential settlers from deciding to come to Illinois. Although Article VI had clearly discouraged slaveholders from coming to Illinois during its territorial stage, Cook saw that, as statehood approached, and with it a chance for Illinois to decide for itself whether or not it wanted slavery, settlers on both sides of the issue were hesitating.

Events began to move quickly. In early December the Illinois legislature convened and Governor Edwards endorsed the push for statehood, calling for a census to be presented at the following year's session. The legislature ignored that instruction and quickly drafted a memorial to Congress asking for statehood. In an attempt to signal to Congress the territory's willingness to comply with the spirit of Article VI, the legislature also passed a bill to repeal indenture on the grounds that the laws creating it had been, essentially, illegal. This was too much for Edwards, who considered the repeal bill a personal affront. After all, he had been responsible for choosing Illinois' territorial laws. Despite assurances that he too opposed slavery, Edwards vetoed the measure and prorogued the session. In little more than a month, however, Cook had managed to ignite a statehood movement and to position himself as the territory's leading antislavery figure. His familial relationship with congressional delegate Nathaniel Pope and his close friendship with Governor Edwards (he later married Edwards's daughter) had likely played a role in the legislature's cooperation in Cook's attempt to repeal indenture. But Edwards's veto signaled that the issue was still highly contentious. The battle lines over slavery and statehood were drawn.[24]

In the months that followed, Illinoisians debated the future of slavery in the pages of the *Intelligencer*. Cook agreed with the writer who argued that "were slavery admitted, many emigrants, who now pass through our territory, on their way to Boon's Lick, and other parts of the Missouri territory, followed by a long concourse of slaves, might settle in Illinois." But he argued that at some future date the state would be filled with people from one part of the country or another, and when it was, he wondered whether residents wished to have their "midnight hours . . . disturbed with the thoughts of house breaking, house burning, and thefts of every kind, committed by his own, or the refugee slaves of others."[25] Another writer feared that proslavery interests were in the majority and that statehood should be postponed because although at present "The wealthy southern planter, will not part with the plantation Gods ... for the blessings of the western woods, while we are a territory, and doubtful as to the future toleration of slavery," a convention now might result in legalized slavery. Why not wait, when "a few years patience, in our present state, will certainly preponderate the scale in favor of humanity and freedom."[26] In the days just prior to the start of the convention, a third position emerged and provided a path to compromise. It was based on the idea that the act of statehood would free Illinois from the constraints of the Northwest Ordinance. A letter in the *Intelligencer* stated:

> That the Ordinance of Congress and the cession of Virginia could only govern us whilst a territory, is self-evident. ... The principle was never doubted in forming the constitutions for the states of Ohio and Indiana, that they might either tolerate or prohibit slavery; and that if the matter were passed over in silence, slaves might then be imported with impunity; for the ordinance for the government of the north western territory would no longer be binding, but merely a dead letter, superceded by the constitution.[27]

This idea could cut both ways. On the one hand it meant, "the people of Illinois themselves are to have the credit for prohibiting the demoniacal practice of slave holding." On the other, proslavery advocates could claim that even if the convention were to ban slavery in the future state, "this obnoxious feature, *in our bill of rights*, may be expunged by our next delegate. ... I am one of those *unbelieving few*, who do not think that all, now, depends on the convention."[28] Here was the key to the slavery debate prior to the convention. Both sides came to the realization that not only could they never reach an agreement before the August convention, but that to do so might be dangerous. Both sides also believed that as a territory they operated under the provisions of the Northwest Ordinance, but at the moment of statehood would be free to resume the contest. A truce was the answer. Edwards, Menard, Cook, and others were already busy buying land in anticipation of statehood. No purpose would be served by jeopardizing the possibility of statehood and the inevitable rise in land prices that would follow. Why not write a constitution that would finesse the issue, leaving the present system largely intact, but not going so far as to antagonize Congress? Better to be safe than sorry. Once admitted to the Union, Illinois' leaders would be free to do as they wished.

The document that emerged from the convention contained the expected prohibition against the introduction of slavery or involuntary servitude in Illinois. However, French-owned slaves were protected, as they had been in the Northwest Ordinance, and existing indenture contracts were to be honored. Male offspring of indentures would be freed when they reached the age of twenty-one and females at eighteen. New indentures were still permitted, but they were limited to one year in duration. Finally, until 1825 slaves could still be imported to work at the Shawneetown saline, where it was thought to be impossible to attract free labor.[29]

When Illinois' constitution reached Washington, concerns over congressional resistance to the sanctioning of any form of servitude proved to be well founded. On November 23, Representative James Tallmadge of New York, in a foreshadowing of the Missouri crisis three months later, rose in opposition to Illinois' admission. Citing Article VI of the Northwest Ordinance, Tallmadge stated that "If the constitution was found to comport with that provision, it ought to be received by Congress; if not, it ought to be rejected." Tallmadge believed it did not "comport." He argued that "The sixth article of the constitution of the new State of Illinois, in each of its three sections contravened this stipulation, either in the letter or the spirit." He compared Illinois' constitution to Indiana's to show "how carefully and scrupulously it [Indiana] had guarded against slavery in any shape, and in the strongest terms reprobated it; lest at some future day amendments to the constitution should admit its introduction, a clause of that constitution forbade any amendment of the sort to be made." In opposition to Tallmadge, Representative Poindexter of Mississippi argued, "it would be impracticable, after admitting the independence of a State, to prevent it from framing or shaping its constitution as it thought proper." Tallmadge answered that he "conceived Congress to be bound by a tie not to be broken" as to the Ordinance's provision "not to permit slavery, in any of the States formed from the Northwest Territory." He also wondered whether Congress would allow a state "to call a convention to-morrow and change its form of government to a monarchy?" William Henry Harrison, representing Ohio, also disagreed with Tallmadge. Dismissing the monarchy question, he addressed the idea of the Northwest Ordinance as a compact between the territories and Congress, saying, "he had always considered it a dead letter." He further claimed that somewhere in the Federalist Papers was a statement by Alexander Hamilton expressing the same opinion. After a few more remarks that were not recorded, the resolution was voted on and passed by a margin of 117–34.[30]

In light of the Missouri crisis that immediately followed, this debate seems rather remarkable. In one afternoon, three positions at the core of the future sectional crisis were articulated. First Tallmadge objected to Illinois' constitution because the Northwest Ordinance compelled Congress to keep slavery out of the territories. Poindexter next countered that a state could write its constitution as it saw fit. Finally, Harrison, a former territorial governor and future president, said the Ordinance was constitutionally irrelevant. Historian Peter Onuf has argued that although the Confederation intended the Ordinance to have a constitutional effect, the terms "constitution," "compact," "charter," "covenant," and "treaty" were to some degree used interchangeably during the Revolutionary era. The Ordinance embodied that ambiguity and "was rapidly 'deconstitutionalized' in the decades before the Civil War."[31] So Harrison's dismissal of the Ordinance as a constitutional document proved prescient. Thus, in the sectional crisis that followed, Tallmadge's assertion of congressional authority—which in Missouri's case had nothing to do with the Northwest Ordinance—was pitted against Poindexter's state's rights argument.

Missouri Statehood

In the fall of 1820 Joseph Charless, whose *Missouri Gazette* had been the first newspaper published in the territory, was preparing to retire. In a farewell letter to his readers he sought to clarify his position in the ongoing Missouri statehood struggle:

> It has been said that the *Gazette* advocated the restriction of Missouri by Congress. The base fabricator of this charge is defied to prove it. Examine the files and they will be found to pursue one uniform course. Open to all communications, the editor has never hesitated to state his opposition to the interference by Congress, but still felt it desirous that some limitation should be put *by the People*, to the importation of slaves.[32]

Charless was, in fact, one of the few prominent restrictionists in Missouri during the long battle for the territory's admission to the Union. His real concern was the possible misconception among his fellow citizens that he might favor the restriction of slavery in Missouri by Congress—an unforgivable sin in 1820—rather than by the people at some future date.

In this distinction lies a significant dimension of Missouri's statehood process. The territory's citizens, already at odds with the federal government over land and trade issues, reacted strongly to congressional attempts to restrict slavery in the future state, but did so as much from principle as from their proslavery inclinations. Missouri's objections to congressional restriction took three lines: that Congress had no power to impose any conditions on admission except that a state's government be republican in character; that Congress was a body of delegated powers and did not possess the power to regulate slavery in a state; and that the 1803 treaty of cession guaranteed the protection of property, which included slaves.[33] These objections combined with the simmering antifederal sentiment in the territory to produce the strong local reaction to the congressional debate noted by historians of the Missouri Compromises, particularly as they relate to the larger stories of the construction of sovereignty in the Illinois Country and the transformation of the Mississippi valley's economy.

As in Illinois, the first rumblings in favor of statehood began in Missouri in late 1817. In January 1818 Missouri's congressional delegate John Scott presented the first of many memorials from sundry inhabitants of the territory, asking for statehood. Among the reasons cited were the desire by Missourians to have a vote in Congress since they were subject to taxation; the fact that Missouri's population was greater than that of Tennessee, Ohio, and Mississippi when they became states; Missouri's thirteen long years as a territory; the governor's veto power over legislation; and the excessive power and lack of oversight of the superior court.[34] Congress, however, took no action on the issue during that session, and in November 1818 Missouri's legislature adopted its own memorial asking Congress for statehood on the basis of the territory's population and large size, which they claimed precluded efficient administration. On February 13, 1819, Congress finally began debate on a bill to grant Missouri statehood, and on that day James Tallmadge proposed his amendment to restrict slavery in the future state. The amendment triggered a political crisis in Congress that lasted for over two years and a political backlash in Missouri itself that lasted even longer.[35]

In the spring of 1819 Missourians responded with surprise and anger to the news that Congress had failed to pass an enabling bill for their territory before adjourning. "These immigrants all took it for granted that Congress had no right to restrict the introduction of slavery into the territory," said the *Niles Register* in a piece about the large numbers of immigrants arriving in Missouri.[36] At the first public meeting held in protest, the tone for the many that followed was set by a resolution stating that Congress was asking Missouri to "stoop to a condition, which degrades them below the rank of free men, and lays the foundation of [a] slavery more abject than that which Congress pretends to be so zealous to reform." Restriction was "a daring stretch of power, an usurpation of our most sacred rights, unprecedented, unconstitutional, and in open violation of the 3rd article of the treaty of cession entered into with France."[37] At another meeting a month later the rhetoric escalated to include an implicit threat:

> That the right of the Missouri territory to be admitted into the union of the states, depends not upon the will of Congress, but upon the treaty of cession, and the principles of the federal constitution.... That the people of this territory have a right to meet in convention by their own authority, and to form a constitution and state government, whenever they shall deem it expedient to do so, and that a second determination on the part of Congress to refuse them admittance upon an equal footing with the original states, will make it expedient to exercise that right.[38]

If some Missourians wanted to take statehood into their own hands, others were confident that, "Once admitted, it is apparent that a convention might be assembled to alter or modify her constitution, and therefore erase the obnoxious feature." Few of these public resolutions and proclamations, however, said much in support of slavery itself. In fact, many of the public meetings, as well as grand jury proclamations and even Fourth of July toasts, contained expressions of ambivalence about slavery's future in Missouri.[39]

Behind many Missourians' position on slavery was a shared concern about the market for land. As in Illinois, most if not all of Missouri's leaders were involved in land speculation. For these men and for many settlers, slavery's future in Missouri had to be analyzed in terms of its effect on immigration and the demand for land. The consensus was that restriction might slow immigration and increase the relative competitiveness of neighboring Illinois. In this light congressional efforts to restrict slavery seemed to be another case of the federal government failing to act in the best interests of Missouri's citizens. A united front against congressional restriction thus emerged quickly and precluded any genuine debate within Missouri about slavery's future.[40]

In March 1820, following the tortuous deliberations that resulted in the first Missouri Compromise, President Monroe signed an enabling bill allowing Missouri to draft a constitution in anticipation of statehood. In the territory the news was "celebrated with ringing of bells, the firing of cannon, illuminations, and transparencies." The campaign to elect delegates for the constitutional convention revealed the degree to which Missourians had closed ranks on the issue of restriction. The only prominent pro-restriction candidate was the former land commissioner John B. C. Lucas, who was "much alarmed at the idea of great slaveholders coming amongst us with their gangs of plantation slaves: assuming an air of nabobs; superciliously looking upon our plain and unassuming farmers." Joseph Charless's *Missouri Gazette* was the only pro-restriction newspaper in the territory. All of the forty-one delegates elected to the June convention were anti-restrictionists, and in fact, the issue played little role in the campaign. Voters instead focused on apportionment, suffrage requirements, the future seat of government, education, the judiciary, banking laws, a bill of rights—and Indian removal.[41]

Many of the West's future leaders were among those elected to meet in St. Louis in June 1820 to write Missouri's constitution. Included were the first US cabinet official from west of the Mississippi River, Edward Bates; two future senators, David Barton and Henry Dodge; four future congressmen, Bates, Dodge, Samuel Hammond, and John Scott; and a politically prominent newspaper editor, Duff Green. Three factions emerged during the convention. The liberals favored frequent elections, no property requirements for suffrage, and elections for judges, sheriffs, and coroners. A conservative faction opposed these measures, and a moderate one mediated between the other two. The constitution they produced was a largely conservative one, with a strong legislature and appointed judges who served for life. Constitutional amendments did not require voter approval, and the constitution itself was not submitted to the people for a vote.[42]

If the constitution adopted on July 19, 1820, demonstrated the continuing influence of Missouri's old guard elite—still referred to as the Junto—the elections held a month later produced a decidedly populist outcome, as only seven delegates to the convention won seats in the assembly. The Junto's candidate for governor, William Clark, was defeated by Alexander McNair, who ran on a platform opposing the new constitution's undemocratic features, including the high salaries paid to state officials and the lifetime appointment of judges. A former Junto supporter, McNair was a militia officer and the register of lands for St. Louis who now opposed the *group's* ongoing efforts to gain confirmation for their large Spanish-era land claims. Clark, meanwhile, carried the baggage associated with his participation in federal efforts to keep white settlers off Indian lands and for his service as a commissioner at the Portage des Sioux treaty conference. Voters also chose William Ashley over the Junto candidate Nathaniel Cook to serve as lieutenant governor. Ashley's services as a militia officer on the frontier during the War of 1812 made him particularly popular with rural voters.[43]

Missouri's first general assembly convened on September 19, 1820, and began to organize and set in motion the machinery of state government. In the selection of two US senators, the Junto benefited from the inability of its opposition to unite behind any one candidate, and two established leaders, David Barton and Thomas Hart Benton, were elected. Benton's close victory over John B. C. Lucas showed the persistence of the Spanish land claims as a potent issue in Missouri politics. Large claimants such as Auguste Chouteau brought great pressure to bear on several of the political novices who had been elected to the assembly. At least one voted for Benton, according to one observer, "because if Judge Lucas was elected senator the French inhabitants would never have the grants to their lands confirmed; that Judge Lucas ... had warred against the confirmation of their claims for fully 20 years; that Benton was friendly to, and would take an active part in passing the laws confirming them in their titles to their lands." Among the other concerns of the first assembly were the location of the state's capitol, the opposition to unpopular features of the constitution, and a structure for state government.[44]

Missouri's senators Barton and Benton, and Representative John Scott, arrived in Washington in November 1820 but were not allowed to take their seats in Congress. The problem was a clause in Missouri's constitution calling for a law "to prevent free negroes and mulattoes from coming to, and settling in, this state, under any pretext whatsoever," which had triggered immediate objections in Congress. Scott, a former territorial delegate, explained his reaction:

> None of us have our seats. I will not act as Delegate; because I take the ground that we are a STATE—and so do all our friends—and were I to act as *Delegate*, it might be construed into an acknowledgement that we are *still a territory.* The consequence is, that the business of Missouri, land claims and all, stand still, till we are disposed of in our state pretensions.[45]

Benton took a hopeful view, writing, "All the friends of Missouri here consider her to be a State in point of fact and in point of right; and expect her to go on calmly and firmly with the operations of her government, preserving all the points of relationship with the government of the United States which her anomalous situation will permit of." But when the problem dragged on into the next congressional session, Benton's newspaper took a harder line. "Our state government is in full and complete.... The territorial government is almost forgotten.... It is [a] matter of fact that we are a state. We both see and feel its operations.... The People of Missouri have also become disgusted with the proceedings of the present session of Congress."[46]

Congress finally hammered out a second compromise in February 1821 demanding that Missouri "by a solemn public act, shall declare the assent of the said state ... that no law shall be passed ... by which any citizen of either of the States in this Union shall be excluded from the enjoyment of any of the privileges and immunities to which such citizen is entitled under the Constitution of the United States." Missourians celebrated the removal of this last barrier to statehood but remained contemptuous of Congress. Few took the new condition seriously, and at the opening of a special session of the state assembly, Governor McNair recommended passage of the required act but with the recommendation that the legislature "carefully avoid[ing] at the same time, everything that might impair our political rights, or draw in question the dignity and independent character of the state.... Our unsettled political condition has already prevented thousands from making our country their home." As always, immigration and land sales remained of paramount concern to Missouri's leaders.[47] The legislature passed an act in June 1821 complying with the language mandated by Congress but including a long, defiant preamble described by an eastern editorialist as "cutting satire." President Monroe chose to ignore any implied insult, and on August 10, 1821, proclaimed Missouri's statehood. The people of Missouri had the last word, however. A published explanation of the design for the new state's coat of arms stated that "The arms of the state of Missouri and of the United States ... denote the connection existing between the two governments, and show that, although connected by a compact, yet we are independent as to internal concerns."[48]

The debate over the nature of Missouri's opposition to slavery restriction became the subject of an ongoing debate by the state's historians that has never been fully resolved. While no one has argued that a majority of the territory's voters wanted to eliminate slavery upon reaching statehood, several believe that the principled resistance to congressional, and more broadly to eastern, meddling resulted in the militancy and unanimity of opposition. Writing in the 1880s, Lucien Carr described congressional efforts to restrict slavery in Missouri as discriminatory and politically motivated, resulting in the alienation of many in the territory "who agreed with them upon the question of slavery." Carr was "struck with the absurdity, inconsistency, and, in view of subsequent decisions, we may add the illegality, that characterized almost every phase of the proceedings of Congress upon this question." A generation later Louis Houck found evidence that many in Missouri believed that absent congressional attempts at restriction, slavery would have been excluded from the new state. Houck's contemporaries, Floyd Shoemaker and Harrison Trexler, did not quite agree, but acknowledged that antipathy for Congress and eastern meddling essentially precluded the possibility of a legitimate debate about the future of slavery in the territory. In the 1970s Arvarh Strickland revisited the issue and agreed that the evidence pointed to a majority supporting slavery, but not in numbers that would explain the degree of concerted and sustained public protests that took place during the controversy.[49] What is clear is the presence in Missouri of a climate hostile to federal authority that predated the statehood process. From this perspective, the years 1819–1821 represent a continuation of the long-running give-and-take between Washington and the people of Missouri over the issues of land, race, and sovereignty.

Dating from the War of Independence, white settlers in the Illinois Country sought physical security against hostile Indians, the protection of property rights, and a system of white political, economic, and social domination. The federal government's systematic efforts to provide for the first two proved largely successful in the years between the Louisiana Purchase and the end of the War of 1812. The result was a flood of immigrants and speculators whose appetite for land overwhelmed the existing institutions for its distribution. The respective statehood processes of Illinois and Missouri thus took place concurrent with the largest and most chaotic land boom yet to occur in the young nation. The result was a continuation of the argument between settlers and the federal government over the terms by which sovereignty would be constructed. Land and trade were now the central issues around which the construction of sovereignty pivoted. The challenges posed by competing European powers or by militarily potent Indians had been eliminated. But if the United States wanted to rule the Illinois Country in an effective manner, with its laws obeyed and its citizens respecting the federal government's power to control the use of violence, two questions still required answers. The first was how and by whom trade with the Indians remaining in the region would be conducted. The second was in what manner and under what terms the lands of Illinois and Missouri would pass into the hands of white settlers. And in those very questions lies proof that a system of white social, political, and economic domination had already emerged in the region.

The first question was answered in these years in favor of John Jacob Astor's American Fur Company. The drive following the War of 1812 to eliminate British interests from the American fur trade resulted in an opening for the well-capitalized and politically well-connected company. Astor had the money to buy out his foreign partners and to trade at prices that threatened both his private competitors and the government trading factories expected to control the majority of the trade. Although Astor joined with other private traders to lobby for the dismantling of the factory system, the ultimate success of this effort only served to increase the relative size and power of the American Fur Company. For all else there were three alternatives: get out of the business; go to work for Astor; or push the trade farther up the Missouri River into the vast reaches of the unsettled (by whites) West. The fur trade in the region, or at least what was left of it as white farmers continued to displace Indians and fur-bearing animals, now belonged to Astor.

The second question, concerning the disposition of land in the Illinois Country, produced a better result for white settlers and the federal government, if not for most Indians. The barrage of demands involving preemption rights, disputed land claims, and the acquisition of Indian lands in the territories were answered by a series of compromises or outright concessions by Washington officials. Federal policy favoring the slow, organized advance of white settlement was jettisoned in favor of aggressive treaty-making and liberalized terms of sale for white settlers. Indians who learned to work within the emerging system were able to exchange their lands for desirable tracts ahead (for the moment) of the tide of immigration. The Cherokees joined white settlers in acquiring lands in the Illinois Country during this period as they exchanged lands in Georgia for lands occupied by the Quapaw and Osage, who both failed to match the Cherokees' expertise in lobbying American officials.[50] The Shawnees and Delawares of the Cape Girardeau area also exchanged their land near the Mississippi River for a tract they had chosen for themselves farther to the west.

The cooperation by the federal government in distributing land on relatively easy terms to the citizens of Illinois and Missouri resulted in the strengthening of US sovereignty in the region. All parties, Indians included, now understood that the only path to secure land ownership was through cooperation with the system of treaty acquisition, survey, and sales administered by the War Department and Land Office. Conflicts continued between all parties as to the pace and terms of the process, but there was no longer any question that from this point forward, secure title to land would be acquired via these institutions.

Although the differences between the statehood processes of Illinois and Missouri must be attributed largely to the respective treatment each received from Congress, the anticipation of that treatment in Illinois and the reaction to it in Missouri had important implications for the future states themselves and for the Union they were joining. In Illinois a leadership that recognized the perils of an attempt to legalize slavery sidestepped the question, though with the understanding within the territory that it would be revisited later. Missourians, in contrast, assumed there would be no congressional opposition to slavery and treated its occurrence as another maddening failure by the federal government to provide the territory with the support and respect it deserved.

The temptation is thus to judge the construction of sovereignty as having been farther along or a greater success in Illinois than in Missouri by the late 1810s. This conclusion, however, must be qualified with the recognition that in both territories white settlers and territorial officials were pursuing very specific agendas concerning land and race. In Illinois the chief impediment to acquiring more land for yeomen and speculators alike was the pace and location of surveying and public sales. There were by this point few Indians in the direct path of white settlement. The majority of the territory's remaining Indians lived far to the north of the next areas to be settled. Statehood was seen as the means by which to raise the price of lands already settled and gain influence in Washington over the Land Office's activities in the new state. Slavery simply did not matter as much as land. As long as French-era property rights to slaves and the indenture system remained intact, the ultimate disposition of the institution could be deferred. It was a fight that the people of Illinois planned to settle among themselves *after* statehood. In this light the Illinois statehood process can be viewed as an embodiment of the emerging system of federalism: sovereignty residing with the people, but mediated through the institutions of their local, state, and national governments. While still a territory, Illinois lacked the authority to legalize slavery; as a state it might.

For Missourians land was also more important than slavery—at least until Congress tried to restrict it. At that point the accumulated weight of Missouri's grievances with the federal government resulted in a vocal and defiant reaction. Slavery then became a line drawn in the sand by a territory that had a more complicated and contentious relationship with the federal government than did Illinois. In Missouri there were still Indians arriving from the East, backed by federal efforts to relocate them west of the Mississippi River. There were also many unresolved Spanish-era land claims that left the disposition of millions of acres of desirable land in question. The image of the federal government and of its appointed officials in the territory was largely negative. Missourians had been left to defend themselves in the recent war and had since been denied the full fruits of their victory. Restricting slavery was out of the question, if mandated by Congress. Federal authority, already in low regard, sunk even lower. The Missouri Compromises were therefore two different though related debates about federalism; one at the national level that ended in compromise and deferred conflict, and another at the local level that ended in defiance.

From another perspective statehood for Illinois and Missouri was almost irrelevant. The lands that had once been called the Illinois Country and would later be thought of as the Mississippi valley were already near the end of a profound transformation that had begun when the first American soldiers to arrive in the 1770s got a look at the soil in the American Bottom. Whether Illinois or Missouri became states or remained territories, whether either or both embraced or rejected slavery, the transformation from furs to farms was nearly complete. White farmers were the future; Indians and white and métis traders were the past. The land itself, some of the most agriculturally productive on the planet, now drove most economic considerations. Even as Astor's American Fur Company tightened its grip on the trade in the region, the locus of the fur trade had already shifted north and west, and those living in Illinois and Missouri knew it. The Indians remaining in Illinois and Missouri were not yet ready to acquiesce—to pick up and run—but they knew better than anyone how few animals remained and how their white and métis trade partners were no longer true partners.

5 / After Statehood: Indian Removal, the Fur Trade, and Slavery

In December 1820 Missouri's state assembly passed a resolution instructing its new senators and representative to ask Congress to extinguish all remaining Indian titles to land in the new state and "to make use of their best Endeavors to prevent the admission of any Indian Tribe to Settle within the Limits of the State of Missouri, that may hereafter be removed from any one of the United States by Any treaty . . . and also to make use of their exertions to remove such tribes as are now living within the boundaries of this State."[1] Congress and the Monroe administration had yet to recognize Missouri statehood—and would not do so for another eight months. Still at odds with Congress over the terms of its ascension to statehood, Missouri's lawmakers nevertheless staked out an aggressive position on Indian removal that flew in the face of federal policies calling for the settlement of eastern tribes in areas west of the Mississippi River, including Missouri.

By the beginning of the 1820s the United States had long since demonstrated the superiority of its imperial model to the European rivals it replaced by delivering to white settlers in the Mississippi valley the physical protection, secure property rights, and white racial supremacy they demanded. In return the Union acquired the attachments and loyalty of the white inhabitants already living in the two new states and of those arriving each month to take up their own farms or businesses. And yet tensions remained between the federal government and those living in Illinois and Missouri, who grew ever more hostile to the idea of sharing any land with any Indians still living in the former Illinois Country—or being relocated there from the east.

Hostility to their very existence in Illinois and Missouri was not the only problem facing Mississippi valley Indians in the 1820s, however. While the American Fur Company dominated what was left of the fur trade in the region, many of the white and métis families involved in the trade were shifting their efforts not only up the Missouri River to the north and west but also along a route that would become known as the Santa Fe Trail, running south and west from Missouri all the way to the Spanish towns of Taos and Santa Fe. In Illinois and Missouri, as the economic rationale for any mutually beneficial relationship between whites and Indians disappeared, white settlers continued to pressure the federal government to adjust its policies to reflect those wishes. Federal officials responded by stepping up the extinguishing of Indian titles and ultimately by finding alternatives to the Mississippi valley as destinations for Indians being removed from eastern states, in a foreshadowing of the formal Indian removal policies that would be implemented by the Jackson administration in the 1830s. Here again, federal officials were adjusting their policies to support the commercial aspirations of frontier citizens who were in turn carrying the flag into the still contested expanses of the continent.

By the early 1820s slavery was a settled issue in Missouri, but not in Illinois, where beginning in 1822 the final contest between those supporting and those opposing slavery began, culminating in the 1824 referendum to call a constitutional convention to revisit the legality of slavery in Illinois. The defeat of the referendum ended the chances of Illinois becoming a slave state and also its potential to trigger a national constitutional crisis by attempting to do so. The region once known as the Illinois Country was now the states of Illinois and Missouri—one a free state and one a slave state—but both now part of a Mississippi valley that had completed its transformation from a fur-based economy to one dominated by commercial agriculture. The fur trade itself, however, would now move—along with many of the families, white, métis, and Indian for whom it was a way of life—deeper into the North American continent, where it would reach near-mythic status from the late 1820s to the 1840s.

The Fur Trade Heads West

As the American Fur Company tightened its grip on the Indian trade in the Upper Great Lakes and Mississippi valley, and government trading factories absorbed much of the rest of the trade, a national depression triggered by a financial panic in 1819 drove down the price of furs and left merchants and traders in Illinois and Missouri in a state of near desperation.[2] Many responded by looking to the southwest and northwest for new opportunities. By doing so they were well positioned when fur prices rebounded and Congress abolished the factories in 1822. The resulting dramatic expansion of the fur trade into the West created problems for federal officials, but also prosperity for some merchants and traders and the opportunity for politicians such as Thomas Hart Benton to use their newly acquired voices in Congress to influence the policies of the federal government.

As the 1820s began, the depression that already gripped the eastern United States was starting to be felt in Illinois and Missouri. No longer arriving were the steady stream of wealthy easterners with ready cash from the sale of their farms. In December 1820 the speculator Justus Post wrote to his son:

> The times are extremely hard here. No cash—destruction is hurrying upon the people in all directions. Had I been endowed with the spirit of prophecy I would have been better prepared for this event; but it does no good to complain. As yet I am better off than thousands of others, for I am not sued.[3]

In 1821 farmers in both states were without markets for crops, and merchants found few buyers for goods acquired on credit from eastern suppliers. The handful of banks that had been established in Illinois and Missouri had all failed, and the states' legislatures rushed to provide relief, including stay laws (to protect landowners from foreclosure) and loan offices, but to no avail. Within months the courts struck down most of the relief measures as unconstitutional, while the people grumbled that the relief efforts seemed to be more for the benefit of speculators than small farmers. As in most business downturns, those who were solvent—such as the American Fur Company—did extremely well, taking advantage of their less fortunate competitors.[4]

The first sign of recovery came at the end of 1821 when William Becknell, a trader from the central Missouri town of Franklin, returned from an expedition to Santa Fe and "dumped heaps of dollars on the sidewalks of Franklin" to demonstrate the incredible success of his venture. Becknell's timing had been fortuitous, to say the least. A number of previous expeditions to Santa Fe dating to the 1790s had resulted in the confiscation of goods by Spanish officials and incarceration for the traders. But Becknell's arrival on the heels of Mexican independence in 1821 meant that he was greeted not by angry government officials, but by buyers eager for manufactured goods. In 1822 Becknell repeated the trip to Santa Fe, as did a number of others during the next two years. Since the value of the manufactured goods brought to Santa Fe exceeded the cost of the furs and mules offered in payment, gold and silver from Mexican mines were used to make up the difference, sending much needed hard currency back to the merchants—and their local economies—who were providing the goods for the trade. Although profits were immense, Becknell and his competitors were attacked on several occasions by hostile Indians, suffering losses in goods and horses while barely escaping with their lives. Protection for the trade caravans thus became an immediate concern, as the potential benefits of the trade for both Missouri and Illinois became clear.[5]

Missouri senator Thomas Hart Benton led the drive in Congress to provide protection for the Santa Fe trade. Backed in his election to the Senate by the St. Louis Junto, Benton upon reaching Congress had come out in favor of reviewing the old, disputed Spanish land titles, abolishing the government trading factories, and privatizing Missouri's lead mines, all key concerns of Missouri's elite.[6] But Benton also correctly sensed the populist direction that Missouri politics was taking and was soon calling for expanded preemption rights for squatters, a graduation policy that provided for reductions in the price of unsold public lands, and federal support of the developing Santa Fe trade. In 1824 he presented a petition from "sundry inhabitants" of Missouri describing the "beneficial trade" as well as the threat posed by hostile Indians "to the commercial and social intercourse so happily begun." Benton requested that the matter be sent to the Indian Affairs Committee, which he chaired. The bill that emerged had three sections. The first called for a commission to mark a road from Missouri to the Mexican border and negotiate with Indians for safe passage; the second authorized the president to negotiate with Mexican authorities to extend the road into Mexico; and the third appropriated $30,000 to pay for it all. President Monroe signed the bill in March 1825 as one of his last official acts, pleasing any number of frontier constituencies, including large merchants; small traders; and farmers, who though not directly involved in the Santa Fe trade, nonetheless enjoyed the benefits of the influx of hard money to the region.[7]

A rebound in fur prices in the summer of 1821 combined with the opening of the Santa Fe trade and the demise of the government trading factories to stimulate a general resurgence in the fur trade. The factory system had been under assault almost since its inception in 1796 and finally succumbed in 1822. A key figure in the factories' demise was the Reverend Jedediah Morse, a Congregationalist minister who had been sent west by the secretary of war in 1820 to assess the general condition of the Indians. Morse was particularly concerned with the pernicious effects of the alcohol trade and believed that effective government control of the entire Indian trade might be the answer. His report, however, concluded that since the government refused to extend credit to the Indians and could not provide high quality goods as cheaply as could private traders and the British, it should abandon the trade altogether. To Morse's voice was added that of Thomas Hart Benton, who helped shepherd through Congress in 1822 bills to dismantle the factory system and tighten the legal prohibitions against the alcohol trade.[8] Benton's success was hailed not only by fur traders and merchants in Missouri and Illinois, but also by John Jacob Astor and his American Fur Company, another longtime critic of the factories. Astor's chief lieutenant Ramsay Crooks spoke for many when he wrote to Benton, "You deserve the unqualified thanks of the community for destroying the pious monster." Within months Astor and Crooks expressed their appreciation by securing Benton's services as an attorney. In the meantime, private traders flocked to William Clark's office in St. Louis to purchase fur-trading licenses.[9]

Prominent among the many attempting to capitalize on the improved prospects for the fur trade was the businessman and politician William Ashley, who partnered with veteran fur trader Andrew Henry to organize a trade expedition up the Missouri River. Trade on the river beyond the borders of Missouri was dominated by the Lakota Sioux, whose reliable ties to British traders allowed them to avoid any contact with Americans that did not serve to reinforce their role as the indispensable middlemen in the region's economy. During the War of 1812, William Clark and Manuel Lisa used lavish gift-giving to prevent the Sioux from taking up arms against the United States, but the Lakota remained firmly opposed to allowing American traders to bypass them on their way to trade with the nations to the north and west. In 1820 General Henry Atkinson had written to Secretary of War Calhoun about conditions on the Missouri River:

You are aware of the importance of sending a body of troops up the Missouri, as early as practicable. The Indians above have been expecting us for two years, and it is more than probable if our traders do not make establishments among them, under the protection & influence of a respectable detachment of troops, they will be so drawn away by British influence that it may be impossible to recall them.[10]

This was a letter that could have been written in 1720 or at any time since, as the pursuit of sovereignty in the West—by any of the imperial contenders—had always been inextricably linked to the Indian fur trade. What made Ashley and Henry's effort important was their plan to bypass the Indians not only geographically (in the case of the Sioux), but also operationally. Their innovation—simple but revolutionary—was to employ semi-independent trappers to collect furs from the wilds of the West instead of acquiring them from Indians in exchange for goods.[11]

The Ashley-Henry partnership, however, faced a number of setbacks in its first season. The first involved acquiring the required license from the War Department to hunt and trap "on the lands of Indians who are unfriendly to us, and under foreign influence." Benjamin O'Fallon, the US Indian agent for the Upper Missouri Agency, favored tight control of the Indian trade and worried in an official letter to Secretary Calhoun that "nothing is better Calculated to disturb the harmony existing between us and the Indians in the vicinity of Council Bluffs." He also complained privately that "There are but few indeed who will promote the views of the Govt and the public interest, unless it be incumbent to do so." But O'Fallon's superior (and uncle) William Clark signaled his support for the Ashley-Henry venture, as did Missouri's three congressional representatives. Calhoun left the matter up to Clark, who chose to issue the license. The expedition set out up the Missouri in the spring of 1823 but was attacked by the Arikaras, a nation that competed with the Sioux for control of the Missouri River trade. Ashley's losses included much of his merchandise as well as twelve dead and eleven critically wounded, more than a quarter of his entire force. In Missouri the attack produced immediate cries for retaliation.[12]

The attack on the Ashley-Henry party brought to national attention a debate that had been simmering in Congress and in the West for several years. The convention of 1818 between the United States and Great Britain had failed to provide a solution to the question of ownership of the Pacific Northwest. Instead it stipulated that any portion of the territory should be viewed as "free and open" to both countries for at least ten years. In Congress Thomas Hart Benton teamed with Virginia congressman John Floyd to argue for an aggressive US policy aimed at removing the British and securing the Pacific Northwest for the United States. Missourians agreed. An editorial in the *St. Louis Enquirer* reflected their usual irascible attitude toward Washington. "If the government of the United States, influenced by the communications derived from interested individuals, will not listen to the proposition of Mr. Floyd, the enterprise of the Missourians will, in the end, accomplish his great object." In fact the British *were* netting the present-day equivalent of several million dollars a year in furs from the Columbia River basin, and the fur trade establishment of Illinois and Missouri knew it. Their support for the Ashley-Henry expedition to trap in a region "which contains a wealth in *Furs* not surpassed by the mines of Peru," so "the rich furs of that region will soon cease to be the exclusive property of the Hudson Bay Company," had been a big reason William Clark and Missouri's congressional delegation had been in favor of issuing the partners a license.[13] As the issue garnered national interest, the *Niles Weekly Register* made its own prediction:

> The eastern and western people [of the United States] are of the same stock; with the former a voyage to the coast of Japan is a common affair; and to cross the Rocky Mountains will soon become as familiar to the other. It is very possible that the citizens of St. Louis on the Mississippi may eat fresh salmon from the waters of the Columbia!—for distance seems as if annihilated by science and the spirit of adventure.[14]

Under pressure for immediate action, the War Department responded by sending Colonel Henry Leavenworth to Ashley's relief.

Unfortunately, Leavenworth's military expedition fared little better than had Ashley's commercial one. This time facing a large force of trained soldiers, the Arikaras still managed to fight Leavenworth's men to a draw. During negotiations the Indians promised to return Ashley's goods, but over the next several days produced only a few rifles and some robes. Leavenworth threatened renewed hostilities but then, deciding that "the Indian[s] had been sufficiently humbled" as to preclude the need "to gratify my troops and make a charge," he returned downriver to explain his actions.[15]

Despite some official support offered by the War Department, Leavenworth became the target of severe criticism as part of the growing national controversy surrounding the western fur trade. Joshua Pilcher of the Missouri Fur Company, which had also recently suffered attacks by Missouri River nations, had contributed men and supplies to Leavenworth's expedition. His comments spoke to the potential long-term implications of Leavenworth's failure:

> You came to restore peace and tranquility to the country & leave an impression which would insure its continuance, your operations have been such as to produce the contrary effect, and to impress the different Indian tribes with the greatest possible contempt for the American characters. You came (to use your own language) to "open and make good this road"; instead of which, you have by the imbecility of your conduct and operations, created and left impossible barriers.[16]

William Ashley joined the chorus of those who demanded that the United States take whatever steps were necessary to ensure that "our citizens whose lawful pursuits call them to that country, will meet with the protection which they have a right to expect from their government." The War Department had no choice but to organize another military expedition in the face of mounting demands by both the western and eastern press to respond to what—given the prevailing assumption that the British were instigating the Indian attacks—had become a clear test of American honor and sovereignty. The ensuing Atkinson-O'Fallon military expedition moved up the Missouri River the following year with an even larger force and negotiated seventeen treaties with the region's Indian nations before returning to St. Louis. Yet Joshua Pilcher's comments proved prescient, as the lands on either side of the Missouri River continued to prove dangerous to white traders until a series of smallpox epidemics in the 1830s broke the power of Indians hostile to US interests.[17]

In light of the ongoing danger to fur traders along the upper Missouri River, the Ashley-Henry plan to contract with white trappers to collect furs without Indian involvement became essentially a matter of necessity. Striking out overland into and across the Rockies, Ashley's men enjoyed great success in the winter of 1823–1824. By the following summer Henry was back in St. Louis, where the *St. Louis Enquirer* greeted his return by declaring, "After an absence of nearly three years, we are happy to announce the safe return of Maj. Henry, with a part of his company, from the Rocky Mountains. He descended the Missouri in boats to St. Louis, with a considerable quantity of valuable furs, &c." Among the benefits of the new system was the rediscovery of the South Pass through the Rockies that would in the future allow settlers to cross the continent to reach Oregon. For William Ashley the new system proved enormously popular, and he was able to replace his losses and clear $80,000 in the next three years before selling his interest in the partnership to the legendary trapper Jedediah Smith.[18]

Closely monitoring all of these developments in the fur trade were the Chouteau family and John Jacob Astor. The Chouteaus' interests in the fur trade were now led by Pierre Chouteau Jr., whose company, Berthold, Chouteau & Pratte, was a major supplier of goods for the western Indian trade. The company also supplied the government with goods for Indian annuities, a part of the trade that Astor's American Fur Company had also entered after the closing of the government trading factories. Astor had long met with resistance from the Illinois and Missouri fur-trading establishment in his efforts to break into the Missouri River trade, but in 1822 Pierre Jr. entered into an arrangement with American Fur to exchange some of its furs for goods imported by the company. Pierre Jr.'s concern with diversifying his marketing and supply base proved beneficial to both parties. In 1823 Astor purchased an interest in the Boston firm Stone & Bostwick, which was a key supplier of manufactured goods to western traders, including the Ashley-Henry partnership. Within three years Pierre Jr.'s reorganized firm, now called B. Pratte & Company, merged with the American Fur Company, making it far and away the largest American fur-trading enterprise and the US analog to the enormous Hudson's Bay Company that operated throughout Canada.[19] As the fur trade establishment pushed the trade deeper into North America, white settlers and land speculators in Illinois and Missouri demanded that the lands that were no longer filled with fur-bearing animals also be cleared of the Indians who remained. Federal policy makers responded by tasking officials in the region with the responsibility to do so.

Indian Removal

During the winter of 1805–1806, Lewis and Clark's Corps of Discovery built a camp in present-day South Dakota that they named Fort Mandan. During the long days of relative inactivity the explorers used the time to update their journals and record a number of observations about the people and places they had encountered on their way up the Missouri River. In the spring before resuming their journey, the explorers sent these materials back to St. Louis to be forwarded to the appropriate officials in Washington. In one of the documents William Clark made possibly the earliest recorded reference to a formal Indian removal policy. "I think two villages, on the Osage river, might be prevailed on to remove to the Arkansas, and the Kansas, higher up the Missouri, and thus leave a sufficient scope of country for the Shawnees, Dillewars, Miames, and Kickapoos." Fifteen years later, as the newly appointed superintendent of Indian affairs at St. Louis, Clark was charged with implementing the policy he had described as a junior officer exploring the uncharted West.[20]

Clark's new job gave him vast powers over an area nearly as large as that encompassed by all of the existing states in the Union. As the government official responsible for the relationships between the United States and thirty-six Indian nations, his duties included issuing licenses and passports to private traders; providing payment to Indians for injuries and injustices inflicted by whites; authorizing the use of military force to arrest lawbreakers; preventing or ending hostilities between Indian nations; removing unauthorized persons from Indian lands and confiscating their property, if appropriate; establishing and marking the boundaries between Indian nations; supervising the distribution of Indian annuities; and conducting treaty councils. Clark knew, however, that the effective exercise of such powers required not only organizational skills and good judgment, but also the cooperation of the white citizenry of the region. This meant that although Clark was not directly beholden to the voters for his position, their support for his performance was crucial.[21]

As had been the case for much of his career, William Clark found himself caught in the middle of a triangle formed by the federal government, white settlers, and Indians. The government and settlers agreed that Clark's goal should be to acquire as much land from the Indians as was possible. But they disagreed as to what to do with that land. Federal officials declared that the "principal object of the negotiation[s] is to acquire lands on the West of the Mississippi, in order to exchange with such of the Indians on this side, as may choose to emigrate to the West." To that end Clark, in just one week in 1821, brought 222 Indian families and their possessions across the Mississippi River for settlement in Missouri. Settlers, of course, wanted all newly acquired Indian lands to be available for immediate purchase. Missouri's Indians, meanwhile, continued to negotiate to retain their rights to hunt, fish, trap, and gather on the lands they were persuaded to relinquish by treaty. William Clark, involved in Indian diplomacy since the 1790s, by now believed that the only solution was to create a vast Indian territory on the Great Plains, reserved in perpetuity for Indians removed from the existing United States. Proposed by Clark in 1821, this was another of his ideas that was ahead of its time.[22]

In 1824 President Monroe signed a bill that created the Bureau of Indian Affairs under the direction of the War Department. Its first head was Thomas McKenney, a former head of the Bureau of Indian Trade. McKenney framed the Indian question as a choice between removal and extinction. Dropped from the policy discussions were any references to the Jeffersonian idea of Indian acculturation and assimilation. The give-and-take between white settlers and the federal government had by now resulted in shifting the debate in a direction that precluded Indians living in close proximity to whites. Federal officials such as Clark had no choice but to pursue Indian lands and leave the question of the ultimate disposition of those lands to their superiors.[23]

Beginning with a trip to Washington in 1824 with an Indian delegation headed by the Sac chief Keokuk, William Clark set out to implement federal policy with results that were nothing less than stunning. While in Washington Clark helped to acquire from the Sacs, Foxes, and Ioways the rights to all of their lands in Missouri for $500 and an annuity. During the treaty negotiations Keokuk asked that a council be called to settle a number of boundary disputes among the Indian nations of the upper Mississippi. This request demonstrated the growing effectiveness of American sovereignty in the West. Keokuk realized that his direct contact with American officials could provide him with an advantage within his nation over his rival Blackhawk, the war chief who, less than a decade later, would famously and tragically challenge American power. Keokuk also saw the potential benefits to using American diplomacy to avoid violence between Indians in an area still relatively free of white settlers. The Indian Bureau responded to his request by authorizing Clark to join with Michigan Territory's governor Lewis Cass in calling for a council at Prairie du Chien for the summer of 1825.[24]

Before that council took place, Clark had other treaties to attend to. The first two were land swaps with the Shawnees and Delawares of southeastern Missouri, who, in exchange for the lands they had acquired when they arrived with Louis Lorimier in the 1780s, received lands farther west, beyond Missouri's borders. These treaties illustrated the futility of Indians choosing to acculturate as the means by which to retain their lands. The Shawnees and Delawares had years earlier taken up white agricultural practices, including slave ownership, but their lands were still considered necessary for use by either eastern tribes or white settlers.²⁵ Clark had actually warned Calhoun in 1823 about a similar situation developing with the Osage and Kansas, who were also attempting to acculturate. "The difficulties of purchasing the lands from those tribes will increase . . . after they have once opened themselves farms." The opposition of a determined Indian delegation proved futile as Clark, in the spring of 1825, completed treaties with the Osage and Kansas that netted the United States an immense tract of land in Missouri, Arkansas, and eastern Kansas in exchange for relatively large annuities. Despite explaining that the cost of the annuities would be recovered by selling as little as a fifth of the land acquired, Clark received a reprimand from Calhoun's replacement John Barbour for exceeding his cost estimates in persuading the Osage and Kansas to part with their land.²⁶

William Clark's busy schedule next took him to the upper Mississippi valley, where he and Lewis Cass convened the Prairie du Chien council in August 1825. This was to be the largest Indian council held since Portage des Sioux a decade earlier, and Clark's preparations included contracting for the delivery of eighty-five thousand pounds of fresh beef and one hundred gallons of whiskey for the Dakota Sioux, Winnebagoes, Menominees, Chippewas, Ottawas, Potawatomis, Sacs, Foxes, and Ioways who attended. Clark opened the council by addressing the nearly two thousand tribal representatives with a message of peace, explaining that he and Governor Cass were there to help the rival nations agree to fixed boundaries for their respective territories. After protracted and sometimes tense negotiations, treaties were signed and gifts distributed in another demonstration of American sovereignty in the former Illinois Country. Although the purpose of the council had been to maintain peace between the rival nations, the surveyors quickly sent by the federal government to mark the negotiated boundaries foreshadowed the land acquisitions to come in an area with few white settlers as yet, but with numerous lead mines worked by Indians who were soon to be overrun by white miners.²⁷

By the close of 1825 William Clark's land acquisitions totaled over one hundred million acres acquired in seventeen different treaties. Clark, partly in response to Secretary Barbour's criticism, traveled to Washington the next year and laid out an ambitious plan to reform US Indian policy. Before leaving office, President Monroe had taken up Clark's idea for a permanent Indian territory and to that proposal Clark now added a number of other recommendations. He called for the appointment of commissioners personally acquainted with the Indians; programs to assist Indians during a transitional period; the establishment of schools in Indian villages; and a switch from the payment of small permanent annuities to larger initial payments, so that the Indians might have more resources with which to abandon their old tribal practices. Clark, whose career in Indian diplomacy stretched back over thirty years to the 1790s, described to Barbour the process Clark himself had been so instrumental in effecting, as well as the type of paternalistic compassion he had come to embody. "While strong and hostile it was our policy and duty to weaken them; now that they are weak and harmless, and most of their lands fallen into our hands, justice and humanity require us to cherish and befriend them."[28] While undoubtedly sincere, Clark's comments described only a portion of the Indians under his jurisdiction. Farther to the west were Indians who were anything but "weak and helpless," and during these same years he was working with military men and private entrepreneurs to extend effective US sovereignty—and commerce—even deeper into the continent he and Meriwether Lewis had explored as young men. In doing so, he was in effect moving back in time to an earlier stage in a process that was all but completed in Illinois and Missouri.

Politics in the New States

The ongoing give-and-take between the federal government and the new states of Illinois and Missouri over issues such as Indian removal and the fur trade represented both a continuity with the territorial period and the increased ability to affect national policy that came with statehood. The two states' representatives clearly influenced federal policy regarding removal and the Indian trade, but the most obvious manifestations of their new clout were the roles played by Illinois' representatives in the Missouri crises. The reliable votes of John McClean in the House and Jesse Thomas and Ninian Edwards in the Senate helped defeat the effort to restrict slavery in Missouri. And it was Thomas who had proposed the amendment eventually adopted as the cornerstone of the first Missouri Compromise.[29]

But increased influence at the national level was accompanied by accountability to the voters of Illinois and Missouri, who were quick to reward or punish elected officials who acted either for or against their wishes. John McClean's votes against slavery restriction for Missouri led directly to his defeat by the antislavery candidate Daniel Cook in the next congressional election, while Cook himself was later defeated in part due to voter displeasure over his vote in the 1824 presidential election decided in the US House of Representatives.[30] As US sovereignty in the former Illinois Country solidified, voters in the new states began to claim the power that belonged to them within the emerging federal system.

The presidential election of 1824 in fact marked a watershed in the state politics of Illinois and Missouri even as it involved the entire Union in the most contested election since that of 1800—the only other decided in the House. In the absence of political parties, voters were free to support any of the four major candidates: William Crawford, Henry Clay, John Quincy Adams, or Andrew Jackson. When the votes were counted, Adams and Clay were the winners in Illinois and Missouri, respectively. Since none of the candidates received a majority of the votes in the electoral college, the contest moved to the House, and in the weeks leading to the crucial vote, the pressure mounted on Representatives Daniel Cook of Illinois and John Scott of Missouri to cast their state's votes to reflect "the will of the people." Cook's situation seemed clear, since Adams had carried the state, but Illinois' system of choosing electors created enough ambiguity to allow Jackson's supporters to claim that Old Hickory deserved Illinois' vote. Cook thought otherwise and cast his vote for John Quincy Adams. Six months later and more than a year before the next congressional election, Joseph Duncan, a farmer and hero of the War of 1812, came out against the until then popular Cook. In 1826 Duncan defeated Cook on a wave of populist backlash that was partly protest against the election of John Quincy Adams, partly support for Andrew Jackson (who in essence had begun the 1828 presidential campaign as soon as the House decided against him in 1825), and partly an anti-elite sentiment that accused Cook and his father-in-law Ninian Edwards of attempting to create a political dynasty in Illinois.[31]

John Scott's fate in Missouri paralleled that of Cook's in Illinois. Since Missouri's choice, Henry Clay, had thrown his support to John Quincy Adams, Scott claimed he was free from his preelection promise to cast his vote for the people's choice. Missouri's senators, David Barton and Thomas Hart Benton, had both been Clay supporters, so it seemed as if Congressman Scott would face no opposition if he decided in favor of Adams. But Benton, as part of his effort to remain in tune with the growing populist sentiment of western voters, came out in favor of his old enemy Andrew Jackson. In 1813 the two had fought on opposing sides in a violent brawl in a Tennessee barroom that had resulted in a gunshot wound to Jackson and several stab wounds to Benton. Now, nearly twelve years later, Benton decided that the people of the West did not want Adams as their president, and so in the words of David Barton, "of all the unnatural coalitions (not to say the most insincere) is that of our Senator Pomposo [Benton], of imperial port and mien, with the General [Jackson]." Sincere or not, Benton made full political use of his decision by publishing a letter to Scott in the *Niles Weekly Register*. Scott's decision was, said Benton, "so inconsistent with your previous conversations, so repugnant to your printed pledges, so amazing to your constituents, so fatal to yourself." In time, Benton's instincts, as well as his prediction about Scott's political future, proved true. Jackson became the political hero of the West, and Benton became the first senator in US history to serve five terms, while Scott and Barton were driven from Missouri politics by the wave of Jacksonian democracy they had not seen coming.[32]

However, the most dramatic example of "the will of the people" in the former Illinois Country took place without a national audience. Slavery, a question settled in Missouri at statehood, had yet to be settled in Illinois where, beginning in 1822, the final battle over its legalization took place over a nearly two-year period. The contest was largely a local one, though its national implications, in hindsight, were potentially cataclysmic.

The Illinois Convention Controversy

Officials in the new state of Illinois had not waited long to pass new legislation strengthening servitude and creating a harsher climate for free blacks. All blacks and mulattoes settling in the state were now required to produce a certificate of freedom. Anyone bringing slaves to Illinois for emancipation was required to post $1,000 bond for each one. Blacks who did not register a certificate of freedom with the clerk of the circuit court could not work legally. Instead, they could be seized, advertised in the papers, and hired out for a term of one year. If no owner appeared during that year, they received a certificate of freedom. Blacks could not be witnesses in court proceedings, except against another black, a mulatto, or an Indian. Economic conditions added to the push for expanded servitude. The depression that followed the panic of 1819 hit Illinois hard. Most of the state's leading men had been involved in both land speculation and frontier banking, and many believed that the exclusion of slavery was a large factor in the state's inability to emerge from the depression.[33]

In 1822 a proslavery legislature clashed openly with the state's new antislavery governor, Edward Coles. Born in Virginia to a prominent family, Coles served as President James Madison's personal secretary before moving to Illinois in 1817. An avowed enemy of slavery, Coles had dramatically freed his own slaves while floating down the Ohio River on his way to Illinois. In fact, his move to Illinois had been made specifically to allow him to combat slavery. In his first address to the state legislature Coles called for a repeal of Illinois' indenture laws and was met by a furious opposition that within weeks proposed a referendum to revise Illinois' constitution—with the specific goal of legalizing slavery.[34]

Irrespective of the proslavery sentiment of its legislature, Coles's election had provided proof of the growing antislavery sentiment in Illinois. The early 1820s were a period of transition in the American antislavery movement, with those like Coles and Cook, who espoused Enlightenment natural rights arguments, being joined by a more religious-based collection of individuals whose opposition to slavery was based on moral grounds. In Illinois the Reverend Thomas Lippincott, born a Quaker in New Jersey, and the Reverend John Mason Peck, a Connecticut-born Congregationalist (turned Baptist), both arrived in Illinois with no intention of acquiescing in the state's system of servitude. Edward Coles was himself directly responsible for the arrival of another group opposed to slavery. Morris Birkbeck was an English Quaker who was introduced to Coles in London by John Quincy Adams. Birkbeck had been considering a move to America, and Coles helped convince him that Illinois was the right place for him to settle. By the early 1820s Birkbeck had attracted several hundred English colonists to the Illinois prairie. One of these men, Elias Pym Fordham, explained that "With minds unbiased and intensely fixed upon its object they have passed by every district that offered peculiar advantages, till they found one that contained an aggregate of all: the climate of Virginia,—the fertility of Ohio,—a commercial communication with the ocean,—Prairies, like those of the Missouri,—the Minerals from the North and East,—and freedom from slavery." Men like Birkbeck and Fordham had helped elect Coles in 1822 and would be needed for the political fight that soon followed.[35]

In the eighteen months between the referendum legislation and the vote itself, the state was convulsed by the slavery question. In the press, editor Henry Eddy's proslavery *Illinois Gazette* squared off against Hooper Warren's antislavery *Edwardsville Spectator*. Congressional incumbent Daniel Cook ran for reelection on an antislavery platform against the proslavery ex-governor Shadrach Bond. Pro-conventionists bolstered their economic argument with the more abstract idea of diffusion. Slaves would be better off in Illinois, they argued, where food was cheap and the climate was milder. Diffusion could also increase the possibility of emancipation and eventual colonization. Those opposing the convention, meanwhile, used the whole gamut of available arguments: slavery was immoral, a sin; slavery was a violation of the principles of the Declaration of Independence; slavery was a quick economic fix that future generations would regret; slavery was an affront and a threat to free labor; slavery brought with it the threat of insurrections; slavery led to a proliferation of free blacks. Nor was the contest merely rhetorical. During the period leading to the referendum, murders increased, as did lesser forms of violence and other criminal activity. Even divorces increased. Governor Coles himself was the target of numerous attacks. He was burned in effigy in front of his own home, and arsonists burned buildings and fruit trees on his farm. He was even sued by the county for emancipating his slaves without posting bond.[36]

But on August 2, 1824, Edward Coles could take comfort from the results of the referendum. Illinois voters defeated the convention initiative by a vote of 6,640 to 4,972. Slavery in Illinois had finally been placed on the road to extinction. Court cases in 1828, 1836, and 1843 progressively weakened any legal basis for servitude in any form. In 1845 the Illinois Supreme Court freed the last descendants of slaves born during its territorial period, and in 1848 the state's second constitution barred any and all forms of slavery.[37] After more than a century of human bondage in one form or another, Illinois was finally free.

The Northwest Ordinance must be considered as largely responsible, as it had influenced Illinois settlement and slavery in three important ways. The first was to discourage slaveholders from choosing to settle in Illinois. In fact, as previously noted, the passage of the ordinance actually drove some slaveholders out of the territory. This problem became so acute that in March 1789, Major John F. Hamtramck wrote to his superior, General Josiah Harmar, that "I am fearful that the Governor will not find many people in the Illinois, as they are daily going on the Spanish side."[38] Despite the questionable assurances given by St. Clair to Illinois slaveholders, and despite the persistent and largely successful evasions of Article VI, the numbers speak for themselves. By the time Illinois and Missouri achieved statehood, Missouri had 10,222 slaves and Illinois only 917. In his memoirs, ex-governor Thomas Ford remembered:

> a tide of Immigrants was pouring into Missouri through Illinois, from Virginia and Kentucky. In the fall of the year every great road was crowded and full of them, all bound for Missouri with their money and long trains of teams and negroes. These were the most wealthy and best educated immigrants from the slave states. Many

of our people who had land and farms to sell looked upon the good fortune of Missouri with envy; whilst the lordly immigrant, as he passed along with his money and droves of negroes, took a malicious pleasure in increasing it by pretending to regret the shortsighted policy of Illinois.[39]

The second important influence of the Ordinance was on the slavery provisions of the constitution drafted by Illinois in 1818. During the convention, an editorial warned that if the delegates chose "to even tolerate slavery of any kind in the state, that it would be rejected by congress upon the same principle, and for the same reason, that it was prohibited by the congress of 1787."[40] The delegates chose not to test Congress on this issue. This was crucial because amending a constitution is a difficult process, with the burden on those who wish for change. It took six long years to even bring before Illinois voters a referendum for a convention to amend. During those six years the composition of settlers in the young state changed.

That shift in the composition of settlers arriving in Illinois was the Ordinance's third important influence. Partly by legal means and partly by perception, Article VI had over time created an expectation that Illinois was to be a free state. On the eve of the 1818 convention, Daniel Cook wrote, "The people of this territory have in general, came to it with an expectation of its being a free state; such was the opinion that the ordinance was intended to produce, and to defeat that expectation would seem to be unfair."[41] Although Cook had a partisan interest in that interpretation, the evidence is overwhelming. In the case of a man such as Morris Birkbeck—who eventually brought several hundred settlers to the state—it cannot be doubted that his expectation of Illinois, formed in conversations with Edward Coles and John Quincy Adams, was that slavery would be unequivocally banned. When he arrived he discovered that "It is not the states alone where slavery is established by law, that are suffering under this outrageous insult upon humanity," but he believed "it is probable that, ere many years have passed, a remedy, mild as the case will admit, must be applied by a wise and strong legislature."[42] Birkbeck himself had much to do with the "remedy" by bringing antislavery settlers to the state, and by taking an active role in the convention fight. Birkbeck's partner, George Flowers, explained how following statehood, "Everybody thought freedom established, and slavery excluded; and under that belief, emigrants from free-states and from Europe came in, and began to make permanent settlements for themselves and their families."[43] Although the referendum battle proves that many still supported slavery, the Ordinance had tipped the balance in favor of people like Birkbeck and Flowers.

With a nod to the moral inspiration provided by the Northwest Ordinance, slavery in Illinois was eliminated because the Ordinance provided an institutional deterrent to legalized slavery that influenced the 1818 constitution and helped insure that a majority of the 11,612 voters who participated in the 1824 referendum were opposed to its legalization. If Article VI had not deterred slaveholders from pouring into Illinois and increasing its population, the statehood movement would have come much sooner, and would likely have posed far greater problems for Congress than the 1818 constitution did. For that reason the Northwest Ordinance should be hailed, as it often was in the nineteenth century, as a remarkable gift from the founders. Had Illinois chosen to become a slave state, a constitutional crisis would have almost certainly ensued—the greatest possible challenge to US sovereignty—and coming on the heels of the Missouri statehood controversy, Congress might have proved unable to thwart Illinois' efforts or to incorporate other new territories into the nation with any restrictions on slavery. For these reasons the Northwest Ordinance deserves far more credit and recognition than it receives for not only providing a blueprint for the expansion of the United States, but for containing slavery and helping to allow the states to ultimately remain united.[44]

The immediate post-statehood periods in Illinois and Missouri demonstrated both continuity with the earlier colonial and territorial histories of the Illinois Country, and the new conditions brought about by full membership in the Union. The give-and-take between the federal government and the people living in the region remained the mechanism by which policies developed in Washington were adjusted or reversed before being implemented in the West. The power of the people as manifested in the ability to elect their own officials, and the influence of those elected officials on national policy-making, resulted in this instance in policies that reinforced the economic transformation of the region from a fur trade–based economy to one centered around commercial agriculture.

The fur trade, long the economic engine of the Illinois Country, continued its decline in the new states of Illinois and Missouri but remained relevant to many of the merchants and traders of those states, who, mired in a depression, looked beyond their local borders for new opportunities.

The reluctance of Indian nations west of the Mississippi valley to accommodate the expansion of American trade into their zones of power provided the basis for continuing conflict and compelled new assertions of American sovereignty, backed ineffectually by military power but effectively by commercial persistence and innovation. In the end the difference between US expansion as driven by arms or by trade became moot. Both served the same purpose and both were to play crucial roles in subduing the Indians and removing the British from the uncharted West.

In the area of Indian policy, the Monroe administration proved itself to be a link between the Jeffersonian idea of assimilation and the Jacksonian policy of forcible removal. In Illinois and Missouri, officials such as William Clark worked hard to execute a federal policy that no longer looked to acculturation and assimilation, but that stopped short of the brutality of the 1830s. The colonial legacy of accommodation between Indians and Europeans in the Illinois Country provided a foundation for a more measured and relatively humane displacement of Indian nations, but the steady influx of white settlers with harsher attitudes toward Indians insured that Clark and his mostly French or métis agents and translators understood the desired outcome. Whether it be wealthy speculators eager to purchase newly acquired lands for resale, or penniless squatters who demanded access to land they could either improve for resale or eventually purchase themselves, the mandate was clear. Federal policy as executed in the West was to provide protection for white settlers as the lands belonging to Indians were systematically acquired for use by whites, while the Indians residing on those lands would be compelled to relocate elsewhere. In addition, the idea of relocating eastern Indian nations on either Illinois or Missouri soil was discarded. The former Illinois Country was to be a racially exclusive society where even métis peoples were no longer welcome. Indians, free blacks, and métis peoples were to have no place in Illinois and Missouri for the foreseeable future. Prominent families such as the Chouteaus, who represented the most direct link to a multiracial, multicultural past, would see their political power, which now required the approval of a majority, dissipate after statehood even as their economic influence continued to grow.[45]

The rise of a populist democracy emerged as the dominant political theme in both Illinois and Missouri in the 1820s. Political leaders such as Thomas Hart Benton launched long, successful careers by recognizing the direction politics—and the region's economy—were heading, while men such as John Scott and Daniel Cook saw their political fortunes plummet when they failed to respond to the "will of the people." This process had been unfolding throughout the Union at various times and in various places since the War of Independence. Its significance in the West, however, derived from the still unsettled nature of the relationship between Washington and white settlers in the Mississippi valley. In this region, where the United States had ruled for more than a generation through appointed officials and the relatively feeble projection of military power, and where the American leaders hoped that people's loyalties and attachments would be to a nascent conception of nationhood, statehood represented the transition from subject to citizen. For this reason the Illinois constitutional referendum marked a watershed in this region. For the vote that took place on that August day can be seen as the last time that federalism—the system of the people's sovereignty as administered through national, state, and local governments—was contested in this area. States' rights would later become a contentious issue elsewhere, and the entire Union would be in peril during the Civil War, but the people of the Illinois Country, by upholding in a free election the provisions of the Northwest Ordinance, had done their part to join the Union.

The principal reason they had done so, however, was economic, not political. Settlers flocking to the West were looking for lands to farm. This was the central motivation that drove all issues. The desire for land—all of the land there was—meant that Indians would have no place in the local economy and therefore no place in society at all. The desire for land also meant that the former Illinois Country would ultimately be divided into one state where farming would flourish with the help of slave labor, and another state where slave labor was specifically excluded, so that yeoman farmers did not have to compete with it.

Conclusion

Among the official witnesses to the March 1804 transfer of Upper Louisiana from Spain to France to the United States was Charles Gratiot, who along with Carlos Delassus, Antoine Soulard, Amos Stoddard, and Meriwether Lewis, witnessed and signed the official transfer documents. It was an eclectic group, testimony to the various imperial and economic forces driving the events surrounding the Louisiana Purchase as well as the region's recent history and future prospects. Delassus and Soulard had both been born in France in the 1760s, with Delassus coming to Spanish Louisiana in the 1790s as an officer in the Spanish army and Soulard that same decade as a refugee from revolutionary France. Stoddard and Lewis, both younger, were born in the colonies—soon to be the states—of Connecticut and Virginia, respectively, and in 1804 had only just arrived in Upper Louisiana. Gratiot was the oldest of this group and the one whose life story perhaps best demonstrates the region's transformation from furs to farms.[1]

Born in Lausanne, Switzerland in 1752, Gratiot was a descendant of French Huguenots whose family sent him to London in the 1760s to be trained as a merchant. Gratiot crossed the Atlantic in 1769 to serve as an apprentice in his uncle's Canadian fur-trading business. In that capacity Gratiot travelled to Michilimackinac, Detroit, and Upper Louisiana before striking out on his own in the 1770s as a merchant in Cahokia, then a part of British Illinois. Gratiot's international fur-trading connections soon helped him to become one of the leading businessmen in the Illinois Country, and in 1778 his support of George Rogers Clark proved crucial to the American takeover of Illinois. In 1781 Gratiot crossed the Mississippi River to resettle in St. Louis, where he soon married Victoire Chouteau, the sister of Auguste and Pierre. Gratiot was now a member of the region's leading family. His commitment to the fur trade during this period included trips to Philadelphia in the 1780s to confer with suppliers as well as a fourteen-month trip to France, Switzerland, and England in the 1790s, where he sought backing to establish a trading house in New Orleans. By this time Gratiot was in his forties, a successful man whose life since his teens had been spent in the fur trade. And yet by the time he put pen to paper at the 1804 transfer of Upper Louisiana, Gratiot had shifted his energies and most of his capital from the declining fur trade to milling, distilling, farming, and land speculation.[2]

Gratiot's actions embodied the shift from furs to farms, and he supported the acquisition of Louisiana by the United States—though not without some reservations—as a means to further prosper as a farmer and land speculator. The arrival of Americans and of US sovereignty promised secure title to lands cleared of Indians, a pool of settlers interested in buying those lands, and a free port—New Orleans—that could serve as a domestic outlet for the agricultural surplus produced on both sides of the Mississippi River. For Charles Gratiot and many like him, the switch to US sovereignty was *not* the catalyst for major changes in their lives and livelihoods, but rather a complementary process that reinforced changes that were already under way. In the years to come Gratiot would not only become a major land speculator but would also embrace the political opportunities created by the Americans' arrival, serving as a justice of the peace, a judge, a clerk of the board of land commissioners, and a member of the St. Louis Board of Trustees.[3]

The communities established by the French in the early eighteenth century were by the eve of the Seven Years War parts of a prosperous, multiethnic, multiracial society with an economy tied to international markets through the Great Lakes and St. Lawrence River and via the Mississippi River and Gulf of Mexico. As such, European powers valued the Illinois Country for its centrality to the eighteenth-century fur trade and for its strategic military location. By looking at the Illinois Country as a whole, I have argued here for the value of an approach to American history that places specific geographic areas at the center of their own histories instead of treating them reflexively as peripheries of an eastern seaboard core. Doing so helps us better appreciate the social, economic, and demographic complexities that existed in various parts of North

America prior to the creation of the United States, and challenges the conventional regional designations that obscure the richness and variety of our local histories.

In the case of the Illinois Country, this is particularly important because the states of Illinois and Missouri had their origins in a single eighteenth-century colonial society and are today both considered parts of the Midwest, yet during the interim spent forty years on opposite sides of an international boundary and sent soldiers to fight on opposite sides during the Civil War. A person born in colonial Cahokia in the early 1760s (who never relocated) would have lived by the age of sixty under the sovereignty of France, Great Britain, Virginia, the Northwest Territory, Indiana Territory, Illinois Territory, and finally, the state of Illinois. For someone living just across the Mississippi River in St. Louis the succession during the same period would have been from France to Spain, back to France (however briefly), and then the District of Louisiana, Missouri Territory, and finally, the state of Missouri. For such people, an analysis of their lives as part of an east-to-west sweep of American history would be misleading, at best. Their stories must be viewed from a local perspective as well as an imperial one to best understand the context for the dramatic events and economic transformation they participated in.

This is not to say that the incorporation of the Illinois Country cannot also be placed within the larger story of the creation and expansion of the United States. For that purpose the year 1763 is an appropriate place to begin. The defeat of the French opened the trans-Appalachian West to American settlers irrespective of British policy to the contrary. Small-scale settlers squatted where they dared, and large speculators formed companies to buy lands from the Indians or to secure grants from the British crown. From the start, the Illinois Country was a prize coveted by prominent men on both sides of the Atlantic. For many, the struggle for American independence was a sideshow to the beginning of history's greatest land rush. Its result meant that land ownership was no longer a matter to be decided in Paris, Madrid, or London, but was temporarily an open question. The 1783 Treaty of Paris gave international sanction to the new nation's claim to the lands between the Appalachians and the Mississippi.[4]

The story of the Illinois Country—what would become the states of Illinois and Missouri—is, however, an example of eighteenth- and early nineteenth-century imperial competition that took place against a backdrop of economic transformation. The peoples, the animals, and even the land itself underwent profound changes during this period, and the result was the shift from furs to farms, from an economy based upon the people and animals living on the land to one based on the land itself. While the imperial competition for the Mississippi valley provided a number of dramatic events that directly affected those living there, the economic transformation from furs to farms not only had the largest impact, but also provided the conditions that favored the successful incorporation of the region by the United States.

In the former Illinois Country the challenge for the new nation was to secure the allegiance of white settlers prior to the point when it developed the capacity to displace the area's Indians by force in order to survey and sell land. Force had been used to clear the Ohio valley of Indians, but the inability to bring force to bear in the Mississippi valley made it necessary to do things differently in Illinois and Missouri. White settlers hardened by a generation of violence valued physical protection over all else and believed the way to guarantee it was through further violence against Indians. White settlers also demanded secure property rights in land and slaves or indentures. Bounty lands and foreign titles had to be quickly confirmed, preemption had to be sanctioned, and political rights had to be liberalized. In both territories the commercial aspirations of prominent Creoles had to be acknowledged, and in Illinois, de facto slavery had to be tolerated. Finally, Missouri's defiance of Congress had to be finessed.

The ability of the federal government to accomplish these tasks grew from the flexibility it demonstrated in frequently adjusting its policies to satisfy the demands of incoming white settlers while concurrently placing the leaders of the already established communities of the Illinois Country into positions of responsibility. The good use made of these human resources began literally from the moment George Rogers Clark arrived in Kaskaskia on the east side of the Mississippi and continued with his brother William's arrival—along with Meriwether Lewis and the Corps of Discovery—on the west side of the river.

The imperial successes enjoyed by the United States during its early national period were neither inevitable nor accomplished primarily through the use of overwhelming force. As much recent scholarship has shown, the settling of the trans-Appalachian West required more than eager settlers supported by the new nation's military.[5] Violence was a big part of the story, but so was diplomacy and compromise. The established societies in the Mississippi valley that became parts of the United States via treaties signed by European powers ultimately "joined the Union" only after the emergence of the system now referred to as federalism.

This system provided for the balancing of national policies with the economic realities of those societies and with the political and cultural demands of the white settlers pouring west during these decades. This is not the story of a strong government or a weak government, but of a deft government that learned quickly that sovereignty did not come "with the stroke of a pen," but rather, was constructed. Most of all, this is a story of a specific geographic place and the forces and events that shaped—and were shaped by—the diverse peoples who, by birth, by choice, or by happenstance, lived out their lives near the banks of the mighty Mississippi River.

Notes

Introduction

1. Floyd C. Shoemaker, "The Louisiana Purchase, 1803, and the Transfer of Upper Louisiana to the United States, 1804," *Missouri Historical Review* 48 (October 1953): 10–13; quote from "Proclamation of Gov. Delassus," in Amos Stoddard, "Papers of Captain Amos Stoddard," Missouri Historical Society, *Glimpses of the Past*, 2 (1935), 86.

2. Shoemaker, "Louisiana Purchase," 11–12. The story of the French flag remains a source of dispute. Most recent historians choose to accept the story that the French flag flew over St. Louis on the night of March 9, 1804, before being replaced by the US flag the next day. Shoemaker, writing earlier but still the most credible source for these events, remained somewhat skeptical about the story; quote from "Proclamation of Capt. Stoddard," in Stoddard, "Papers," 86; "Stoddard To His Mother Mrs. Samuel Benham," June 16, 1804, ibid., 112–13.

3. Clarence Alvord, *The Illinois Country, 1673–1818* (Springfield: Illinois Centennial Commission, 1920; reprint (Urbana: University of Illinois Press, 1987); Richard White, *The Middle Ground: Indians, Empires, and Republics in the Great Lakes Region, 1650–1815* (Cambridge, UK: Cambridge University Press, 1991); Kathleen DuVal, *The Native Ground: Indians and Colonists in the Heart of the Continent* (Philadelphia: University of Pennsylvania Press, 2006); Eric Hinderaker, *Elusive Empires: Constructing Colonialism in the Ohio Valley, 1673–1800* (Cambridge, UK: Cambridge University Press, 1997), 9, 37–38, 47–54, 87–88; James E. Davis, *Frontier Illinois* (Bloomington: Indiana University Press, 1998); Carl Ekberg, *Francois Valle and His World: Upper Louisiana Before Lewis and Clark* (Columbia: University of Missouri Press, 2002); Helen Hornbeck Tanner et al., eds., *Atlas of Great Lakes Indian History* (Norman: University of Oklahoma Press, 1987), 31–121; Stephen Aron, *American Confluence: The Missouri Frontier from Borderland to Border State* (Bloomington: Indiana University Press, 2006). The term *Big Rivers* was used to describe the area by M. J. Morgan,

Land of Big Rivers: French & Indian Illinois, 1699–1778 (Carbondale: Southern Illinois University Press, 2010).

4. Arthur Whitaker, *The Spanish-American Frontier, 1783–1795* (1927; reprint, Gloucester, MA: Peter Smith, 1962); Arthur Whitaker, *The Mississippi Question 1795–1803: A Study in Trade, Politics, and Diplomacy* (1934; reprint, Gloucester, MA: Peter Smith, 1962); Thomas Abernethy, *The Burr Conspiracy* (New York: Oxford University Press, 1954); J. Leitch Wright, *Britain and the American Frontier 1783–1815* (Athens: University of Georgia Press, 1975); Samuel Flagg Bemis, *Pinckney's Treaty: America's Advantage From Europe's Distress, 1783–1800* (1926; reprint, New Haven: Yale University Press, 1960).

5. White, *Middle Ground*; DuVal, *Native Ground*; Hinderaker, *Elusive Empires*; Cayton, *Frontier Indiana*; Ekberg, *Francois Valle*; Aron, *American Confluence*; R. Douglas Hurt, *Nathan Boone and the American Frontier* (Columbia: University of Missouri Press, 1998); John Mack Faragher, "'More Motley than Mackinaw': From Ethnic Mixing to Ethnic Cleansing on the Frontier of the Lower Missouri, 1783–1830," in *Contact Points: American Frontiers from the Mohawk Valley to the Mississippi, 1750–1830*, ed. Andrew Cayton and Frederika Teute (Chapel Hill: University of North Carolina Press, 1998), 304–26; Morgan, *Land of Big Rivers*; Jay Gitlin, *The Bourgeois Frontier: French Towns, French Traders & American Expansion* (New Haven: Yale University Press, 2010); Peter J. Kastor, *The Nation's Crucible: The Louisiana Purchase and the Creation of America* (New Haven: Yale University Press, 2004).

6. Shannon Lee Dawdy, *Building the Devil's Empire: French Colonial New Orleans* (Chicago: University of Chicago Press, 2008); J. Frederick Fausz, *Founding St. Louis: First City of the New West* (Charleston, SC: History Press, 2011); Patricia Cleary, *The World, the Flesh, and the Devil: A History of Colonial St. Louis* (Columbia, University of Missouri Press, 2011); Kenneth J. Banks, *Chasing Empire across the Sea: Communications and the State in the French Atlantic, 1713–1763* (Montreal: McGill-Queen's University Press, 2003); Janice E. Thomson, *Mercenaries, Pirates, and Sovereigns* (Princeton, NJ: Princeton University Press, 1994).

7. Alexander Davidson and Bernard Stuve, *A Complete History of Illinois from 1673–1873* (Springfield: Illinois Journal Company, 1874); Alvord, *The Illinois Country*; Solon Buck, *Illinois in 1818* (Springfield: Illinois Centennial Commission, 1917; reprint, Urbana: University of Illinois Press, 1967); Lucien Carr, *Missouri: A Bone of Contention* (Boston: Houghton Mifflin, 1888); E. M. Violette, *A History of Missouri* (1918; reprint, St. Louis: State Publishing, 1955); Louis Houck, *History of Missouri from Earliest Explorations and Settlements until the Admission of the State into the Union*. 3 vols. (Chicago: R.R. Donnelley & Sons, 1908).

8. Beverley Bond Jr., *The Civilization of the Old Northwest: A Study of Political, Social, and Economic Development, 1788–1812* (New York: Macmillan, 1934); Ray Allen Billington, *Westward Expansion: A History of the American Frontier*, 4th edition (New York: Macmillan, 1974); R. Carlyle Buley, *The Old Northwest: Pioneer Period, 1815–1840*, 2 vols. (Indianapolis: Indiana Historical Society, 1950); John Barnhart, *Valley of Democracy: The Frontier versus the Plantation in the Ohio Valley, 1775–1818* (Bloomington: Indiana University Press, 1953); Francis S. Philbrick, *The Rise of the West, 1754–1830* (New York: Harper & Row, 1965); Reginald Horsman, *The Frontier in the Formative Years, 1783–1815* (New York: Holt, Rinehart, and Winston, 1970).

9. LeRoy Hafen, ed., *French Fur Traders & Voyageurs in the American West* (Lincoln: University of Nebraska Press, 1995); Julie Winch, *The Clamorgans: One Family's*

History of Race in America (New York: Hill and Wang, 2011); Gitlin, *The Bourgeois Frontier*; Peterson, Jacqueline, and Jennifer S. H. Brown, eds., *The New Peoples: Being and Becoming Métis in North America* (Lincoln: University of Nebraska Press, 1985).

10. Richard Buel Jr., *America on the Brink: How the Political Struggle over the War of 1812 Almost Destroyed the Young Republic* (New York: Palgrave Macmillan, 2005); Albert Z. Carr, *The Coming of War: An Account of the Remarkable Events Leading to the War of 1812* (Garden City, NY: Doubleday, 1960); Reginald Horsman. *The Causes of the War of 1812* (New York: A.S. Barnes, 1962); John K. Mahon, *The War of 1812* (1972; reprint, New York: Da Capo, 1991); Julius W. Pratt, *Expansionists of 1812* (1925; reprint, Gloucester, MA: Peter Smith, 1957).

11. William Cronon, *Changes in the Land: Indians, Colonists, and the Ecology of New England* (New York: Hill and Wang, 1983); Peterson and Brown, eds., *The New Peoples*; Gregory Evans Dowd, *A Spirited Resistance: The North American Indian Struggle for Unity, 1745–1815* (Baltimore: Johns Hopkins University Press, 1992), 65–147; Daniel Richter, *Facing East from Indian Country: A Native History of Early America* (Cambridge, MA: Harvard University Press, 2001), 165–66; Daniel H. Usner Jr., *Indians, Settlers, and Slaves in a Frontier Exchange Economy* (Chapel Hill: University of North Carolina Press, 1992); Tanis C. Thorne, *The Many Hands of My Relations: French and Indians on the Lower Missouri* (Columbia: University of Missouri Press, 1996); Colin G. Calloway, *New Worlds for All: Indians, Europeans, and the Remaking of Early America* (Baltimore: Johns Hopkins University Press, 1997); James H. Merrell, *Into the American Woods: Negotiations on the Pennsylvania Frontier* (New York: W.W. Norton, 1999); DuVal, *Native Ground*; John P. Bowes, *Exiles and Pioneers: Eastern Indians in the Trans-Mississippi West* (Cambridge, UK: Cambridge University Press, 2007).

12. David M. Friedenberg, *Life, Liberty, and the Pursuit of Land: The Plunder of Early America* (Buffalo: Prometheus Books, 1992), 305–307; Horsman, *The Frontier in the Formative Years*; Bowes, *Exiles and Pioneers*; Robert M. Owens, *Mr. Jefferson's Hammer: William Henry Harrison and the Origins of American Indian Policy* (Norman: University of Oklahoma Press, 2007).

13. Glover Moore, *The Missouri Controversy, 1819–1821* (Lexington: University Press of Kentucky, 1966).

14. Adam Rothman, *Slave Country: American Expansion and the Origins of the Deep South* (Cambridge, MA: Harvard University Press, 2005); Matthew Mason, *Slavery & Politics in the Early American Republic* (Chapel Hill: University of North Carolina Press, 2006); John Craig Hammond, *Slavery, Freedom, and Expansion in the Early American West* (Charlottesville: University of Virginia Press, 2007).

15. John Reynolds, *Reynolds' History of Illinois: My Own Times: Embracing also the History of My Life* (Belleville, IL: B. H. Perryman and H. L. Davison, 1855; reprint, Chicago: Chicago Historical Society, 1879), 132.

16. Paul Finkelman, "Slavery and the Northwest Ordinance: A Study in Ambiguity," *Journal of the Early Republic* 6 (Winter 1986): 343–70; Paul Finkelman, "Evading the Ordinance: The Persistence of Bondage in Indiana and Illinois," *Journal of the Early Republic* 9 (Spring 1989): 21–51; William W. Freehling, *The Road to Disunion: Secessionists at Bay, 1776–1854* (New York: Oxford University Press, 1990), 138–42.

17. James E. Davis, *Frontier Illinois* (Bloomington: Indiana University Press, 1999), 160–68.

18. Robert Pierce Forbes, *The Missouri Compromise and Its Aftermath: Slavery and the Meaning of America* (Chapel Hill: University of North Carolina Press, 2007); Moore, *The Missouri Controversy*; Don Fehrenbacher, *Sectional Crisis and Southern Constitutionalism*, Comprising *The South and Three Sectional Crises* and *Constitutions and Constitutionalism in the Slaveholding South* (Baton Rouge: Louisiana State University Press, 1995).

19. Floyd Calvin Shoemaker, *Missouri's Struggle for Statehood, 1804-1821* (1916; reprint, New York: Russell & Russell, 1969); William E. Foley, *The Genesis of Missouri: From Wilderness Outpost to Statehood* (Columbia: University of Missouri Press, 1989), 293-98; Faragher, "More Motley Than Mackinaw," 304-26.

20. Pierre Chouteau to Thomas Jefferson, 31 January 1805, Chouteau Collection, Box 7, Pierre Chouteau, Sr. Letterbook, Missouri Historical Society.

21. Gitlin, *Bourgeois Frontier*, 12.

1 / The Colonial Eighteenth Century in the Illinois Country

1. Among the many good sources for the early history of the Illinois Country are Clarence Alvord, *The Illinois Country, 1673-1818* (Springfield: Illinois Centennial Commission, 1920; reprint, Urbana: University of Illinois Press, 1987); Carl J. Ekberg, *French Roots in the Illinois Country: The Mississippi Frontier in Colonial Times* (Urbana: University of Illinois Press, 1998); W. J. Eccles, *The French in North America 1500-1783* (Markham, Ontario: Fitzhenry & Whiteside, 1998).

2. For descriptions of the Osage and their relationship to the French in the Illinois Country, see Willard H. Rollings, *The Osage: An Ethnohistorical Study of Hegemony on the Prairie Plains* (Columbia: University of Missouri Press, 1992); William Foley, *The Genesis of Missouri from Wilderness Outpost to Statehood* (Columbia: University of Missouri Press, 1989); Kathleen DuVal, *The Native Ground: Indians and Colonists in the Heart of the Continent* (Philadelphia: University of Pennsylvania Press, 2006); Stephen Aron, *American Confluence: The Missouri Frontier from Borderland the Border State* (Bloomington: Indiana University Press, 2006).

3. Alvord, *The Illinois Country*, 324-28, 380-86; Arthur Whitaker, *The Spanish-American Frontier, 1783-1795* (1927; reprint, Gloucester, MA: Peter Smith, 1962).

4. David Lavender, *The Fist in the Wilderness* (1964; reprint, Lincoln: University of Nebraska Press, 1998), ch. 2-4; Hiram Chittenden, *A History of the American Fur Trade of the Far West* (1902; reprint, Stanford, CA: Academic Reprints, 1954): 1:71-82.

5. James E. Davis, *Frontier Illinois* (Bloomington: Indiana University Press, 1998), 40-41, 13-14.

6. Winstanley Briggs, "Le Pays des Illinois," *William and Mary Quarterly* 48 (January 1990): 30-56; Aron, *American Confluence*, 35.

7. Works that place the eighteenth-century Mississippi valley within an Atlantic World perspective include: Aron, *American Confluence*; Patricia Cleary, *The World, the Flesh, and the Devil: A History of Colonial St. Louis* (Columbia: University of Missouri Press, 2011); Shannon Lee Dawdy, *Building the Devil's Empire: French Colonial New Orleans* (Chicago: University of Chicago Press, 2008); J. Frederick Fausz, *Founding St. Louis: First City of the New West* (Charleston, SC: History Press, 2011); Robert Morrissey, *Empire by Collaboration: Indians, Colonists, and Governments in Colonial Illinois Country* (Philadelphia: University of Pennsylvania Press, 2015).

8. Histories of the French Empire in North America start with the works of Francis Parkman and progress to those of W. J. Eccles, among others. Recently, however, historians have begun to question the entire idea of a French inland empire in North America. See Michael Witgen, *An Infinity of Nations: How the Native New World Shaped Early North America* (Philadelphia: University of Pennsylvania Press, 2012).

9. DuVal, *Native Ground*, 4–5; Tanis C. Thorne, *The Many Hands of My Relations: French and Indians on the Lower Missouri* (Columbia: University of Missouri Press, 1996), 81–82.

10. Aron, *American Confluence*, 3, 24; DuVal, *Native Ground*, 8, 103; Briggs, "Le Pays des Illinois," 51; Davis, *Frontier Illinois*, 44–45.

11. M. J. Morgan, *Land of Big Rivers: French & Indian Illinois, 1699–1778* (Carbondale: Southern Illinois University Press, 2010), 191.

12. Quote from Foley, *Genesis of Missouri*, 26. This trope is the source of the title and is brilliantly developed in the introduction to Colin G. Calloway's *The Scratch of a Pen: 1763 and the Transformation of North America* (Oxford: Oxford University Press, 2006), where he credits Francis Parkman for its origin. Francis Parkman, *Montcalm and Wolfe: The French and Indian War* (1884; reprint, New York: Da Capo, 1995), 535.

13. Some historians are beginning to question the entire idea of a French empire in North America. Michael Witgen's *Infinity of Nations* argues for the idea of a Native New World in the North American interior instead of a French empire.

14. Davis, *Frontier Illinois*, 56–61; Alvord, *The Illinois Country*, 256–66. Two excellent modern treatments of Pontiac's Rebellion are Gregory Dowd, *War under Heaven: Pontiac, the Indian Nations, & the British Empire* (Baltimore: Johns Hopkins University Press, 2002); David Dixon, *Never Come to Peace Again: Pontiac's Uprising and the Fate of the British Empire in North America* (Norman: University of Oklahoma Press, 2005).

15. Walter S. Dunn Jr., *Frontier Profit and Loss: The British Army and the Fur Traders, 1760–1764* (Westport, CT: Greenwood Press, 1998), 148–49; Davis, *Frontier Illinois*, 58–59.

16. Foley, *Genesis of Missouri*, 31–32; Aron, *American Confluence*, 59.

17. William E. Foley and C. David Rice, *The First Chouteaus: River Barons of Early St. Louis* (Urbana: University of Illinois Press, 1983), 1–9; Aron, *American Confluence*, 63; Foley, *Genesis of Missouri*, 33, 38–40; Carl J. Ekberg and Sharon K. Person, *St. Louis Rising: The French Regime of Louis St. Ange de Bellerive* (Urbana: University of Illinois Press, 2015).

18. J. Frederick Fausz, *Founding St. Louis: First City of the New West* (Charleston, SC: History Press, 2011), 41–47.

19. Ibid., 48; James Julian Coleman Jr., *Gilbert Antoine de St. Maxent: The Spanish-Frenchman of New Orleans* (New Orleans: Pelican, 1968), 19.

20. Fausz, *Founding St. Louis*, 67–68; Patricia Cleary, *The World, the Flesh, and the Devil: A History of Colonial St. Louis* (Columbia: University of Missouri Press, 2011), 85–99. In their recent *St. Louis Rising*, Carl Ekberg and Sharon Person challenge the long-accepted founding story of St. Louis, arguing that the fourteen-year-old Auguste Chouteau could never have commanded the men who began the building of St. Louis. Instead, they argue that Laclède and Chouteau likely joined a number of men relocating from the east side of the Mississippi to found the new town. They also take issue with Laclède's naming of St. Louis, concluding that it is impossible

154 / NOTES

to know who actually gave the town its name. Ekberg and Person, *St. Louis Rising*, 58–60, 107–108.

21. The most thorough examination of the British occupation of Illinois and its consequences remains Clarence Carter, *Great Britain and the Illinois Country, 1763–1774* (1910; reprint, Honolulu: University Press of the Pacific, 2004), particularly ch. 2–4.

22. Walter S. Dunn, *People of the American Frontier: The Coming of the American Revolution* (Westport, CT: Praeger, 2005), 6–8, 7–75, 166–69.

23. The Camden-Yorke opinion was issued by the British government in response to a complaint by the British East India Company about the difficulties involved in gaining Crown approval for land purchases in India. Lindsay G. Robertson, *Conquest by Law: How the Discovery of America Dispossessed Indigenous Peoples of Their Lands* (Oxford: Oxford University Press, 2005), 7–11. The dispute in America about the legality of individuals buying land from Indians was not settled until the Supreme Court ruling in *Johnson v. M"Intosh* (1823) that finally dashed the hopes of the two companies whose claims were kept alive for nearly half a century. For the circumstances surrounding Virginia's eventual cession of its western lands, see Peter Onuf, "Toward Federalism: Virginia, Congress, and the Western Lands," *William and Mary Quarterly* 34 (July 1977): 353–74.

24. Davis, *Frontier Illinois*, 63–64.

25. Clark to [Patrick Henry?], 1777, *George Rogers Clark Papers, 1771–1781*, ed. James Alton James (Springfield: Illinois State Historical Library, 1912), 1:30–32.

26. William Nester, *George Rogers Clark: "I Glory in War"* (Norman: University of Oklahoma Press, 2012), 65–66; Thomas Abernethy, *Western Lands and The American Revolution* (New York: Russell & Russell, 1959), 193–98. Historians differ as to whether Clark conceived of the plan to invade Illinois and then sought backing, or Henry and his fellow speculators were behind it from the start. For example, Abernethy favors the latter explanation while Davis, *Frontier Illinois*, 69–70, supports the former.

27. Alvord, *The Illinois Country*, 323–31; James Alton James, *The Life of George Rogers Clark* (1928; reprint, New York: Greenwood Press, 1969), 127–30; R. David Edmunds, *The Potawatomis: Keepers of the Fire* (Norman: University of Oklahoma Press, 1978), 101–10. Following the British recapture of Vincennes in the fall of 1778, Clark led his men on an epic winter march across the waterlogged trail linking Kaskaskia to Vincennes, where he recaptured the town and took prisoner the notorious British officer, Henry Hamilton, known as the "hair buyer." The best account of the entire campaign is in Clark's own words, George Rogers Clark, *The Conquest of the Illinois*, ed. Milo Milton Quaife (1920; reprint, Carbondale: Southern Illinois University Press, 2001.

28. Davis, *Frontier Illinois*, 77–79; Shirley Christian, *Before Lewis and Clark: The Story of the Chouteaus, the French Dynasty That Ruled America's Frontier* (New York: Farrar, Straus and Giroux, 2004), 80–84; Frederick A. Hodes, *Beyond the Frontier: A History of St. Louis to 1821* (Tucson: Patrice Press, 2004), 195; James, *The Life of George Rogers Clark*, 123.

29. Alvord, *The Illinois Country*, 358–78; James, *The Life of George Rogers Clark*, 163–68, 176.

30. Foley, *Genesis of Missouri*, 38–47. Still valuable for understanding the

complexities of the effect of the American Revolution on Spain's holdings is Arthur Whitaker, *The Spanish-American Frontier: 1783-1795* (1927; reprint).

31. Among the essential discussions of the diplomacy that ended the American Revolution and the subsequent problems in the West are Abernethy, *Western Lands*, 274-87; Albert Z. Carr, *The Coming of War: An Account of the Remarkable Events Leading to the War of 1812* (Garden City, NY: Doubleday, 1960), 17-57; Francis S. Philbrick, *The Rise of the West, 1754-1830* (New York: Harper & Row, 1965), 64-79, 134-62; J. Leitch Wright Jr., *Britain and the American Frontier 1783-1815* (Athens: University of Georgia Press, 1975), 1-37.

32. Carr, *The Coming of War*, 67; Nicolas de Finiels, *An Account of Upper Louisiana* (Columbia: University of Missouri Press, 1989), 81.

33. Most of the memorials and petitions sent from Illinois are found in French and English in Clarence W. Alvord, ed., *Cahokia Records, 1778-1790* (Springfield: Illinois State Historical Library, 1907), and Clarence W. Alvord, *Kaskaskia Records 1778-1790* (Springfield: Illinois State Historical Library, 1909); John Barnhart, *Valley of Democracy: The Frontier versus the Plantation in the Ohio Valley, 1775-1818* (Bloomington: Indiana University Press, 1953), 54, 59-60.

34. Davis, *Frontier Illinois*, 82-89.

35. Alvord, *Illinois Country*, 417. For the Kentucky land situation, see Stephen Aron, *How the West Was Lost: The Transformation of Kentucky from Daniel Boone to Henry Clay* (Baltimore: Johns Hopkins University Press, 1996).

36. John Reynolds, *The Pioneer History of Illinois, Containing the Discovery in 1673, and the History of the Country to the Year 1818, When the State Government Was Organized* (1852; reprint, Ann Arbor: University Microfilms, 1968), 116-18, 160-65, 291-94.

37. Alvord, *The Illinois Country*, 339; Arthur Boggess, *The Settlement of Illinois 1778-1830* (Chicago: Chicago Historical Society, 1908), 40-70.

38. Alvord, *Illinois Country*, 358.

39. Ibid., 36-62; Father Gibault to the Bishop of Quebec, 6 June 1786, *Kaskaskia Records*, ed. Clarence Alvord, 542.

40. Alvord, *Illinois Country*, 363.

41. Harmar to the Secretary of War, 24 November 1787, Smith, *St. Clair Papers*, 2:32. Descriptions of the French as indolent and not ready for democracy were also frequent after the Louisiana Purchase.

42. Howard C. Rice, *Barthelemi Tardiveau: A French Trader in the West* (Baltimore: Johns Hopkins Press, 1938), 2-3; Alvord, *Illinois Country*, 371.

43. Rice, *Barthelemi Tardiveau*, 7-12; Boggess, *Settlement of Illinois*, 57.

44. St. Clair to Luke Decker, Smith, *St. Clair Papers*, 1:206, 2:318-19, 2:176; Davis, *Frontier Illinois*, 101.45. Rice, *Barthelemi Tardiveau*, 13-15, 25-26.

46. Barthelemi Tardiveau to St. John de Crevecoeur, 7 October 1789, Rice, *Barthelemi Tardiveau*, 35.

47. Ibid., 40-48; Carl Ekberg, *A French Aristocrat in the American West: The Shattered Dreams of De Lassus de Luzières* (Columbia: University of Missouri Press, 2010), 31-49, 61-72. Ekberg's account of Tardiveau's failed plan introduces another colorful character from this period, De Lassus de Luzières, a French aristocrat who fled his country's revolution in hopes of finding safety and success in the United States. His involvement with Tardiveau and Carondelet led to De Lassus moving his family from the United States to Upper Louisiana.

48. Foley, *Genesis of Missouri*, 99; Carl J. Ekberg, *Stealing Indian Women: Native Slavery in the Illinois Country* (Urbana: University of Illinois Press, 2007), 54–63, 81, 91–94.

49. "Virtutis, Veritatisque Amicus" to Bernardo de Gálvez, 12 June and 23 June 1780, and the People of Illinois to Gálvez, 1780, *The Spanish in the Mississippi Valley, 1762–1804*, ed. John F. McDermott (Urbana: University of Illinois Press, 1965), 363–72.

50. A wealth of correspondence between Spanish officials in Louisiana concerning the various commercial and military threats they faced can be found in *The Spanish Regime in Missouri*, ed. Louis Houck, 2 vols. (Chicago: R.R. Donnelley, 1908), and in *Before Lewis and Clark: Documents Illustrating the History of the Missouri, 1785–1804*, ed. A. P. Nasitir, 2 vols. (1952; reprint, Lincoln: University of Nebraska Press, 1990).

51. Foley, *Genesis of Missouri*, 64–65; John Sugden, *Tecumseh: A Life* (New York: Henry Holt, 1997), 52; John Bowes, *Exiles and Pioneers: Eastern Indians in the Trans-Mississippi West* (Cambridge, UK: Cambridge University Press, 2007), 19–52.

52. Thorne, *The Many Hands of My Relations*, 80–81; Landon Y. Jones, *William Clark and the Shaping of the West* (New York: Hill and Wang, 2004), 45; Sugden, *Tecumseh*, 53–55. One of Lorimier's sons was among those chosen by Meriwether Lewis to attend West Point. Foley, *Genesis of Missouri*, 141. There is some disagreement about Lorimier's ethnicity, with some believing him to be the métis child of an Indian mother. The evidence leans toward Lorimier as French-Canadian but is not conclusive.

53. Esteban Miró to Francisco Cruzat, 15 May 1787, *Spain in the Mississippi Valley*, ed. Lawrence Kinnaird (Washington, DC: Government Printing Office, 1946), 2:201; Foley, *Genesis of Missouri*, 63, 68–69.

54. Proclamation by Governor Miro, *St. Clair Papers*, 122–23; Hamtramck to Harmar, 29 July 1789, *Outpost On The Wabash 1787–1791*, ed. Gayle Thornbrough (Indianapolis: Indiana Historical Society, 1957), 178–83; Foley, *Genesis of Missouri*, 60–63; Bowes, *Exiles*, 25–29.

55. Carondelet to Branceforte, 7 June 1796, Nasitir, *Before Lewis and Clark*, 2:440.

56. Frederick Hodes, *Beyond the Frontier*, 267; Carondelet to Trudeau, 27 May 1794, 1:212; Trudeau to Carondelet, 28 September, 1793, 197–99; Trudeau to Carondelet, 24 April 1794, 207–208; Trudeau to Carondelet, 27 May 1794, 214–216; Trudeau to Carondelet, 31 May 1794, 214; Carondelet to Clamorgan, 22 July 1794, 236–37, Nasitir, *Before Lewis and Clark*.

57. Jon Kukla, *A Wilderness So Immense: The Louisiana Purchase and the Destiny of America* (New York: Knopf, 2003), 166.

58. Clark's title from Kukla, *A Wilderness So Immense*, 176; Clark himself advanced $4,680 for the proposed attack. James, *The Life of George Rogers Clark*, 425; George Rogers Clark to Genet, 1794, *The American Historical Review* 18, no. 4 (July 1913): 782.

59. William E. Foley and C. David Rice, *The First Chouteaus: River Barons of Early St. Louis* (Urbana: University of Illinois Press, 1983), 52–55; Thorne, *Many Hands of My Relations*, 104–106.

60. W. Raymond Wood, *Prologue to Lewis and Clark: The Mackay and Evans Expedition* (Norman: University of Oklahoma Press, 2003); Lavender, *The Fist in the Wilderness*, 37–38.

61. Minutes of the Council of State, 27 May 1789, Nasitir, *Before Lewis and Clark*, 2:432–39; Foley, *Genesis of Missouri*, 74–75; Whitaker, *The Spanish-American Frontier*;

Samuel Bemis, *Pinckney's Treaty: America's Advantage from Europe's Distress, 1783-1800* (1926; reprint, New Haven: Yale University Press, 1960).

62. The second clause of the Jay Treaty classified residents of border areas at the time of the 1796 surrender of the British forts to be American citizens unless they chose otherwise. Lavender, *Fist in the Wilderness*; Foley, *Genesis of Missouri*, 76-77.

63. Foley, *Genesis of Missouri*, 77-80. Within the vast literature dealing with the Louisiana Purchase are a number of thorough treatments of the Spanish retrocession. Noteworthy are Frederic Austin Ogg, *The Opening of the Mississippi: A Struggle for Supremacy in the American Interior* (1904; reprint, New York: Haskell House, 1969); Carr, *The Coming of War*; Marshall Sprague, *So Vast, So Beautiful A Land: Louisiana and the Purchase* (Boston: Little, Brown, 1974); and Alexander de Conde, *This Affair of Louisiana* (New York: Charles Scribner's Sons, 1976).

64. One expression of the Indians' attitudes toward Americans came from the citizens of Kaskaskia: "The name of an American among them is a disgrace, because we have no superior: our horses, horned cattle and corn are stole . . . for ever since the cession of this territory to Congress we have been neglected as an abandoned people," Thornbrough, *Outpost on the Wabash*, 190-91; Patrick Griffin, *American Leviathan: Empire, Nation, and Revolutionary Frontier* (New York: Hill and Wang, 2007). Griffin casts the growing racial hatred of whites for Indians during these years as driven by a gradual rejection of the "stadial" theory of development, which posited stages of development for people based on the assumption of an innate moral capacity. Where white settlers had once viewed Indians as simply at a lower stage of development and capable of improvement, they now saw them as innately savage—as irredeemable. In light of this change in attitude and in the absence of any effective sovereignty, a Hobbesian state of nature ensued on the frontier.

65. Reynolds, *Pioneer History of Illinois*, 153. Supporting the idea that white settlers were no longer differentiating between Indians is the fact that John Reynolds, a white settler himself during this period, rarely refers to Indians with any specificity as to tribe or nation.

66. George Rogers Clark to Richard H. Lee, received 8 June 1786, Boggess, *The Settlement of Illinois*, 48; Reynolds, *Pioneer History of Illinois*, 185-88.

67. Kathleen DuVal, *The Native Ground: Indians and Colonists in the Heart of the Continent* (Philadelphia: University of Pennsylvania Press, 2006). DuVal argues persuasively throughout the book that Europeans (mostly French) in parts of the Illinois Country did, in fact, become incorporated into a "native ground" dominated by Indians—during the eighteenth century. This argument refines traditional notions of European colonization or the more recent conceptualization of a middle ground of accommodation between groups. Richard White, *The Middle Ground: Indians, Empires, and Republics in the Great Lakes Region, 1650-1815* (Cambridge, UK: Cambridge University Press, 1991).

68. J. B. Martigny to Monsieur [Galvez?], 30 October 1779, Nasitir, *Before Lewis and Clark*, 1:71. It should be noted that Spanish officials were also forced to ignore violations of the ban on Indian slavery, although the desire to which they actually wished to eliminate the practice is subject to debate. See Ekberg, *Stealing Indian Women*.

69. Arthur St. Clair to George Washington, [No date], 1790, *St. Clair Papers*, 2:175-76.

70. John Weaver, *The Great Land Rush and the Making of the Modern World, 1650-1900* (Montreal & Kingston: McGill-Queen's University Press, 2003), 49.

71. Witgen, *Infinity*, 343–45; Thorne, *Many Hands*, 134–37.

2 / The Louisiana Purchase, Territorial Government, and Contested Lands

1. Petition to Congress From Inhabitants of the Illinois Country, 10 January 1799, *The Territorial Papers of the United States*, ed. Clarence Carter (Washington, DC: US Government Printing Office, 1934–75), 3:10–13.

2. Casa Calvo to Delassus, 30 December 1800, *Before Lewis and Clark: Documents Illustrating the History of the Missouri, 1785–1804*, ed. A. P. Nasitir (1952; reprint, Lincoln: University of Nebraska Press, 1990), 2:627–28; Robidoux and Others to Governor of Louisiana, 8 December 1800, ibid., 624–27; Concession by Salcedo to Lisa and Others, 12 June 1802, ibid., 687–89; Salcedo to Delassus, 19 June 1802, ibid., 689–90; Delassus to Salcedo, 28 August 1802, ibid., 705–706; Richard Oglesby, *Manuel Lisa and the Opening of the Missouri Fur Trade of the Far West* (Norman: University of Oklahoma Press, 1963), 23–24; Willard H. Rollings, *The Osage: An Ethnohistorical Study of Hegemony on the Prairie Plans* (Columbia: University of Missouri Press, 1992), 193–96.

3. The secret Treaty of San Ildefonso ceding Louisiana to France was signed October 1, 1800. Word of the retrocession did not reach St. Louis until June 1802 although Jefferson learned of it in December 1801. Shirley Christian, *Before Lewis and Clark: The Story of the Chouteaus, the French Dynasty That Ruled America's Frontier* (New York: Farrar, Straus and Giroux, 2004), 106–108; Dumas Malone, *Jefferson the President: First Term, 1801–1805* (Boston: Little, Brown, 1970), 248. On October 18, 1802, a proclamation was published closing the American deposit at New Orleans. Arthur Whitaker, *The Mississippi Question 1795–1803: A Study in Trade, Politics, and Diplomacy* (1934; reprint, Gloucester, MA: Peter Smith, 1962), 189.

4. Jefferson to Livingston, 18 April 1802, *Thomas Jefferson: Writings* (New York: Library of America, 1984), 1104–107; Jefferson to Pierre Samuel du Pont de Nemours, 25 April 1802; de Nemours to Jefferson, 30 April 1802; de Nemours to Jefferson, 12 May 1802; Jefferson to de Nemours, 1 February 1803, *Correspondence between Thomas Jefferson and Pierre Samuel du Pont de Nemours 1798–1817*, ed. Dumas Malone (New York: Da Capo, 1970), 46–79.

5. Thomas Jefferson, *Notes on the State of Virginia*, in *Jefferson: Writings* (New York: Library of America, 1984), 132.

6. Jefferson's Message to Congress, 18 January 1803, *Letters of the Lewis and Clark Expedition with Related Documents 1783–1854*, ed. Donald Jackson (Urbana: University of Illinois Press, 1978), 1:10–13.

7. Albert Gallatin to Thomas Jefferson, 13 April 1803, *Letters of Lewis & Clark*, 1:32–33.

8. Jefferson to William Henry Harrison, 27 February 1803, *Messages and Letters of William Henry Harrison*, ed. Logan Esarey (New York: Arno, 1975): 1:69–73; Dumas Malone, *Jefferson the President: First Term 1801–1805* (Boston: Little, Brown, 1970), 269–70.

9. Governor Harrison to the President, 30 December 1801, *The Territorial Papers of the United States*, ed. Clarence Carter (Washington: US Government Printing Office, 1934–75), 7:42–43.

10. Thomas Jefferson to de Nemours, 1 November 1803, Malone, *Correspondence*, 79.

11. The official transfer of Louisiana from France to the United States took place

in New Orleans on December 20, 1803. The best account of the ceremonies in New Orleans and in St. Louis can be found in Floyd C. Shoemaker, "The Louisiana Purchase, 1803, and the Transfer of Upper Louisiana to the United States, 1804," *Missouri Historical Review* 48 (October 1953): 10–15.

12. One contemporary described Louisiana as "A great waste, a wilderness unpeopled with any beings except wolves and wandering Indians," Fabricus in Boston, *Columbian Centinel*, 13 July 1803, quoted in Malone, *Jefferson the President: First Term* (Boston: Little, Brown, 1970), 297. Among the best accounts of the imperial fur trade competition are David Lavender, *The Fist in the Wilderness* (1964; reprint, Lincoln: University of Nebraska Press, 1998); John Denis Haeger, *John Jacob Astor: Business and Finance in the Early Republic* (Detroit: Wayne State University Press, 1991); and Richard Oglesby, *Manuel Lisa and the Opening of the Missouri Fur Trade of the Far West* (Norman: University of Oklahoma Press, 1963).

13. Samuel W. Thomas, "William Clark's 1795 and 1797 Journals and Their Significance." *Bulletin of the Missouri Historical Society* 25 (1969): 279–95.

14. Thomas T. Davis to the President (Jefferson), 5 October 1803, Carter, *Territorial Papers* 13:7–8; George Muter and Benjamin Sebastian to John Breckinridge, 12 December 1803, ibid., 11–12; Moses Austin to James Richardson, 2 August 1803, Louisiana Purchase Transfer Papers, *Missouri Historical Society*.

15. Lewis to Auguste Chouteau, 4 January 1804, Jackson, *Letters of the Lewis and Clark*, 1:161; Clark's List of Questions, ibid., 157–61; Lewis to Clark, 2 May 1804, ibid., 177–78; Clark to William Croghan, 15 January 1804, ibid., 164; Clark to Croghan, 2 May 1804, ibid., 178.

16. Lewis to Jefferson, 28 December 1803, Jackson, *Letters of the Lewis and Clark Expedition*, 1:148–55. Jefferson's plan for an Indian preserve west of the Mississippi is best explained in his letter to William Henry Harrison, 27 February 1803, Esarey, *Messages and Letters*, 1:69–73.

17. Captain Stoddard's Address to the People of Upper Louisiana, 10 March 1804, "Transfer of Upper Louisiana: Papers of Captain Amos Stoddard," Missouri Historical Society, *Glimpses of the Past* 2 (1935): 87–91.

18. Stoddard to His Mother Mrs. Samuel Benham, 16 June 1804, "Papers of Captain Stoddard," 112.

19. William C. C. Claiborne and James Wilkinson to Stoddard, 16 January 1804, "Papers of Captain Stoddard," 80; Amos Stoddard to General Dearborn, 15 March 1804, ibid., 92–93; Stoddard to William Claiborne, 26 March 1804, ibid., 98; Financial Records of the Lewis and Clark Expedition, 5 August 1807, Jackson, *Letters of the Lewis and Clark Expedition*, 2:419–31.

20. Stoddard to Claiborne, 26 March 1804, "Papers of Captain Stoddard," 98; Stoddard to Dearborn, 3 June 1804, ibid., 110–11.

21. Dearborn to Stoddard, 8 May 1804, "Papers of Captain Stoddard," 101.

22. William E. Foley, *The Genesis of Missouri: From Wilderness Outpost to Statehood* (Columbia: University of Missouri Press, 1989), 149–53.

23. Amos Stoddard to William Claiborne, 19 May 1804, Amos Stoddard Papers, Missouri Historical Society, folder 7; Foley, *Genesis of Missouri*, 149–53.

24. Christian, *Before Lewis and Clark*, 23; Lewis to Clark, 18 February 1804, Jackson, *Letters of the Lewis and Clark Expedition*, 1:167–68; Foley, *Genesis*, 141; Lewis to Jefferson, 18 May 1804, Jackson, *Letters of the Lewis and Clark Expedition*, 1:192–94.

25. Jefferson to the Osage, ibid., 200–202.

26. The Secretary of War (Dearborn) to Pierre Chouteau, 17 July 1804, Carter, *Territorial Papers*, 13:31–32; Albert Gallatin to Jefferson, 20 August 1804, quoted in Foley and Rice, *The First Chouteaus*, 109–10.

27. Committee of the Town of St. Louis to Stoddard, 4 August 1804, "Papers of Captain Stoddard," 116–17.

28. Jean-Baptiste Vallé to Charles Delassus, 19 March 1804, quoted in Carl J. Ekberg, *Colonial St. Genevieve: An Adventure on the Mississippi Frontier* (Gerald, MO: Patrice Press, 1985), 84.

29. Minutes of a Meeting at St. Louis, 14 September 1804, Carter, *Territorial Papers*, 13:44; Representation and Petition of the Representatives Elected by the Freemen of the Territory of Louisiana, *American State Papers*, misc. 1 (Washington, DC: Gales & Seaton, 1832–1861), 400–404.

30. Foley, *Genesis of Missouri*, 151.

31. Ibid., 154–55; Proclamation by Governor Harrison, 1 October 1804, Carter, *Territorial Papers*, 13:51–52; Harrison to Jefferson, 6 November 1804, Esarey, *Messages and Letters*, 1:110–11.

32. Harrison to Jefferson, 6 November 1804, in Esarey, *Messages and Letters*, 1:110–11; James Neal Primm, *Lion of the Valley: St. Louis, Missouri, 1764–1980*, 3rd edition (St. Louis: Missouri Historical Society Press, 1998), 74–76; Memorandum by the Secretary of the Treasury re Claims to the Dubuque Lead Mines, 7 January 1807, Carter, *Territorial Papers*, 14:73–74.

33. Pierre Chouteau to Henry Dearborn, 2 March 1805, quoted in Christian, *Before Lewis and Clark*, 128.

34. See Chastain, *First Chouteaus*, for the most complete account of Pierre Chouteau's remarkable career.

35. Report of House Committee on Petitions From St. Clair and Randolph Counties, 24 November 1803, in Carter, *Territorial Papers*, 7:157–58.

36. J. P. Dunn Jr., *Indiana: A Redemption from Slavery* (Boston: Houghton, Mifflin, 1899), 325–54; Andrew R. L. Cayton, *Frontier Indiana* (Bloomington: Indiana University Press, 1996), 236–39.

37. Harrison to the Secretary of War, 25 March 1802, Minutes of Indian Conference, 17 September 1802, Esarey, *Messages*, 1:47, 56–57; Secretary of the Treasury to the President, 22 June 1803, Carter, *Territorial Papers*, 7:116. Jefferson and Gallatin were deeply involved in monitoring the leasing of the salt springs. Many letters between them include exchanges on lease terms, prices, distribution, profits to the lessees, etc.

38. Secretary of the Treasury to John Badollet and Michael Jones, 9 July 1804, in Carter, *Territorial Papers*, 7:205–208; for Vincennes and Kaskaskia commissions, Michael Jones to the Secretary of the Treasury, 19 August 1804, ibid., 212–14; Secretary of the Treasury to Michael Jones, 26 September 1804, ibid., 218–19; Jared Mansfield to the Secretary of the Treasury, 13 October 1804, ibid., 223–25; Secretary of Treasury to Harrison, 10 July 1804, Esarey, *Messages*, 1:101–102.

39. Memorial to Congress by Inhabitants of St. Clair and Randolph Counties, 12 December 1804, Carter, *Territorial Papers*, 7:243–47; Memorial to the President by Citizens of St. Charles, 30 December 1805, ibid., 13:360–61; Minutes of a Meeting at St. Louis, 14 September 1804, ibid., 43–46; Samuel Hammond to the Secretary of War,

29 December 1805, ibid., 352–55; James Wilkinson to the Officials of Louisiana, 22 August 1805, *Letters of Lewis & Clark*, 1:167.

40. Foley, *Genesis*, 147–58, 170–74; Lucien Carr, *Missouri: A Bone of Contention* (Boston: Houghton, Mifflin, 1888), 82–86.

41. John Rice Jones to Judge Davis, 21 January 1804, for first word of fraud and mention of Lewis & Clark knowing about it and informing Jefferson, Carter, *Territorial Papers*, 7:168–69.

42. For a thorough treatment of Wilkinson's intrigues with Spanish officials, see James Jacobs, *Tarnished Warrior: Major-General James Wilkinson* (New York: Macmillan, 1938), 77–83, 94–98, 99–103, 128–29, 133–38, 149–51, 183–90, 205–206. A good modern treatment of Wilkinson's notorious career is Andro Linklater's *An Artist in Treason: The Extraordinary Double Life of James Wilkinson* (New York: Walker, 2009).

43. For Zebulon Pike's expedition, see Jacobs, *Tarnished Warrior*, 221; James Wilkinson to the Secretary of War, 15 June 1805, in Carter, *Territorial Papers*, 13:135–36; Governor Wilkinson to Secretary of State, 28 July 1805, ibid., 172–75; Governor Wilkinson to the Secretary of State, 24 August 1805, ibid., 189–91; Governor Wilkinson to the Secretary of War, 8 September 1805, ibid., 204–207. Wilkinson's closing of the Mississippi River was protested as violating both the Jay Treaty and the 1802 Act to regulate Indian trade. He admitted to Dearborn in his November 8 letter that his "conduct . . . has been somewhat extrajudicial," but thought extreme measures were called for.

44. Governor Wilkinson to the Secretary of War, 22 September 1805, Carter, *Territorial Papers*, 13:227–30; John B. Treat to the Secretary of War, 15 November 1805, Carter, *Territorial Papers*, 13:276–85.

45. Rufus Easton to the President, 17 January 1805, Carter, *Territorial Papers*, 13:82, for lead mines bill; Resolution On Lead Mines In The Territory, 21 November 1804, ibid., 73: For Austin and Smith T's long-running feud, the best source is Dick Steward, *Frontier Swashbuckler: The Life and Legend of John Smith T* (Columbia: University of Missouri Press, 2000).

46. Jacobs, *Tarnished Warrior*, 219. His partner in this venture was one of his officers, and one aspect of the deal may have been Wilkinson's need to entice the man to accept an otherwise unattractive frontier post. For the Austin-Wilkinson feud, see the Rufus Easton Papers, Missouri Historical Society, folder 4, as well as several letters in Carter, *Territorial Papers*, 13.

47. Governor Wilkinson to the Secretary of State, 7 September 1805, Carter, *Territorial Papers*, 13:195–96; Governor Wilkinson to James Madison, 21 September 1805, ibid., 219–20; The Secretary of War to Governor Wilkinson, 16 October 1805, ibid., 239–40.

48. A complete account of Aaron Burr's western intrigues is found in Thomas Abernethy, *The Burr Conspiracy* (New York: Oxford University Press, 1954). For the career of James Wilkinson in the 1790s, see Jacobs, *Tarnished Warrior*. For a good overview of the region's imperial struggles in this period, see the classics, Whitaker's *The Spanish-American Frontier* and Bemis's *Pinckney's Treaty*, as well as more recent works such as Jon Kukla's *A Wilderness So Immense: The Louisiana Purchase and the Destiny of America* (New York: Knopf, 2003).

49. J. P. Dunn Jr., *Indiana: A Redemption from Slavery* (Boston: Houghton, Mifflin, 1899), 319–24; Jefferson to Harrison, 28 April 1805, Esarey, *Messages*, 1:126–27.

50. Harrison's Address to the General Assembly, 29 July, Esarey, *Messages*, 1:153–54.

51. Jefferson's Message to Congress, 18 January 1803, *Letters of Lewis and* Clark, 1:10–13; John B. Treat to Secretary of War, 15 November 1805, Carter, *Territorial Papers*, 13:276–84.

52. Petition to Congress by Inhabitants of Randolph and St. Clair Counties, 2 December 1805, Carter, *Territorial Papers*, 7:317–23; Petition to Congress by Inhabitants of the Territory, 25 December 1805, ibid., 13:327–28.

53. James E. Davis, *Frontier Illinois* (Bloomington: Indiana University Press, 1998), 120; Foley, *Genesis*, 248. The idea that western lands would drain population from eastern states had been around since the end of the Revolution.

54. For the Easton case, see Presentment of the Grand Jury of the Territory, October term, 1805, and Governor Wilkinson to the Secretary of State, 6 November 1805, Carter, *Territorial Papers*, 13:248–51, 253–65; William Carr quote from Carr Papers, Missouri Historical Society.

55. Lucien Carr, *Missouri: A Bone of Contention* (Boston: Houghton Mifflin, 1888), 40–41.

56. Judge Lucas to the Secretary of the Treasury, 12 November 1805, Carter, *Territorial Papers*, 13:269–70; Samuel Hammond to the Secretary of War, 29 December 1805, ibid., 352–55; William C. Carr to the Attorney General, 24 December 1805, ibid., 319–24.

57. The President to Samuel Smith, 4 May 1806, Carter, *Territorial Papers*, 13:504–505; Bill to Extend the Powers of the Surveyor General to the Territory, 21 February 1806, ibid., 448–49; Jared Mansfield to the Secretary of the Treasury, 14 June 1806, ibid., 519–20.

58. Silas Bent to Jared Mansfield, 22 September 1806, Carter, *Territorial Papers*, 14:8–9; The Governor of Indiana Territory to Jared Mansfield, 19 April 1806, ibid., 13:492; Antoine Soulard to Governor Wilkinson, 30 June 1806, ibid., 522–35; Antoine Soulard to the Land Commissioners, 5 November 1806, Carter, ibid., 14:29–34.

59. James Wilkinson to Jefferson, 23 December 1805, *Letters of Lewis and Clark*, 1:272–75; James Wilkinson to Henry Dearborn, 8 October 1805, ibid., 261–62.

60. Clark to Hugh Heney, 20 July 1806, Jackson, *Letters of Lewis & Clark*, 1:309–13. Perversely, Wilkinson also worked to undermine American interests, writing in March 1803 to Spanish officials and urging them to send an expedition to arrest the explorers in what may or may not have been Spanish territory. Jackson, *Letters of Lewis and Clark*, 2:686–687.

61. Message to the Legislature, 17 August 1807, Esarey, *Messages*, 1:229–36. Two good sources for British policy with regard to the fur trade in this period are Colin Calloway, *Crown and Calumet: British-Indian Relations, 1783–1815* (Norman: University of Oklahoma Press, 1987), and J. Leitch Wright Jr., *Britain and the American Frontier, 1783–1815* (Athens: University of Georgia Press, 1975).

62. Harrison to Secretary of War, 11 July 1807, Esarey, *Messages*, 1:222–25; The Prophet to Harrison, [August] 1807, ibid., 251.

63. Message to the Shawnee Prophet, 24 June 1808, William Henry Harrison Papers, Indiana Historical Society Library. The relationships between Harrison, The Prophet, and Tecumseh are best explained in John Sugden, *Tecumseh: A Life*; R. David Edmunds, *The Shawnee Prophet*; Freeman Cleaves, *Old Tippecanoe: William Henry Harrison and His Time* (1939; reprint, Newtown, CT: American Political Biography

Press, 2000); and Cayton, *Frontier Indiana*. For a good overview of Britain's Indian policy during this period, see Timothy Willig's *Restoring the Chain of Friendship: British Policy and the Indians of the Great Lakes, 1783-1815* (Lincoln: University of Nebraska Press, 2008).

64. Meriwether Lewis to William Henry Harrison, 26 May 1808, William Henry Harrison Papers, Indiana Historical Society Library; Oglesby, *Manuel Lisa*, 50-53; William Clark to the Secretary of War, 23 September 1808, Carter, *Territorial Papers*, 14:224-28; Landon Y. Jones, *William Clark and the Shaping of the West* (New York: Hill and Wang, 2004), 167-69. For the Osage perspective on the 1808 treaty, Kathleen DuVal, *The Native Ground: Indians and Colonists in the Heart of the Continent* (Philadelphia: University of Pennsylvania Press, 2006), 200-205; Rollings, *The Osage*, 222-30.

65. Dunn, *Indiana*, 305-83; Foley, *Genesis*, 203-14; Clarence Alvord, *The Illinois Country, 1673-1818* (Springfield: Illinois Centennial Commission, 1920; reprint, Urbana: University of Illinois Press, 1987), 428-33.

66. Governor Lewis to the Secretary of War, 20 August 1808, Carter, *Territorial Papers*, 14:212-19; Governor Lewis to the Secretary of War, 1 July 1808, ibid., 196-203; Jefferson to Harrison, December 22, 1808, Esarey, *Messages*, 1:322-23.

67. Carter, *Territorial Papers*, 14, contains correspondence relating to the various actions taken by Governor Lewis in 1808-1809.

68. The Secretary of War to Governor Lewis, 15 July 1809, Carter, *Territorial Papers*, 14:285-86.

69. William Carr to Charles Carr, 25 August 1809, Carr Papers, MHS. The death of Meriwether Lewis has been the source of ongoing historiographical debate for many years, although the consensus clearly falls on the side of Lewis having taken his own life.

70. Pierre Chouteau Jr. to Secretary of War, 1 September 1809, Carter, *Territorial Papers*, 14:317-18; Pierre Chouteau Jr. to the Secretary of War, 14 December 1809, ibid., 315-19; Pierre Chouteau Jr. to William Eustis, 28 September 1809, in *The Life and Papers of Frederick Bates*, ed. Thomas Maitland Marshall (New York: Arno, 1975), 2:86-92.

71. Alvord, *The Illinois Country*, 430-35; Ninian Edwards, *History of Illinois, from 1778-1833, and Life and Times of Ninian Edwards* (Springfield: Illinois State Journal Co., 1870; reprint, New York: Arno, 1975), 27-36; Governor Edwards to James Gilbreath, 28 June 1809, Carter, *Territorial Papers*, 16:47-48.

72. Alvord, *Illinois Country*, 417-22. Fraudulent and floating claims are the subject of dozens of letters between territorial and federal officials during this period. Some examples are from Carter, *Territorial Papers*, 7, 21 January 1804, 5 May 1806, 16 August 1806, 14 October 1807, 17 July 1808; examples from Carter, *Territorial Papers*, vol. 14, 4 January 1806, 24 January 1806, 13 February 1806; and from Carter, *Territorial Papers*, vol. 16, 6 September 1810, 8 September 1810, 31 October 1810.

73. To Albert Gallatin, 22 July 1808, Marshall, *Life and Papers of Frederick Bates*, 2:7-11.

74. Problems concerning land surveys were also the subject of a great deal of correspondence during this period. Examples from Carter, *Territorial Papers*, vol. 7, 13 October 1804, 13 March 1805, 4 October 1806, 18 January 1807, 22 May 1807, 25 June 1808; examples from Carter, *Territorial Papers*, vol. 14, 30 July 1810, 18 October 1810;

and from Carter, *Territorial Papers*, vol. 16, 4 March 1808, 24 February 1810, 26 April 1810, 3 February 1811.

75. The internal problems within the land commissions themselves are well documented. Some examples are: Bates to Gallatin, 14 July 1807, Marshall, *Life and Papers of Frederic Bates*, 1:158–61; Bates to Gallatin, 28 August 1808, ibid., 2: 20–22; Bates to Gallatin, 25 December 1808, ibid., 47–54; Bates to Benjamin Howard, 8 May 1811, ibid., 178–79; James L. Donaldson to the Secretary of the Treasury, 26 April 1806, Carter, *Territorial Papers*, 13:493–501; Petition to Congress by the Citizens of the Territory, 2 January 1808, Carter, *Territorial Papers*, 14:161–63; William C. Carr to the Secretary of the Treasury, 23 November 1810, ibid., 425.

76. Judge Lucas to the Secretary of the Treasury, 13 February 1810, Carter, *Territorial Papers*, 14:375–76.

77. The Land Commissioners to the Secretary of the Treasury, 15 March 1810, Carter, *Territorial Papers*, 14:378–85; Elias Rector to Jared Mansfield, 26 April 1810, Carter, *Territorial Papers*, 16:96–97.

78. Jefferson to Harrison, 22 December 1808, Esarey, *Messages*, 1:322–23; Bemis, *Jay's Treaty*, for a thorough treatment of the treaty's provisions and implications.

79. Among the numerous letters between territorial and federal officials concerning Indian depredations and the fears of a general war are: William Clark to the Secretary of War, 12 September 1810 and 28 September 1810, Carter, *Territorial Papers*, 14:412–15, 415–16; Nicholas Boilvin to the Secretary of War, 5 March 1811, ibid., 16:154–57; Governor Edwards to the Secretary of War, 27 June 1811, 6 July 1811, 11 August 1811, and 28 September, 1811, ibid., 162–63, 164–66, 169–71, 174–75; Matthew Irwin to the Secretary of War, 19 January 1812, ibid., 184–85; William Henry Harrison to Secretary of War, 6 June 1811, Esarey, *Messages*, 1:512–17.

3 / From Tippecanoe to Portage des Sioux

1. David Lavender, *The Fist in the Wilderness* (1964; reprint, Lincoln: University of Nebraska Press, 1998), 185–87.

2. Volumes 14–17 of *The Territorial Papers of the United States*, ed. Clarence Carter (Washington: US Government Printing Office, 1934–75), contain numerous pieces of correspondence outlining the diplomatic efforts of territorial officials to use diplomacy to curb the violence in the Illinois Country during the war years.

3. See the same volumes as previously for dozens of petitions and memorials sent from the Illinois Country to Washington, protesting the perceived lack of federal support for the war effort in this region. Many of these will appear in subsequent footnotes.

4. Clarence Alvord, *The Illinois Country, 1673–1818* (Springfield: Illinois Centennial Commission, 1920; reprint, Urbana: University of Illinois Press, 1987), 431–32. As per the Northwest Ordinance, Illinois was allowed to advance to the second stage on the word of Governor Edwards, once its population reached 5,000 adult males. The 1805 act that organized Louisiana's territorial government did not include the same provision and so required a specific act of Congress. William Foley, *The Genesis of Missouri: From Wilderness Outpost to Statehood* (Columbia: University of Missouri Press, 1989), 211, 223.

5. Foley, *Genesis*, 210; Petition to Congress by the Inhabitants of the Territory,

24 March 1812, Carter, *Territorial Papers*, 16:204; Governor Edwards to Richard M. Johnson, 14 March 1812, ibid, 199-200; Arthur Boggess, *The Settlement of Illinois 1778-1830* (Chicago: Chicago Historical Society, 1908), 5:112.

6. The most thorough account of fighting in Illinois during this period is found in Gillum Ferguson, *Illinois in the War of 1812* (Urbana: University of Illinois Press, 2012); for Missouri, see R. Douglas Hurt, *Nathan Boone and the American Frontier* (Columbia: University of Missouri Press, 1998).

7. Albert Z. Carr, *The Coming of War: An Account of the Remarkable Events Leading to the War of 1812* (Garden City, NY: Doubleday, 1960), 321-24. Reginald Horsman, *The Causes of the War of 1812* (New York: A.S. Barnes, 1962) is among those arguing for domestic politics on both sides driving the conflict. On p. 244 he explicitly states that American leaders would not have gone to war had Parliament rescinded the hated Order in Council (which it did, but the news did not reach the United States until after a declaration of war had been voted). Political machinations by a weakening Federalist Party are cited as the primary cause of the war in Roger H. Brown, *The Republic in Peril: 1812* (1964; reprint, New York: W.W. Norton, 1971) and Richard Buel Jr., *America on the Brink: How the Political Struggle over the War of 1812 Almost Destroyed the Young Republic* (New York: Palgrave Macmillan, 2005). The need for a changing society to both prove and renew itself is cited as the main impetus for war in Steven Watts, *The Republic Reborn: War and the Making of Liberal America, 1790-1820* (Baltimore: Johns Hopkins University Press, 1987).

8. Colin G. Calloway, *Crown and Calumet: British-Indian Relations, 1783-1815* (Norman: University of Oklahoma Press, 1987), 227-28; Timothy D. Willig, *Restoring the Chain of Friendship: British Policy and the Indians of the Great Lakes, 1783-1815* (Lincoln: University of Nebraska Press, 2008); Thomas Forsyth to Governor Edwards, 13 July 1812, Carter, *Territorial Papers*, 16:250.

9. Willard H. Rollings, *The Osage: An Ethnohistorical Study of Hegemony on the Prairie Plains* (Columbia: University of Missouri Press, 1992), 220-22, 233-35.

10. Robert M. Owens, *Mr. Jefferson's Hammer: William Henry Harrison and the Origins of American Indian Policy* (Norman: University of Oklahoma Press, 2007), 135-36; Calloway. *Crown and Calumet*, 55-56; R. David. Edmunds, *The Potawatomis: Keepers of the Fire* (Norman: University of Oklahoma Press, 1978), 164-67; John Sugden. *Tecumseh: A Life* (New York: Henry Holt, 1997), 170-73.

11. Edmunds, *The Potawatomis*, 130-32; Sugden, *Tecumseh*, 172; Calloway, *Crown and Calumet*, 206; Carr, *Coming of War*, 294.

12. Edmunds, *The Potawatomis*, 164-65; Lavender, *Fist in the Wilderness*, 188-89.

13. Alvord, *The Illinois Country*, 439; Milo Milton Quaife, *Chicago and the Old Northwest, 1673-1835* (1913; reprint, Urbana: University of Illinois Press, 2001), 301-305; Calloway, *Crown and Calumet*, 135.

14. George C. Sibley to Governor Clark, 28 November 1812, Carter, *Territorial Papers*, 14:712-14; John Denis Haeger, *John Jacob Astor: Business and Finance in the Early Republic* (Detroit: Wayne State University Press, 1991), 96-98.

15. A Petition to the Secretary of War From the Inhabitants of Arkansas District, received 14 April 1812, Carter, *Territorial Papers*, 14:544-45; Petition to Congress by the Territorial Legislature, 30 November 1812, ibid., 16:271-72; Governor Edwards to the Secretary of War, 21 July 1812, ibid., 244-47; Governor Howard to the Secretary of War, 20 September 1812, Carter, ibid., 14:593-94.

16. Ninian W. Edwards, *History of Illinois, from 1778–1833, and Life and Times of Ninian Edwards* (1870; reprint, New York: Arno, 1975), 69–72, 84; R. Douglas Hurt, *Nathan Boone and the American Frontier* (Columbia: University of Missouri Press, 1998), 82–94.

17. Lavender, *Fist in the Wilderness*, 180, 183; Thomas Forsyth to Governor Edwards, 13 July 1812, Carter, *Territorial Papers*, 16:250; Edmunds, *Potawatomis*, 164–65, 193–94.

18. Landon Y. Jones, *William Clark and the Shaping of the West* (New York: Hill and Wang, 2004), 208; Joseph Charless to the Secretary of War, 7 February 1813, Carter, *Territorial Papers*, 14:629–30; Governor Howard to the Secretary of War, 6 March 1813, ibid., 640–45; Shadrach Bond and Edward Hempstead to the Secretary of War, 18 January 1813, ibid., 16:290–91.

19. John Reynolds, *The Pioneer History of Illinois, Containing the Discovery in 1673, and the History of the Country to the Year 1818, When the State Government Was Organized* (1852; reprint, Ann Arbor: University Microfilms, 1968), 404; Alvord, *Illinois Country*, 442.20. Governor Howard to the Secretary of War, 10 January 1813, Carter, *Territorial Papers*, 14:614–21; Governor Howard to the Secretary of War, 12 April 1813, ibid., 657–662; Governor Edwards to the Secretary of War, 12 April 1813, Carter, ibid., 16:312–15; Daniel Bissell to the Secretary of War, 30 March 1813, Daniel Bissell Papers, *Missouri Historical Society*, box 1, folder 3.

21. Alvord, *Illinois Country*, 445–46; Governor Clark to the Secretary of War, 12 September 1813, Carter, *Territorial Papers*, 14:697–98; Benjamin Howard to the Secretary of War, 28 October 28, 1813, ibid., 370–72; Edmunds, *Potawatomis*, 201.

22. James E. Davis, *Frontier Illinois* (Bloomington: Indiana University Press, 1998), 149; Edmunds, *Potawatomis*, 198; Governor Clark to the Secretary of War, 2 February 1814, Carter, *Territorial Papers*, 14:738–39.

23. Governor Clark to the Secretary of War, 2 February 1814, Carter, *Territorial Papers*, 14:739; Delegate Hempstead to the Secretary of War, 22 March 1814, ibid., 744; The Secretary of War to Benjamin Howard, 20 April 1814, ibid., 750; Governor Clark to the Secretary of War, 4 May 1814, ibid., 762–63; Governor Clark to the Secretary of War, 5 June 1814, ibid., 768–69; Governor Clark to the Secretary of War, 31 July 1814, ibid., 781–82; Lavender, *Fist in the Wilderness*, 210–11.

24. Governor Clark to the Secretary of War, 28 March 1814, Carter, *Territorial Papers*, 14:746–47; William Russell to the Secretary of War, 14 December 1814, ibid., 800–801; Jones, *William Clark*, 218, Foley, *Genesis of Missouri*, 232.

25. Acting Governor Bates to Governor Howard, 27 February 1814, Carter, *Territorial Papers*, 14:638; Pierre Chouteau to the Secretary of War, 5 March 1813, ibid., 639–40; Pierre Chouteau to the Secretary of War, 20 May 1813, ibid., 671–72; Acting Governor Bates to Pierre Chouteau, 4 March 1813, ibid., 673–74; Delegate Hempstead to the Secretary of War, 14 June 1813, ibid., 676.

26. Secretary Pope to Delegate Stephenson, 20 October 1814, Carter, *Territorial Papers*, 17:35; Foley, *Genesis of Missouri*, 231. William Clark's popularity in Missouri peaked with his expedition to capture Prairie du Chien and declined thereafter as citizens became increasingly frustrated with Indian diplomacy as opposed to military conquest.

27. Rollings, *The Osage*, 233. The Osage rejected overtures from Tecumseh to join his pan-Indian confederation because they did not see all whites as enemies or

all Indians as friends. This theme is best developed in Kathleen DuVal, *The Native Ground: Indians and Colonists in the Heart of the Continent* (Philadelphia: University of Pennsylvania Press, 2006), 205–207.

28. Governor Clark to the Secretary of War, 20 August 1814, Carter, *Territorial Papers*, 14:786–87; Richard Oglesby, *Manuel Lisa and the Opening of the Missouri Fur Trade of the Far West* (Norman: University of Oklahoma Press, 1963), 151–55; Jones, *William Clark*, 222–23.

29. "Let the north as well as the south be JACKSONIZED!!!," *Missouri Gazette*, 28 May 1814; Memorial to Congress From the Legislative Assembly, 26 December 1814, Carter, *Territorial Papers*, 14:810; Petition to Congress by US Missouri Rangers, 17 December 1814, ibid., 806.

30. William Russell to the Secretary of War, 14 December 1814, Carter, *Territorial Papers*, 14:804.

31. Governor Edwards to Shadrach Bond, 11 January 1814, Carter, *Territorial Papers*, 16: 409–11.

32. Foley, *Genesis of Missouri*, 232–33; The Secretary of War to the Indian Commissioners, 11 March 1815, Carter, *Territorial Papers*, 15:14; Christian Wilt to Joseph Hertzog, 13 March 1815, quoted in Foley, *Genesis of Missouri*, 233.

33. William Russell to the Secretary of War, 12 March 1815, Carter, *Territorial Papers*, 15:15–16; William Russell to the Secretary of War, 24 April 1815, ibid., 48; The Secretary of War to the Indian Commissioners, 11 March 1815, ibid., 14; Foley, *Genesis of Missouri*, 233.

34. The Treaty of Greenville followed Anthony Wayne's victory in 1794 at the Battle of Fallen Timbers. The Treaty of Fort Jackson followed Andrew Jackson's victory at the Battle of Horseshoe Bend. Governor Edwards to the Secretary of State, 13 April 1815, Carter, *Territorial Papers*, 17:169; William Russell to the Secretary of War, 29 May 1815, ibid., 15: 57–58; Daniel Bissell to Andrew Jackson, 2 July 1815, Daniel Bissell Papers, *Missouri Historical Society*, box 1, folder 3.

35. Jones, *William Clark*, 227–28; William E. Foley, *Wilderness Journey: The Life of William Clark* (Columbia: University of Missouri Press, 2004), 204–205; *Missouri Gazette*, 10 June 1815, quoted in Hurt, *Nathan Boone and the American Frontier*, 104–105.

36. Hurt, *Nathan Boone and the American Frontier*, 106; Jones, *William Clark*, 228; Foley, *Wilderness Journey*, 206; Lavender, *Fist in the Wilderness*, 226–27.

37. Secretary of War to Andrew Jackson, 12 June 1815, Carter, *Territorial Papers*, 15:62–63; Daniel Bissell to Andrew Jackson, 15 July 1815, ibid., 68–70.

38. Hurt, *Nathan Boone and the American Frontier*, 106–107; Indian Commissioners to the Secretary of War, 17 June 1816, Carter, *Territorial Papers*, 17:352–56.

39. Foley, *Genesis of Missouri*, 234.

40. Proclamation of Public-Land Sales, 25 April 1814, Carter, *Territorial Papers*, 16:416–17; Proclamation of Land Sales at St. Louis and Franklin, 30 April 1818, ibid., 15:385–86; William Rector to Edward Tiffin, 20 April 1815, ibid., 34–35.

41. Nicholas Boilvin to Edward Tiffin, 12 January 1816, Carter, *Territorial Papers*, 17:281–83; Governor Edwards to the Secretary of State, 3 March 1816, ibid., 308–310; Governor Edwards to the Secretary of War, 18 November 1816, ibid., 430–37; Haeger, *John Jacob Astor*, 180–81, 189–92.

42. Raymond Hammes, "Land Transactions in Illinois Prior to the Sale of Public

Domain," *Journal of the Illinois State Historical Society* (Summer 1984): 101–14; Boggess, *Settlement of Illinois*, 102; Foley, *Genesis of Missouri*, 251–52; Resolution of the Territorial Assembly, 22 January 1816, Carter, *Territorial Papers*, 15:108–109.

43. Resolutions of the Territorial Assembly, 22 January 1816, Carter, *Territorial Papers*, 15:105–107, 108–109; Alexander McNair to the Secretary of State, 27 January 1816, ibid., 110–11; Alexander McNair to Josiah Meigs, 27 January 1816, ibid., 111–12; Memorial to Congress by the Legislative Assembly, 13 February 1816, Carter, *Territorial Papers*, 17:299–300; Benjamin Stephenson to the Secretary of War, 16 August 1816, ibid., 377–78; The Secretary of War to Ambrose Whitlock, 10 September 1816, ibid., 391–92; Alexander McNair to Josiah Meigs, 20 June 1816, Carter, *Territorial Papers*, 15: 148–49.

44. John Mack Faragher, "'More Motley than Mackinaw': From Ethnic Mixing to Ethnic Cleansing on the Frontier of the Lower Missouri, 1783–1833," in *Contact Points: American Frontiers from the Mohawk Valley to the Mississippi, 1750–1830*, ed. Andrew Cayton and Frederika Teute (Chapel Hill: University of North Carolina Press, 1998), 320–26; Foley, *Genesis of Missouri*, 234–37.

45. William L. Lovely to the Secretary of War, 27 May 1815, Carter, *Territorial Papers*, 15:49–50; Richard Graham to the Secretary of War, 4 September 1816, ibid., 17:384–85; The Indian Commissioners to the Secretary of War, 9 September 1816, ibid., 387–89.

46. The Secretary of War to the Indian Commissioners, 27 May 1816, Carter, *Territorial Papers*, 15:136–38.

47. DuVal, *The Native Ground*, 208–209; William Clark to the President, 10 April 1811, Carter, *Territorial Papers*, 14: 445–46; William Russell to Delegate Hempstead, 1 November 1813, ibid., 72–21; The Indian Commissioners to the Secretary of War, 17 June 1816, ibid., 17:136–38; Richard Graham to the Secretary of War, 8 July 1816, ibid., 359–60.

48. Governor Clark to the Secretary of War, 30 September 1816, Carter, *Territorial Papers*, 15:177–78; Memorial to Congress by the Territorial Assembly, 25 January 1816, ibid., 195–96; Petition of the Inhabitants of Missouri Territory, [No date], ibid., 182–83.

49. Haeger, *John Jacob Astor*, 180–99; William Puthuff to Lewis Cass, 20 June 1816, quoted in ibid., 196; William Puthuff to Lewis Cass, 14 May 1816, quoted in ibid., 195.

4 / Statehood for Illinois and Missouri

1. *Annals of Congress*, 15th Cong., 2nd sess., 1: 305–11; Solon J. Buck, *Illinois in 1818* (Springfield: Illinois Centennial Commission, 1917; reprint, Urbana: University of Illinois Press, 1967), 313–15.

2. Tallmadge quoted in Robert Pierce Forbes, *The Missouri Compromise and Its Aftermath: Slavery and the Meaning of America* (Chapel Hill: University of North Carolina Press, 2007), 35–36; Clarence Carter, ed., *The Territorial Papers of the United States* (Washington, DC: US Government Printing Office, 1934–75), 15:742.

3. The best book-length account of the national scope of the Missouri statehood controversy is Robert Forbes's *The Missouri Compromise and Its Aftermath*. Recent examinations of the political problems posed by slavery in the West include John Craig Hammond, *Slavery, Freedom, and Expansion in the Early American West*

(Charlottesville: University of Virginia Press, 2007) and Matthew Mason, *Slavery & Politics in the Early American Republic* (Chapel Hill: University of North Carolina Press, 2006).

4. Resolution of the Territorial Assembly, 2 January 1817, Carter, *Territorial Papers*, 15:224–25; Resolution of the Territorial Assembly, 24 January 1817, ibid., 234–36.

5. Delegate Pope to the Secretary of State, 1 March 1817, Carter, *Territorial Papers*, 17:485–86; Governor Edwards to the Acting Secretary of War, 12 May 1817, ibid., 503–507; The Secretary of War to Governor Clark, 8 May 1818, ibid., 15:390.

6. Charles Jouett to the Governor of Michigan Territory, 1 February 1817, Carter, *Territorial Papers*, 17:478–79; Governor of Michigan Territory to Charles Jouett, 21 July 1817, ibid., 524–26; Governor Edwards to the Acting Secretary of War, 12 May 1817, ibid., 506.

7. Governor Clark to the Secretary of War, 1 July 1818, Carter, *Territorial Papers*, 15:405–406; Kathleen DuVal, *The Native Ground: Indians and Colonists in the Heart of the Continent* (Philadelphia: University of Pennsylvania Press, 2006), 217–26.

8. Proclamation of Land Sales at St. Louis and Franklin, 30 April 1818, Carter, *Territorial Papers*, 15:385; Josiah Meigs to Thomas A. Smith, 8 September 1818, ibid., 432; William Rector to Josiah Meigs, 24 August 1818, ibid., 428; Memorial to Congress by the Territorial Assembly, 8 January 1819, ibid., 495; Henry Carroll to Josiah Meigs, 18 October 1818, ibid., 440–44.

9. Memorial to Congress by the Territorial Assembly, 4 January 1819, Carter, *Territorial Papers*, 15:489; Memorial to Congress by the Territorial Assembly, 22 January 1819, ibid., 502; Landon Y. Jones, *William Clark and the Shaping of the West* (New York: Hill and Wang, 2004), 237; Governor Edwards to William Rector, 18 January 1818, Carter, *Territorial Papers*, 17:576.

10. Thomas A. Smith and Charles Carroll to Josiah Meigs, 23 March 1820, Carter, *Territorial Papers*, 15:599; Attorney General to the Secretary of the Treasury, 19 June 1820, ibid., 621; Secretary of War to Henry Atkinson, 21 July 1820, ibid., 629; Delegate Scott to the Secretary of War, 21 September 1820, ibid., 645.

11. Governor Edwards to the Acting Secretary of War, 21 February 1817, Carter, *Territorial Papers*, 17:483–85; Thomas L. McKenney to the Acting Secretary of War, 19 March 1817, ibid., 492–93; Thomas L. McKenney to the Acting Secretary of War, 6 May 1817, ibid., 499–500; Governor Clark to the Secretary of War, 11 May 1818, ibid., 15:392; John Denis Haeger, *John Jacob Astor: Business and Finance in the Early Republic* (Detroit: Wayne State University Press, 1991), 184–85, 189–92.

12. David Lavender, *Fist in the Wilderness* (1964; reprint, Lincoln: University of Nebraska Press, 1998), 260, 280–83; Haeger, *John Jacob Astor*, 189–95. Despite employing "foreign" traders and boatmen, Astor's company was not a front for British interests but instead among the most successful companies in the United States at this time.

13. Lavender, *Fist in the Wilderness*, 279; Talbot Chambers to Thomas A. Smith, 10 May 1818, Carter, *Territorial Papers*, 17:588; Thomas L. McKenney to the Secretary of War, 21 August 1818, ibid., 600.

14. Lavender, *Fist in the Wilderness*, 277; Secretary of War to Governor Clark, 3 March 1819, Carter, *Territorial Papers*, 15:520; Thomas L. McKenney to George Sibley, 21 June 1821, ibid., 734; Memorial to Congress from the Missouri Baptist Convention, 24 October 1818, ibid., 448.

15. *Illinois Intelligencer*, 2 September 1818.

16. An Act to prevent the Migration of free Negroes and Mullattoes into this Territory and for other purposes, 8 December 1813, Francis Philbrick, *The Laws of Illinois Territory: 1809-1818* (Springfield: Illinois State Historical Library, 1950), 91-92.

17. An Act concerning negroes and Mullattoes, 22 December 1814, ibid., 157-58.

18. Davis, *Frontier Illinois*, 159; Boggess, *Settlement of Illinois*, 91-92; Merton Dillon, "Sources of Early Antislavery Thought in Illinois," *Journal of the Illinois State Historical Society* 50 (1957): 34-56.

19. N. Dwight Harris, *The History of Negro Servitude in Illinois, and of the Slavery Agitation in That State, 1719-1864* (Chicago: A.C. McClurg, 1904), 11-13.

20. For insight into the preoccupation of prominent Illinoisans with land speculation, see especially Daniel Cook to Ninian Edwards, Washington, 6 February 1817, Ninian Edwards Papers, Chicago Historical Society, folder 4; there are also numerous similar letters in Clarence Carter, *The Territorial Papers of the United States*, vols. 7, 13-1.

21. William Brown, "Memoir of the Late Hon. Daniel P. Cook," Ninian W. Edwards, *History of Illinois, from 1778-1833, and Life and Times of Ninian Edwards* (Springfield: Illinois State Journal Co., 1870; reprint, New York: Arno, 1975), 253-55; Daniel Cook to Ninian Edwards, Washington, 2 October 1817, *The Edwards Papers*, ed. E. B. Washburne (Chicago: Fergus, 1884), 139-41.

22. Daniel Cook, "To James Monroe, President of the United States of America, *The National Register*, 13 September 1817 and 20 September 1817. For a comprehensive discussion of the possibility of compensated emancipation, see Betty Fladeland, "Compensated Emancipation: A Rejected Alternative," *Journal of Southern History* 42, no. 2 (May 1976): 169-86.

23. Daniel Cook writing as "A Republican," *The Western Intelligencer*, 27 November 1817; Thomas Ford, *A History of Illinois: From Its Commencement as a State in 1818 to 1847* (1854; reprint, Urbana: University of Illinois Press, 1995), 30-31.

24. Illinois Legislature, Journal of the House, Second Session of Third General Assembly (Kaskaskia: Berry and Blackwell, 1818).

25. Edward Coles writing as "Agis," *The Western Intelligencer*, 1 July 1818; Daniel Cook writing as "A Republican," *The Western Intelligencer*, 1 April 1818.

26. "Caution," *The Western Intelligencer*, 15 April 1818.

27. "One of the People," *The Western Intelligencer*, 6 May 1818.

28. "One of the People," *The Western Intelligencer*, 6 May 1818; "A Citizen," *The Illinois Intelligencer*, 24 June 1818.

29. Emil Verlie, *Illinois Constitutions* (Springfield: Illinois State Historical Library, 1919), 1:25-47.

30. *The Annals of Congress*, 16th Cong., 2nd. sess., 306-11; Don Fehrenbacher, *The South and Three Sectional Crises* (Baton Rouge: Lousiana State University Press, 1980), 14-15; Glover Moore, *The Missouri Controversy, 1819-1821* (Lexington: University Press of Press, 1966), 34.

31. Peter Onuf, *Statehood and Union: A History of the Northwest Ordinance* (1987; reprint, Bloomington: Indiana University Press, 1992), xvii-xxi.

32. *Missouri Gazette*, 13 September 1820, quoted in Floyd Shoemaker, *Missouri's Struggle for Statehood, 1804-1821* (1916; reprint, New York: Russell & Russell, 1969), 102.

33. Shoemaker, *Missouri's Struggle for Statehood*, 110.

34. Ibid., 37–39; Louis Houck, *History of Missouri from Earliest Explorations and Settlements until the Admission of the State into the Union* (Chicago: R.R. Donnelley & Sons, 1908), 3: 243–44.

35. Shoemaker, *Missouri's Struggle for Statehood*, 37–39, 41, 55–57; Houck, *History of Missouri*, 3: 243–44.

36. Quoted in Houck, *History of Missouri*, 3:150.

37. *Missouri Gazette*, 19 May 1819, and *St. Louis Enquirer*, 12 May 1819, quoted in Shoemaker, *Missouri's Struggle for Statehood*, 83.

38. Ibid., 85–86.

39. Shoemaker, *Missouri's Struggle for Statehood*, 88–89. Shoemaker's documentation is important because Clarence Carter notes in his *Territorial Papers*, 15:690n70 that many petitions and memorials emanating from Missouri during this period are missing.

40. Historian John Moses wrote in *Illinois, Historical and Statistical*, 2 vols. (Chicago: Fergus, 1889): 323, that "The settlement of Missouri at this time by wealthy and respectable immigrants from the South, passing through Illinois with their flocks and herds and slaves and their well-equipped wagons drawn by fine horses, who would doubtless, as it was asserted, remain in Illinois but for the constitutional anti-slavery restriction, was used as a strong argument in favor of its abrogation." He quotes a Judge Gillespie who spoke of a settler on his way to Missouri who said, " well sir, your *sile* is mighty *fartil*, but a man can't own niggers here; gol durn you."

41. John B. C. Lucas quoted in Glover Moore, *The Missouri Controversy, 1819–1821* (Lexington: University Press of Kentucky, 1966), 265; Shoemaker, *Missouri's Struggle for Statehood*, 120, William E. Foley, *The Genesis Of Missouri: From Wilderness Outpost to Statehood* (Columbia: University of Missouri Press, 1989), 294–95.

42. Shoemaker, *Missouri's Struggle for Statehood*, 135, 148–49; Foley, *Genesis of Missouri*, 296–97.

43. Richard M. Clokey, *William H. Ashley: Enterprise and Politics in the Trans-Mississippi West* (Norman: University of Oklahoma Press, 1980), 52; Foley, *Genesis of Missouri*, 296–97; Shoemaker, *Missouri's Struggle for Statehood*, 261–62.

44. Clokey, *William H. Ashley*, 52–54; John F. Darby quoted in Houck, *History of Missouri*, 3:53–54. Many of the claims in question were eventually confirmed, although not until the mid-1830s. One of Benton's votes came from a man who rose from his deathbed to cast the vote before dying a few hours later. William Nisbet Chambers, *Old Bullion Benton: Senator from the New West* (Boston: Little, Brown, 1956), 99–100.

45. Shoemaker, *Missouri's Struggle for Statehood*, 290.

46. Ibid., 292–93, 297–98.

47. Ibid., 300, 310.

48. Theodore Dwight quoted in Moore, *Missouri Controversy*, 168; Houck, *History of Missouri*, 3: 270–72.

49. Lucien Carr, *Missouri: A Bone of Contention* (Boston: Houghton Mifflin, 1888), 139–62; Houck, *History of Missouri*, 3:250; Shoemaker, *Missouri's Struggle for Statehood*, 81–113; Harrison Trexler, *Slavery In Missouri 1804–1865* (Baltimore: Johns Hopkins Press, 1914), 105; Arvarh E. Strickland, "Aspects of Slavery in Missouri, 1821," *Missouri Historical Review* 65 (July 1971): 512–16.

50. Kathleen DuVal challenged the traditional narrative of dispossessed Indians helpless in the face of white expansion in "Debating Identity, Sovereignty, and

Civilization: The Arkansas Valley after the Louisiana Purchase," *Journal of the Early Republic* 26 (Spring 2006): 25–58.

5 / After Statehood

1. Resolution, 12 December 1820, Clarence E. Carter, *The Territorial Papers of the United States* (Washington, DC: US Government Printing Office, 1934–75), 15:682.

2. David Lavender, *The Fist in the Wilderness* (1964; reprint, Lincoln: University of Nebraska Press, 1998), 302.

3. Justus Post to John Post, 19 December 1820, Justis Post Papers, Missouri Historical Society, St. Louis.

4. Dale Morgan, ed., *The West of William H. Ashley, 1822–1838* (Denver: Old West Publishing, 1964), li; William Chambers, *Old Bullion Benton: Senator from the New West* (Boston: Little, Brown, 1956), 105–106; Perry McCandless, *A History of Missouri, 1820–1860* (Columbia: University of Missouri Press, 1971), 2:23–28; James Neal Primm, *Lion of the Valley: St. Louis, Missouri, 1764–1980*, 3rd edition, (St. Louis: Missouri Historical Society Press, 1998), 119.

5. Edwin C. McReynolds, *Missouri: A History of the Crossroads State* (Norman: University of Oklahoma Press, 1962), 92–98; Primm, *Lion of the Valley*, 131.

6. Benton failed to persuade Congress to privatize Missouri's lead mines, but succeeded in getting the state's disputed Spanish claims switched to Missouri's federal district court, where judges sympathetic to local sentiment made the decisions. His efforts to champion preemption and graduation persisted for years. Chambers, *Old Bullion Benton*, 110–14.

7. The road was completed all the way to Santa Fe by 1826, greatly increasing the volume of trade, although Indian attacks persisted until 1830. Chambers, *Old Bullion Benton*, 127–28; Jay Buckley, *William Clark: Indian Diplomat* (Norman: University of Oklahoma Press, 2008), 156–57; McReynolds, *Missouri*, 102–103.

8. Morgan, *The West of William Ashley*, lii; Buckley, *William Clark*, 153–54; Chambers, *Old Bullion Benton*, 110–11; Lavender, *Fist in the Wilderness*, 324–30. The bill to thwart the alcohol trade contained several loopholes that were predictably exploited by many private traders.

9. Ramsay Crooks to Thomas Benton, 31 December 1822, quoted in Cambers, *Old Bullion Benton*, 111; Foley, *Wilderness Journey*, 231.

10. Buckley, *William Clark*, 4, 17–18; General Henry Atkinson to Secretary of War John Calhoun, 24 November 1820, quoted in Morgan, *The West of William Ashley*, lii; ibid.

11. Richard M. Clokey, *William H. Ashley: Enterprise and Politics in the Trans-Mississippi West* (Norman: University of Oklahoma Press, 1980), 62–68.

12. Benjamin O'Fallon, U.S. Indian Agent, Upper Missouri Agency, to John C. Calhoun, Secretary of War, St. Louis, 9 April 9, 1822, Morgan, *The West of William H. Ashley*, 6; Benjamin O'Fallon, U.S. Indian Agent, Upper Missouri Agency, to Ramsay Crooks, at St. Louis, Fort Atkinson, 10 July 1822, ibid., 17–18; Clokey, *William H. Ashley*, 78–82, 88–91, 94–98.

13. Clokey, *William H. Ashley*, 82–84; *St. Louis Enquirer*, 13 April 1822, Morgan, *The West of William H. Ashley*, 6–7; *St. Louis Enquirer*, 9 April 1822, quoted in Jones, *William Clark*, 267; ibid., 272; *St. Louis Enquirer*, reprinted in *Missouri Intelligencer*, Franklin, 17 September 1822, Morgan, *The West of William H. Ashley*, 19.

14. *Niles Weekly Register*, 16 November 1822.
15. Clokey, *William H. Ashley*, 106–11; Buckley, *William Clark*, 159.
16. Joshua Pilcher to Henry Leavenworth, 26 August 1823, printed in *Missouri Republican*, 15 October 1823, quoted in Clokey, *William H. Ashley*, 11–12.
17. Clokey, *William H. Ashley*, 164, 116; William H. Ashley to the Editors of the *St. Louis Enquirer*, 17 November 1823, in Morgan, *The West of William H. Ashley*, 63–64.
18. Clokey, *William H. Ashley*, 116; *St. Louis Enquirer*, 30 August 1824, in Morgan, *The West of William H. Ashley*, 87; Jones, *William Clark*, 127.
19. Shirley Christian, *Before Lewis and Clark: The Story of the Chouteaus, the French Dynasty That Ruled America's Frontier* (New York: Farrar, Straus and Giroux, 2004), 252, 262–63. Pierre Jr. eventually acquired control of the American Fur Company and spent most of the rest of his life in New York where, like John Jacob Astor, he made another fortune in real estate. William E. Foley and C. David Rice, *The First Chouteaus: River Barons of Early St. Louis* (Urbana: University of Illinois Press, 1983), 189.
20. William Clark, Estimate of Eastern Indians, in Gary E. Moulton, ed., *The Journals of the Lewis and Clark Expedition* (Lincoln: University of Nebraska Press, 1983–2001), 3:391. Previously, US officials worked to acquire title to Indian lands for occupation by white settlers with little or no regard for where the displaced Indians might end up. Clark's already vast experience on the frontier taught him that the eastern tribes pushed west by white settlers would inevitably need lands already occupied by others, who would in turn need somewhere else to go; Jay Buckley, *William Clark: Indian Diplomat* (Norman: University of Oklahoma Press, 2008), 146.
21. Buckley, *William Clark*, 146–47; William Foley, *Wilderness Journey: The Life of William Clark* (Columbia: University of Missouri Press, 2004), 227–31.
22. Secretary of War John C. Calhoun, quoted in Buckley, *William Clark*, 132; ibid., 26, 142; Landon Jones, *William Clark and the Shaping of the West* (New York: Hill and Wang, 2004), 261.
23. Jones, *William Clark*, 273, 279–80.
24. Foley, *Wilderness Journey*, 236–37; Jones, *William Clark*, 276–77; Buckley, *William Clark*, 210–11; R. Douglas Hurt, *Nathan Boone and the American Frontier* (Columbia: University of Missouri Press, 1998), 121–22.
25. Jones, *William Clark*, 280.
26. William Clark to John Calhoun, 8 December 1823, quoted in Jones, *William Clark*, 280; ibid., 280–81; Foley, *Wilderness Journey*, 241.
27. Buckley, *William Clark*, 172–74; Foley, *Wilderness Journey*, 239; Jones, *William Clark*, 281–83; Hurt, *Nathan Boone*, 122. Lewis Cass, a strong temperance advocate, objected to the use of whiskey in the negotiations, and to the chagrin of the Indians, much (but not all) of the whiskey brought by Clark was ceremoniously dumped on the ground.
28. Jones, *William Clark*, 285–86; Buckley, *William Clark*, 163–67; William Clark to James Barbour, 1 March 1826, quoted in Foley, *Wilderness Journey*, 242.
29. Thomas Calvin Pease, *The Frontier State, 1818–1848* (Springfield, Illinois Centennial Commission: 1918; reprint, Urbana: University of Illinois Press, 1987), 71–72.
30. McCandless, *History of Missouri*, 74–78; Pease, *The Frontier State*, 105–108.
31. Pease, *The Frontier State*, 105–108.
32. Chambers, *Old Bullion Benton*, 50–52; David Barton to Silas Bent, 2 February 1825, quoted in ibid., 129; Thomas Hart Benton to John Scott, 8 February 1825,

printed in *Niles Weekly Register*, March 26, 1825; McCandless, *History of Missouri*, 77–87.

33. Pease, *The Frontier State*, 47.

34. Merton Dillon, "Sources of Early Antislavery Thought in Illinois," *Journal of the Illinois State Historical Society* 53 (Spring 1957): 36–50. The most thorough treatment of the career of Edward Coles and its effect on the national antislavery movement can be found in Suzanne Guasco, *Confronting Slavery: Edward Coles and the Rise of Antislavery Politics in Nineteenth-Century America* (DeKalb: Northern Illinois University Press, 2013).

35. Clarence Alvord, *Governor Edward Coles, Collections of the Illinois State Historical Library* (Springfield: Illinois State Historical Library, 1920), 15:138–39, 153, 314, 332–37, 366–69; Dillon, "Sources of Early Antislavery Thought," 36–50; Elias Pym Fordham, *Personal Narrative of Travels in Virginia, Maryland, Pennsylvania, Ohio, Indiana, Kentucky; and of a Residence in the Illinois Territory: 1817–1818*, ed. Frederic Ogg (Cleveland: Arthur H. Clark, 1906), 122–23.

36. James Simeone, *Democracy and Slavery in Frontier Illinois: The Bottomland Republic* (DeKalb: Northern Illinois University Press, 2000); Pease, *Frontier State*, 70–92.

37. Harris, *Negro Servitude*, 99–119.

38. Maj. John F. Hamtramck to Gen. Josiah Harmar, 28 March 1789, Draper Collection, Harmar Papers 1, 17–18, quoted in Arthur Boggess, *The Settlement of Illinois 1778–1830* (Chicago: Chicago Historical Society, 1980), 63–64.

39. Ford, *History of Illinois*, 30–31.

40. Daniel Cook writing as "Independence," *Illinois Intelligencer*, 19 August 1818.

41. Daniel Cook writing as "Independence," *Illinois Intelligencer*, 29 July 1818.

42. Morris Birkbeck, *Letters From Illinois* (1818; reprint, New York: Da Capo, 1970), 102–103.

43. George Flower, *History of the English Settlement in Edwards County Illinois, founded in 1817 and 1818 by Morris Birkbeck and George Flower, Chicago Historical Society's Collection* (Chicago: Fergus Printing, 1909), 1:156.

44. Although in the nineteenth century many agreed with former Illinois governor John Reynolds that "I have never had any doubt but slavery would now exist in Illinois if it had not been prevented by this famous Ordinance," few recent historians seem to agree. David Brion Davis did when he recognized that due to the Ordinance "the principle that slavery should be excluded from the virgin West became the core of an antislavery and Republican party ideology that obscured the economic benefits of coerced labor and transformed the meaning of national interest." Peter Onuf also came close in his treatment of the history of the Ordinance. He concluded that over time the Ordinance was translated into a "higher law," which, during the Illinois convention battle, was "invoked . . . as a source of moral obligation: it epitomized the wisdom and foresight of the founding Fathers and was, therefore, an infallible guide for Illinois voters." John Reynolds, *My Own Times: Embracing also the History of My Life* (Chicago: Chicago Historical Society, 1879), 1:132. The memoirs were written in the early 1850s but were lost for many years. David Brion Davis, "The Significance of Excluding Slavery from the Old Northwest in 1787," *Indiana Magazine of History* 84 (March 1988): 75–89; Peter Onuf, *Statehood and Union: A History of the Northwest Ordinance* (1987; reprint, Bloomington: Indiana University Press, 1992), 125.

45. Foley and Rice, *The First Chouteaus*, 197.

Conclusion

1. Louisiana Purchase Transfer Papers Collection, 1783–1953, Missouri Historical Society; Charles Gratiot Papers, 1769–1933, Missouri Historical Society; *Dictionary of Missouri Biography*, ed. Lawrence O. Christensen, William E. Foley, Gary R. Kremer, Kenneth H. Winn (Columbia: University of Missouri Press, 1999), 237, 347–48, 484, 712, 724.

2. Frederick A. Hodes, *Beyond the Frontier: A History of St. Louis to 1821* (Tucson: Patrice Press, 2004), 211, 304; James Primm, *Lion of the Valley: St. Louis, Missouri, 1764–1980* (St. Louis: Missouri Historical Society Press, 1981), 50–51; William E. Foley, *The Genesis of Missouri: From Wilderness Outpost to Statehood* (Columbia: University of Missouri Press, 1989), 172–73.

3. Charles Gratiot Papers, 1769–1933, Missouri Historical Society.

4. Placing land in the center of the Revolutionary era also helps to recast the Articles of Confederation and the Constitution as treaties between potentially hostile powers. This idea and its relationship to the concept of federalism is pursued in Peter Onuf and Nicholas Onuf, *Federal Union, Modern World: The Law of Nations in an Age of Revolutions, 1776–1814* (Madison, WI: Madison House 1993) and in David C. Hendrickson, *Peace Pact: The Lost World of the American Founding* (Lawrence: University Press of Kansas, 1997).

5. Among the recent works making this argument are Peter J. Kastor, *The Nation's Crucible: The Louisiana Purchase and the Creation of America* (New Haven: Yale University Press, 2004); Kathleen DuVal, *The Native Ground: Indians and Colonists in the Heart of the Continent* (Philadelphia: University of Pennsylvania Press, 2006); Stephen Aron, *American Confluence: The Missouri Frontier from Borderland to Border State* (Bloomington: Indiana University Press, 2006); Jay Gitlin, *The Bourgeois Frontier: French Towns, French Traders and American Expansion* (New Haven: Yale University Press, 2010). An impressive and modern case for the older narrative can be found in Patrick Griffin, *American Leviathan: Empire, Nation, and Revolutionary Frontier* (New York: Hill and Wang, 2007).

Selected Bibliography

Primary Sources

Manuscript Sources

Chicago Historical Society, Chicago: Ninian Edwards Papers; French America, Kaskaskia, and Louisiana Papers, 1635–1848; Elias Kent Kane MSS.

Illinois State Archives, Springfield: Raymond H. Hammes Collection of Illinois Records, 1678–1827; RG 100 (Records of the territorial government, 1809–18); RG 101 (Official papers of Illinois governors); Executive Documents and Governor's Letter Books, 1790–1834; Governor's Correspondence, 1814–40.

Illinois State Historical Library, Springfield: Pierre Menard Collection; Jesse B. Thomas Papers.

Indiana Historical Society Library, Indianapolis: William Henry Harrison Papers (Clanin Collection); Northwest Territory Papers.

Missouri Historical Society, St. Louis: Bates Family Papers; Daniel Bissell Papers; William C. Carr Papers; Chouteau Family Papers; Clark Family Collection; Rufus Easton Papers; Charles Gratiot Papers; Louisiana Purchase Transfer Papers Collection; John B. C. Lucas Family Papers, John B. C. Lucas Papers; Justis Post Papers; Amos Stoddard Papers.

Randolph County Courthouse, Chester, Il.: The Kaskaskia Manuscripts.

Newspapers

Illinois Intelligencer
Missouri Gazette
Niles Weekly Register

St. Louis Enquirer
Western Intelligencer

Published Primary Sources

Alvord, Clarence W., ed. *Cahokia Records, 1778–1790.* Vol. 2, *Collections of the Illinois State Historical Library.* Springfield: Illinois State Historical Library, 1907.

———. *Governor Edward Coles.* Vol. 15, *Collections of the Illinois State Historical Library.* Springfield: Illinois State Historical Library, 1920.

———. *Kaskaskia Records 1778–1790.* Vol. 5, *Collections of the Illinois State Historical Library.* Springfield: Illinois State Historical Library, 1909.

American State Papers. Washington, DC: Government Printing Office, 1832–1861.

Annals of the Congress of the United States, 1789–1824. Washington, DC, 1834–1856.

Bates, Frederick. *The Life and Papers of Frederick Bates.* Edited by Thomas Maitland Marshall. 2 vols. St. Louis: Missouri Historical Society, 1926.

Beck, Lewis C. *A Gazetteer of the States of Illinois and Missouri.* 1823. Reprint, New York: Arno, 1975.

Billon, Frederic Louis. *Annals of St. Louis in Its Early Days under the French and Spanish Dominations, 1764–1804.* 1886. Reprint, New York: Arno Press and the New York Times, 1971.

———. *Annals of St. Louis in Its Territorial Days, From 1804 to 1821.* 1888. Reprint, New York: Arno, 1971.

Birkbeck, Morris. *Letters from Illinois.* 1818. Reprint, New York: Da Capo, 1970.

Brackenridge, Henry Marie. *Recollections of Persons and Places in the West.* Philadelphia: J.B. Lippincott, 1868.

Carter, Clarence, ed. *The Territorial Papers of the United States.* 26 vols. Washington, DC: United States Government Printing Office, 1934–75.

Clark, George Rogers. *The Conquest of the Illinois.* Edited by Milo Milton Quaife. 1920. Reprint, Carbondale: Southern Illinois University Press, 2001.

———. "George Rogers Clark to Genet, 1794." *American Historical Review*, vol. 18, no. 4 (July 1913): 780–83.

Clark, William. *Dear Brother: Letters of William Clark to Jonathan Clark.* Edited by James J. Holmberg. New Haven: Yale University Press, 2002.

de Finiels, Nicolas. *An Account of Upper Louisiana.* 1803. Edited by Carl J. Ekberg and William E. Foley. Columbia: University of Missouri Press, 1989.

de Laussat, Pierre Clément. *Memories of My Life.* Edited by Robert D. Bush. 1831. Reprint, Baton Rouge: Louisiana State University Press, 1978.

Dunn, Jacob Piatt. "Slavery Petitions and Papers." In *Indiana Historical Society Publications.* Vol. 2. Indianapolis: Bowen-Merrill, 1895.

Edwards, Ninian W. *The Edwards Papers.* Edited by E. B. Washburne. Chicago: Fergus, 1884.
———. *History of Illinois, from 1778-1833, and Life and Times of Ninian Edwards.* Springfield: Illinois State Journal Co., 1870. Reprint, New York: Arno, 1975.
Esarey, Logan, ed. *Messages and Letters of William Henry Harrison.* 2 vols. Indianapolis: Indiana Historical Commission, 1922.
Flint, Timothy. *Recollections of the Last Ten Years Passed in Occasional Residences and Journeyings in the Valley of the Mississippi.* 1826. Reprint, New York: Da Capo, 1968.
Flower, George. *History of the English Settlement in Edwards County.* 2nd edition. Chicago: Fergus, 1909.
Ford, Thomas. *A History of Illinois: From Its Commencement as a State in 1818 to 1847.* 1854. Reprint, Urbana: University of Illinois Press, 1995.
Fordham, Elias Pym. *Personal Narrative of Travels in Virginia, Maryland, Pennsylvania, Ohio, Kentucky; and of a Residence in the Illinois Territory: 1817-1818.* Edited by Frederic Austin Ogg. Cleveland: Arthur H. Clark, 1906.
George Rogers Clark to Genet, 1794, *The American Historical Review* 18, no. 4 (July 1913): 782.
Greene, Evarts B., and Clarence Walworth Alvord, eds. *The Governors' Letter-Books, 1818-1834.* Vol. 4, *CISHL.* Springfield: Illinois State Historical Library, 1909.
Houck, Louis, ed. *The Spanish Regime in Missouri.* 2 vols. Chicago: R.R. Donnelley, 1908.
Illinois Legislature, Journal of the House, Second Session of Third General Assembly. Kaskaskia: Berry and Blackwell, 1818.
Jackson, Donald, ed. *Letters of the Lewis and Clark Expedition with Related Documents, 1783-1854.* 2 vols. Urbana: University of Illinois Press, 1978.
James, James Alton, ed. *George Rogers Clark Papers.* Vol. 8, *CISHL.* Springfield: Illinois State Historical Society, 1912.
Jefferson: Writings. New York: Library of America, 1984.
Kinniard, Lawrence, ed. "Clark-Leyba Papers." *American Historical Review* 41, no. 1 (Oct. 1935): 92-112.
———. *Spain in the Mississippi Valley.* 3 vols. Washington, DC: Government Printing Office, 1946.
Malone, Dumas, ed. *Correspondence between Thomas Jefferson and Pierre Samuel du Pont de Nemours, 1798-1817.* 1930. Reprint, New York: Da Capo, 1970.
Mason, Edward G., ed. *Early Chicago and Illinois.* Chicago: Fergus, 1890.
McDermott, John Francis, ed. *The Early Histories of St. Louis.* St. Louis: Historical Documents Foundation, 1952.
Moulton, Gary E., ed. *The Journals of the Lewis and Clark Expedition.* 3 vols. Lincoln: University of Nebraska Press, 1983-2001.
Morgan, Dale, ed. *The West of William H. Ashley, 1822-1838.* Denver: Old West Publishing, 1964.

Nasatir, Abraham P., ed. *Before Lewis and Clark: Documents Illustrating the History of the Missouri, 1785–1804*. 2 vols. 1952. Reprint, Lincoln: University of Nebraska Press, 1990.

Nash, Linda Clark. *The Journals of Pierre-Louis de Lorimier 1777–1795*. Montreal: Baraka, 2012.

Norton, Margaret Cross, ed. *Illinois Census Returns, 1810 and 1818*. 1935. Reprint, Baltimore: Genealogical Publishing, 1969.

Peck, John Mason. *Forty Years of Pioneer Life: Memoir of John Mason Peck, D.D.* Edited by Rufus Babcock. 1864. Reprint, Carbondale: Southern Illinois University Press, 1965.

Philbrick, Francis, ed. *The Laws of Indiana Territory, 1801–1809*. Vol. 21, *CISHL*. Springfield: Illinois State Historical Library, 1930.

Pope, Nathaniel. *The Laws of Illinois Territory, 1809–1818*. Vol. 25, *CISHL*. Springfield: Illinois State Historical Library, 1950.

Reynolds, John. *The Pioneer History of Illinois, Containing the Discovery in 1673, and the History of the Country to the Year 1818, When the State Government Was Organized*. 1852. Reprint, Ann Arbor: University Microfilms, 1968.

———. *Reynolds' History of Illinois: My Own Times: Embracing also the History of My Life*. Belleville, IL: B. H. Perryman and H. L. Davison. Reprint, Chicago: Chicago Historical Society, 1879.

Smith, William Henry, ed. *The St. Clair Papers*. 2 vols. Cincinnati: Robert Clarke, 1882.

Stoddard, Amos. "Papers of Captain Amos Stoddard." In Missouri Historical Society, *Glimpses of the Past*, 2 (1935): 78–122.

———. *Sketches, Historical and Descriptive, of Louisiana*. Philadelphia: Mathew Carey, 1812.

The Territorial Papers of the United States. Edited by Clarence Edwin Carter. 28 vols. Washington, DC: Government Printing Office, 1934–75.

Thornbrough, Gayle, ed. *The Correspondence of John Badollet and Albert Gallatin, 1804–1836*. Indianapolis: Indiana Historical Society, 1961.

———. *Outpost on the Wabash, 1787–1791*. Indianapolis: Indiana Historical Society, 1957.

Verlie, Emil Joseph, ed. *Illinois Constitutions*. Vol. 1. Springfield: Illinois State Historical Library, 1919.

Secondary Sources

Books

Abernethy, Thomas. *The Burr Conspiracy*. New York: Oxford University Press, 1954.

———. *Western Lands and The American Revolution*. New York: Russell & Russell, 1959.

Adler, Jeffrey S. *Yankee Merchants and the Making of the Urban West: The Rise and Fall of Antebellum St. Louis.* Cambridge, UK: Cambridge University Press, 1991.

Allen, John Logan. *Lewis and Clark and the Image of the American Northwest.* 1975. Reprint, New York: Dover, 1991.

Alvord, Clarence. *Governor Edward Coles,* Volume 1 of Biographical Series; Collections of the Illinois State Historical Library, vol. 15. Springfield: Illinois State Historical Library, 1920.

———. *The Illinois Country, 1673–1818.* Springfield: Illinois Centennial Commission, 1920. Reprint, Urbana: University of Illinois Press, 1987.

Aron, Stephen. *American Confluence: The Missouri Frontier from Borderland to Border State.* Bloomington: Indiana University Press, 2006.

———. *How the West Was Lost: The Transformation of Kentucky from Daniel Boone to Henry Clay.* Baltimore: Johns Hopkins University Press, 1996.

Balesi, Charles. *The Time of the French in the Heart of North America 1673–1818.* Chicago: Alliance Française Chicago, 1991.

Banks, Kenneth J. *Chasing Empire Across the Sea: Communications and the State in the French Atlantic, 1713–1763.* Montreal: McGill-Queen's University Press, 2003.

Banner, Stuart. *How the Indians Lost Their Land: Law and Power on the Frontier.* Cambridge, MA: Belknap Press of Harvard University Press, 2005.

Barnhart, John. *Valley of Democracy: The Frontier versus the Plantation in the Ohio Valley, 1775–1818.* Bloomington: Indiana University Press, 1953.

Barnhart, John D., and Dorothy L. Riker. *Indiana to 1816: The Colonial Period.* 1971. Reprint, Indianapolis: Indiana Historical Society, 1994.

Beckwith, Paul. *Creoles of St. Louis.* St. Louis: Nixon-Jones, 1893.

Belting, Natalia Maree. *Kaskaskia Under the French Regime.* 1948. Reprint, Carbondale: Southern Illinois University Press, 2003.

Bemis, Samuel Flagg. *Jay's Treaty: A Study in Commerce and Diplomacy.* New Haven: Yale University Press, 1962.

———. *Pinckney's Treaty: America's Advantage from Europe's Distress, 1783–1800.* 1926. Reprint, New Haven: Yale University Press, 1960.

Berwanger, Eugene. *The Frontier Against Slavery: Western Anti-Negro Prejudice and the Slavery Extension Controversy.* 1967. Reprint, Urbana: University of Illinois Press, 2002.

Billington, Ray Allen. *Westward Expansion: A History of the American Frontier.* 4th edition. New York: Macmillan, 1974.

Boewe, Charles. *Prairie Albion: An English Settlement in Pioneer Illinois.* 1962. Reprint, Carbondale: Southern Illinois University Press, 1999.

Boggess, Arthur Clinton. *The Settlement of Illinois, 1778–1830.* Vol. 5, *CHSC.* Chicago: Chicago Historical Society, 1908.

Bogue, Allan G. *From Prairie to Corn Belt: Farming on the Illinois and Iowa Prairies in the Nineteenth Century.* Chicago: University of Chicago Press, 1963.

Bond, Beverley Jr. *The Civilization of the Old Northwest: A Study of Political, Social, and Economic Development, 1788–1812.* New York: Macmillan, 1934.

Bowes, John P. *Exiles and Pioneers: Eastern Indians in the Trans-Mississippi West.* Cambridge, UK: Cambridge University Press, 2007.

Brown, Margaret. *History As They Lived It: A Social History of Prairie du Rocher, Illinois.* Tucson, AZ: Patrice Press, 2005.

Brown, Roger H. *The Republic in Peril: 1812.* 1964. Reprint, New York: W.W. Norton, 1971.

Buck, Solon J. *Illinois in 1818.* Springfield: Illinois Centennial Commission, 1917. Reprint, Urbana: University of Illinois Press, 1967.

Buckley, Jay. *William Clark: Indian Diplomat.* Norman: University of Oklahoma Press, 2008.

Buel, Richard Jr. *America on the Brink: How the Political Struggle Over the War of 1812 Almost Destroyed the Young Republic.* New York: Palgrave Macmillan, 2005.

Buley, R. Carlyle. *The Old Northwest: Pioneer Period, 1815–1840.* 2 vols. Indianapolis: Indiana Historical Society, 1950.

Buss, James. *Winning the West with Words: Language and Conquest in the Lower Great Lakes.* Norman: University of Oklahoma Press, 2011.

Calloway, Colin G. *Crown and Calumet: British-Indian Relations, 1783–1815.* Norman: University of Oklahoma Press, 1987.

———. *New Worlds for All: Indians, Europeans, and the Remaking of Early America.* Baltimore: Johns Hopkins University Press, 1997.

———. *The Scratch of a Pen: 1763 and the Transformation of North America.* Oxford: Oxford University Press, 2006.

Carr, Albert Z. *The Coming of War: An Account of the Remarkable Events Leading to the War of 1812.* Garden City, NY: Doubleday, 1960.

Carr, Lucien. *Missouri: A Bone of Contention.* Boston: Houghton Mifflin, 1888.

Carter, Clarence. *Great Britain and the Illinois Country, 1763–1774.* 1910. Reprint, Honolulu: University Press of the Pacific, 2004.

Caughey, John Walton. *Bernardo de Gálvez in Louisiana, 1776–1783.* 1934. Reprint, Gretna, LA: Pelican, 1972.

Cayton, Andrew. *Frontier Indiana.* 1996. Reprint, Bloomington: Indiana University Press, 1998.

Cayton, Andrew, and Peter Onuf. *The Midwest and the Nation: Rethinking the History of an American Region.* Bloomington: Indiana University Press, 1990.

Chambers, William Nisbet. *Old Bullion Benton: Senator from the New West.* Boston: Little, Brown, 1956.

Chittenden, Hiram. *A History of the American Fur Trade of the Far West.* 2 vols. 1902. Reprint, Stanford, CA: Academic Reprints, 1954.

Christensen, Lawrence O., William E. Foley, Gary R. Kremer, and Kenneth H.

Winn, eds., *Dictionary of Missouri Biography*. Columbia: University of Missouri Press, 1999.

Christian, Shirley. *Before Lewis and Clark: The Story of the Chouteaus, the French Dynasty That Ruled America's Frontier*. New York: Farrar, Straus and Giroux, 2004.

Cleary, Patricia. *The World, the Flesh, and the Devil: A History of Colonial St. Louis*. Columbia: University of Missouri Press, 2011.

Cleaves, Freeman. *Old Tippecanoe: William Henry Harrison and His Time*. 1939. Reprint, Newtown, CT: American Political Biography Press, 2000.

Clokey, Richard M. *William H. Ashley: Enterprise and Politics in the Trans-Mississippi West*. Norman: University of Oklahoma Press, 1980.

Coleman, James Julian Jr. *Gilbert Antoine de St. Maxent: The Spanish-Frenchman of New Orleans*. New Orleans: Pelican, 1968.

Cronon, William. *Changes in the Land: Indians, Colonists, and the Ecology of New England*. New York: Hill and Wang, 1983.

Dary, David. *The Santa Fe Trail: Its History, Legends, and Lore*. New York: Penguin, 2000.

Davidson, Alexander, and Bernard Stuve. *A Complete History of Illinois from 1673-1873*. Springfield: Illinois Journal Company, 1874.

Davis, David Brion. *Challenging the Boundaries of Slavery*. Cambridge, MA: Harvard University Press, 2003.

Davis, James E. *Frontier Illinois*. Bloomington: Indiana University Press, 1998.

Dawdy, Shannon Lee. *Building the Devil's Empire: French Colonial New Orleans*. Chicago: University of Chicago Press, 2008.

De Conde, Alexander. *This Affair of Louisiana*. New York: Charles Scribner's Sons, 1976.

Dixon, David. *Never Come to Peace Again: Pontiac's Uprising and the Fate of the British Empire in North America*. Norman: University of Oklahoma Press, 2005.

Dowd, Gregory Evans. *A Spirited Resistance: The North American Indian Struggle for Unity, 1745-1815*. Baltimore: Johns Hopkins University Press, 1992.

———. *War under Heaven: Pontiac, the Indian Nations, & the British Empire*. Baltimore: Johns Hopkins University Press, 2002.

Dunn, Jacob P. *Indiana: A Redemption from Slavery*. Boston: Houghton Mifflin, 1888.

Dunn, Walter S. Jr. *Frontier Profit and Loss: The British Army and the Fur Traders, 1760-1764*. Westport, CT: Greenwood, 1998.

———. *People of the American Frontier: The Coming of the American Revolution*. Westport, CT: Praeger, 2005.

DuVal, Kathleen. *The Native Ground: Indians and Colonists in the Heart of the Continent*. Philadelphia: University of Pennsylvania Press, 2006.

Eblen, Jack Ericson. *The First and Second United States Empires: Governors and

Territorial Government, 1784–1912. Pittsburgh: University of Pittsburgh Press, 1968.

Eccles, W. J. *The French in North America, 1500–1783*. Markham, Ontario: Fitzhenry & Whiteside, 1998.

Edmunds, R. David. *The Potawatomis: Keepers of the Fire*. Norman: University of Oklahoma Press, 1978.

———. *The Shawnee Prophet*. Lincoln: University of Nebraska Press, 1983.

Ekberg, Carl J. *Colonial Ste. Genevieve: An Adventure on the Mississippi Frontier*. Gerald, MO: Patrice Press, 1985.

———. *Francois Valle and His World: Upper Louisiana Before Lewis and Clark*. Columbia: University of Missouri Press, 2002.

———. *A French Aristocrat in the American West: The Shattered Dreams of De Lassus de Luzières*. Columbia: University of Missouri Press, 2010.

———. *French Roots in The Illinois Country: The Mississippi Frontier in Colonial Times*. Urbana: University of Illinois Press, 2000.

———. *Stealing Indian Women: Native Slavery in the Illinois Country*. Urbana: University of Illinois Press, 2007.

Ekberg, Carl J., and Sharon K. Person. *St. Louis Rising: The French Regime of Louis St. Ange de Bellerive*. Urbana: University of Illinois Press, 2015.

Etcheson, Nicole. *The Emerging Midwest: Upland Southerners and the Political Culture of the Old Northwest, 1787–1861*. Bloomington: Indiana University Press, 1996.

Faragher, John Mack. *Daniel Boone: The Life and Legend of an American Pioneer*. New York: Henry Holt, 1992.

———. *Sugar Creek: Life on the Illinois Prairie*. New Haven: Yale University Press, 1986.

Fausz, J. Frederick. *Founding St. Louis: First City of the New West*. Charleston, SC: History Press, 2011.

Fehrenbacher, Don. *Sectional Crisis and Southern Constitutionalism*, comprising *The South and Three Sectional Crises* and *Constitutions and Constitutionalism in the Slaveholding South*. Baton Rouge: Louisiana State University Press, 1995.

Ferguson, Gillum. *Illinois in the War of 1812*. Urbana: University of Illinois Press, 2012.

Fischer, David Hackett, and James C. Kelly. *Bound Away: Virginia and the Westward Movement*. Charlottesville: University Press of Virginia, 2000.

Foley, William E. *The Genesis of Missouri: From Wilderness Outpost to Statehood*. Columbia: University of Missouri Press, 1989.

———. *A History of Missouri: Volume I, 1673–1820*. 1971. Reprint, Columbia: University of Missouri Press, 1999.

———. *Wilderness Journey: The Life of William Clark*. Columbia: University of Missouri Press, 2004.

Foley, William E., and C. David Rice. *The First Chouteaus: River Barons of Early St. Louis*. Urbana: University of Illinois Press, 1983.

Forbes, Robert Pierce. *The Missouri Compromise and Its Aftermath: Slavery and the Meaning of America*. Chapel Hill: University of North Carolina Press, 2007.

Frazier, Harriet. *Slavery and Crime in Missouri, 1773–1865*. Jefferson, NC: McFarland, 2001.

Freehling, William W. *The Road to Disunion*. Vol. I, *Secessionists at Bay, 1776–1854*. New York: Oxford University Press, 1990.

Friedenberg, David. *Life, Liberty, and the Pursuit of Land: The Plunder of Early America*. Buffalo: Prometheus Books, 1992.

Friend, Craig. *Kentucke's Frontiers*. Bloomington: Indiana University Press, 2010.

Furstenberg, François. *When the United States Spoke French: Five Refugess Who Shaped a Nation*. New York: Penguin, 2014.

Gates, Paul. *Landlords and Tenants on the Prairie Frontier: Studies of American Land Policy*. Ithaca, NY: Cornell University Press, 1973.

Gilpin, Alec R. *The War of 1812 in the Old Northwest*. East Lansing, MI: Michigan State University Press, 1958.

Gitlin, Jay. *The Bourgeois Frontier: French Towns, French Traders and American Expansion*. New Haven: Yale University Press, 2010.

Griffin, Patrick. *American Leviathan: Empire, Nation, and Revolutionary Frontier*. New York: Hill and Wang, 2007.

Guasco, Suzanne. *Confronting Slavery: Edward Coles and the Rise of Antislavery Politics in Nineteenth-Century America*. DeKalb: Northern Illinois University Press, 2013.

Haeger, John Denis. *John Jacob Astor: Business and Finance in the Early Republic*. Detroit: Wayne State University Press, 1991.

Hafen, LeRoy, ed. *French Fur Traders & Voyageurs in the American West*. Lincoln: University of Nebraska Press, 1995.

Hammond, John Craig. *Slavery, Freedom, and Expansion in the Early American West*. Charlottesville: University of Virginia Press, 2007.

Harris, N. Dwight. *The History of Negro Servitude in Illinois, and of the Slavery Agitation in That State, 1719–1864*. Chicago: A.C. McClurg, 1904.

Harrison, Lowell H. *George Rogers Clark and the War in the West*. Lexington: University Press of Kentucky, 1976.

Hartley, Robert E. *Lewis and Clark in the Illinois Country: The Little-Told Story*. Westminster, CO: Sniktau, 2002.

Hauck, Philomena. *Bienville: Father of Louisiana*. Lafayette: University of Southwestern Louisiana, 1998.

Havighurst, Walter. *Wilderness For Sale: The Story of the First Western Land Rush*. New York: Hastings House, 1956.

Hendrickson, David C. *Peace Pact: The Lost World of the American Founding.* Lawrence: University Press of Kansas, 1997.
Hinderaker, Eric. *Elusive Empires: Constructing Colonialism in the Ohio Valley, 1673–1800.* Cambridge, UK: Cambridge University Press, 1997.
Hodes, Frederick A. *Beyond the Frontier: A History of St. Louis to 1821.* Tucson, AZ: Patrice Press, 2004.
Hollrah, Paul. *History of St. Charles County, Missouri (1765–1885).* 1885. Reprint, Patria, 1997.
Horsman, Reginald. *The Causes of the War of 1812.* New York: A.S. Barnes, 1962.
———. *The Frontier in the Formative Years, 1783–1815.* New York: Holt, Rinehart, and Winston, 1970.
Houck, Louis. *History of Missouri from Earliest Explorations and Settlements until the Admission of the State into the Union.* 3 vols. Chicago: R.R. Donnelley & Sons, 1908.
Howard, Robert P. *Illinois: A History of the Prairie State.* Grand Rapids, MI: William B. Eerdmans, 1972.
Hurt, R. Douglas. *Agriculture and Slavery in Missouri's Little Dixie.* Columbia: University of Missouri Press, 1992.
———. *Nathan Boone and the American Frontier.* Columbia: University of Missouri Press, 1998.
Hyde, Anne. *Empires, Nations, and Families: A New History of the North American West, 1800–1860.* New York: Harper Collins, 2011.
Jackson, Donald. *Thomas Jefferson and the Rocky Mountains: Exploring the West from Monticello.* 1981. Reprint, Norman: University of Oklahoma Press, 2002.
Jacobs, James Ripley. *Tarnished Warrior: Major-General James Wilkinson.* New York: Macmillan, 1938.
James, James Alton. *The Life of George Rogers Clark.* 1928. Reprint, New York: Greenwood Press, 1969
Jennings, Sister Marietta. *A Pioneer Merchant of St. Louis, 1810–1820: The Business Career of Christian Wilt.* 1939. Reprint, New York: AMS, 1968.
Jones, Landon Y. *William Clark and the Shaping of the West.* New York: Hill and Wang, 2004.
Jortner, Adam. *The Gods of Prophetstown: The Battle of Tippecanoe and the Holy War for the American Frontier.* Oxford: Oxford University Press, 2012.
Kaplan, Lawrence S. *Thomas Jefferson: Westward the Course of Empire.* Wilmington, DE: SR Books, 1999.
Kastor, Peter J. *The Nation's Crucible: The Louisiana Purchase and the Creation of America.* New Haven: Yale University Press, 2004.
Keating, Ann. *Rising Up from Indian Country: The Battle of Fort Dearborn and the Birth of Chicago.* Chicago: University of Chicago Press, 2012.
Kellogg, Louise Phelps. *The British Regime in Wisconsin and the Northwest.* New York: Da Capo, 1971.

Kukla, Jon. *A Wilderness So Immense: The Louisiana Purchase and the Destiny of America*. New York: Knopf, 2003.

Lavender, David. *The Fist in the Wilderness*. 1964. Reprint, Lincoln: University of Nebraska Press, 1998.

Limerick, Patricia. *The Legacy of Conquest: The Unbroken Past of the American West*. New York: W.W. Norton, 1987.

Linklater, Andro. *An Artist in Treason: The Extraordinary Double Life of James Wilkinson*. New York: Walker, 2009.

Mahon, John K. *The War of 1812*. 1972. Reprint, New York: Da Capo, 1991.

Malone, Dumas. *Jefferson the President: First Term, 1801-1805*. Boston: Little, Brown, 1970.

Marshall, Thomas Maitland, ed. *The Life and Papers of Frederick Bates*. New York: Arno, 1975).

Mason, Matthew. *Slavery & Politics in the Early American Republic*. Chapel Hill: University of North Carolina Press, 2006.

Matson, Nehemiah. *French and Indians of Illinois River*. 1874. Reprint, Carbondale: Southern Illinois University Press, 2001.

McCandless, Perry, ed. *A History of Missouri: Volume II, 1820-1860*. Columbia: University of Missouri Press, 1971, 2000.

McCoy, Drew. *The Elusive Republic: Political Economy in Jeffersonian America*. Chapel Hill: University of North Carolina Press, 1980.

McCurdy, Frances. *Stump, Bar, and Pulpit: Speechmaking on the Missouri Frontier*. Columbia: University of Missouri Press, 1969.

McDermott, John, ed. *Old Cahokia: A Narrative and Documents Illustrating the First Century of Its History*. Belleville, IL: Beuchler, 1949.

———. *The Spanish in the Mississippi Valley, 1762-1804*. Urbana: University of Illinois Press, 1974.

McReynolds, Edwin C. *Missouri: A History of the Crossroads State*. Norman: University of Oklahoma Press, 1962.

Merrell, James H. *Into the American Woods: Negotiations on the Pennsylvania Frontier*. New York: W.W. Norton, 1999.

Meyer, Douglas K. *Making the Heartland Quilt: A Geographical History of Settlement and Migration in Early-Nineteenth-Century Illinois*. Carbondale: Southern Illinois University Press, 2000.

Moore, Glover. *The Missouri Controversy, 1819-1821*. Lexington: University Press of Kentucky Press, 1966.

Morgan, M. J. *Land of Big Rivers: French & Indian Illinois, 1699-1778*. Carbondale: Southern Illinois University Press, 2010.

Morrissey, Robert. *Empire by Collaboration: Indians, Colonists, and Governments in Colonial Illinois Country*. Philadelphia: University of Pennsylvania Press, 2015.

Moses, John. *Illinois, Historical and Statistical*. 2 vols. Chicago: Fergus, 1889.

Murphy, Lucy. *A Gathering of Rivers: Indians, Métis, and Mining in the Western Great Lakes, 1737–1832.* Lincoln: University of Nebraska Press, 2000.

Nester, William. *George Rogers Clark: "I Glory in War."* Norman: University of Oklahoma Press, 2012.

Norall, Frank. *Bourgmont: Explorer of the Missouri, 1698–1725.* Lincoln: University of Nebraska Press, 1988.

Nugent, Walter. *Habits of Empire: A History of American Expansion.* New York: Alfred A. Knopf, 2008.

Nute, Grace Lee. *The Voyageur.* 1931. Reprint, St. Paul: Minnesota Historical Society Press, 1987.

Ogg, Frederic Austin. *The Opening of the Mississippi: A Struggle For Supremacy in the American Interior.* 1904. Reprint, New York: Haskell House, 1969.

Oglesby, Richard. *Manuel Lisa and the Opening of the Missouri Fur Trade of the Far West.* Norman: University of Oklahoma Press, 1963.

Onuf, Peter. *Jefferson's Empire: The Language of American Statehood.* Charlottesville: University of Virginia Press, 2000.

———. *The Origins of the Federal Republic: Jurisdictional Controversies in the United States 1775–1787.* Philadelphia: University of Pennsylvania Press, 1983.

———. *Statehood and Union: A History of the Northwest Ordinance.* 1987. Reprint, Bloomington: Indiana University Press, 1992.

Onuf, Peter, and Nicholas Onuf. *Federal Union, Modern World: The Law of Nations in an Age of Revolutions, 1776–1814.* Madison, WI: Madison House, 1993.

Owens, Robert M. *Mr. Jefferson's Hammer: William Henry Harrison and the Origins of American Indian Policy.* Norman: University of Oklahoma Press, 2007.

Parkman, Francis. *The Conspiracy of Pontiac.* 1851. Reprint, New York: Library of America, 1991.

———. *LaSalle and the Discovery of the Great West.* 1865. Reprint, New York: Modern Library, 1999.

———. *Montcalm and Wolfe: The French and Indian War.* 1884. Reprint, New York: Da Capo, 1995.

Pease, Theodore Calvin. *The Frontier State, 1818–1848.* Springfield: Illinois Centennial Commission, 1918. Reprint, Urbana: University of Illinois Press, 1987.

———. *George Rogers Clark and the Revolution in Illinois, 1763–1787.* Springfield: Illinois State Historical Library, 1929.

Peterson, Jacqueline, and Jennifer S. H. Brown, eds. *The New Peoples: Being and Becoming Metis in North America.* Lincoln: University of Nebraska Press, 1985.

Philbrick, Francis S. *The Rise of the West, 1754–1830.* New York: Harper & Row, 1965.

Power, Richard Lyle. *Planting Corn Belt Culture: The Impress of the Upland Southerner and Yankee in the Old Northwest.* Indianapolis: Indiana Historical Society, 1953.

Pratt, Julius W. *Expansionists of 1812.* 1925. Reprint, Gloucester, MA: Peter Smith, 1957.

Primm, James Neal. *Lion of the Valley: St. Louis, Missouri, 1764–1980.* 3rd edition. St. Louis: Missouri Historical Society Press, 1998.

Prucha, Francis. *American Indian Policy in the Formative Years.* 1962. Reprint, Lincoln: University of Nebraska Press, 1970.

———. *The Sword of the Republic: The United States Army on the Frontier, 1783–1846.* New York: Macmillan, 1969.

Quaife, Milo Milton. *Chicago and the Old Northwest, 1673–1835.* 1913. Reprint, Urbana: University of Illinois Press, 2001.

Rice, Howard C. *Barthelemi Tardiveau: A French Trader in the West.* Baltimore: Johns Hopkins Press, 1938.

Richter, Daniel. *Facing East from Indian Country: A Native History of Early America.* Cambridge, MA: Harvard University Press, 2001.

Robertson, Lindsay G. *Conquest by Law: How the Discovery of America Dispossessed Indigenous Peoples of Their Lands.* Oxford: Oxford University Press, 2005.

Rohrbough, Malcolm. *The Land Office Business: The Settlement and Administration of American Public Lands, 1789–1837.* 1968. Reprint, New York: Oxford University Press, 1971.

———. *The Trans-Appalachian Frontier: People, Societies, and Institutions, 1775–1850.* New York: Oxford University Press, 1978.

Rollings, Willard H. *The Osage: An Ethnohistorical Study of Hegemony on the Prairie Plains.* Columbia: University of Missouri Press, 1992.

Ronda, James P. *Lewis and Clark among the Indians.* 1984. Reprint, Lincoln: University of Nebraska Press, 2002.

Rothman, Adam. *Slave Country: American Expansion and the Origins of the Deep South.* Cambridge, MA: Harvard University Press, 2005.

Rushforth, Brett. *Bonds of Alliance: Indigenous and Atlantic Slaveries in New France.* Chapel Hill: University of North Carolina Press, 2012.

Sadosky, Leonard. *Revolutionary Negotiations: Indians, Empires, and Diplomats in the Founding of America.* Charlottesville: University of Virginia Press, 2009.

Saunt, Claudio. *West of the Revolution: An Uncommon History of 1776.* New York: W.W. Norton, 2014.

Shoemaker, Floyd Calvin. *Missouri's Struggle for Statehood, 1804–1821.* 1916. Reprint, New York: Russell & Russell, 1969.

Simeone, James. *Democracy and Slavery in Frontier Illinois: The Bottomland Republic.* DeKalb: Northern Illinois University Press, 2000.

Smith, Henry Nash. *Virgin Land: The American West as Symbol and Myth.* 1950. Reprint, Cambridge, MA: Harvard University Press, 1978.
Sprague, Marshall. *So Vast, So Beautiful A Land: Louisiana and the Purchase.* Boston: Little, Brown, 1974.
Stepenoff, Bonnie. *From French Community to Missouri Town: Ste. Genevieve in the Nineteenth Century.* Columbia: University of Missouri Press, 2006.
Stevens, Wayne Edson. *The Northwest Fur Trade, 1763–1800.* Urbana: University of Illinois, 1928.
Steward, Dick. *Frontier Swashbuckler: The Life and Legend of John Smith T.* Columbia: University of Missouri Press, 2000.
Sublette, Ned. *The World That Made New Orleans: From Spanish Silver to Congo Square.* Chicago: Lawrence Hill, 2009.
Sugden, John. *Tecumseh: A Life.* New York: Henry Holt, 1997.
Tanner, Helen Hornbeck et al., eds. *Atlas of Great Lakes Indian History.* Norman: University of Oklahoma Press for the Newberry Library, 1987.
Thomson, Janice E. *Mercenaries, Pirates, and Sovereigns.* Princeton, NJ: Princeton University Press, 1994.
Thorne, Tanis C. *The Many Hands of My Relations: French and Indians on the Lower Missouri.* Columbia: University of Missouri Press, 1996.
Todd, Charles S., and Benjamin Drake. *Sketches of the Civil and Military Services of William Henry Harrison.* 1840. Reprint, New York: Arno, 1975.
Treat, Payson. *The National Land System, 1785–1820.* 1910. Reprint, New York: Russell & Russell, 1967.
Trexler, Harrison. *Slavery in Missouri, 1804–1865.* Baltimore: Johns Hopkins Press, 1914.
Usner, Daniel H. Jr. *Indians, Settlers, and Slaves in a Frontier Exchange Economy.* Chapel Hill: University of North Carolina Press, 1992.
Valencius, Conevery Bolton. *The Health of the Country: How American Settlers Understood Themselves and Their Land.* New York: Basic Books, 2002.
Van Atta, John R. *Securing the West: Politics, Public Lands, and the Fate of the Old Republic, 1785–1850.* Baltimore: Johns Hopkins University Press, 2014.
Vestal, Stanley. *The Missouri.* New York: Farrar and Rinehart, 1945.
Violette, E. M. *A History of Missouri.* 1918. Reprint, St. Louis: State Publishing, 1955.
Wade, Richard C. *The Urban Frontier: Pioneer Life in Early Pittsburgh, Cincinnati, Lexington, Louisville, and St. Louis.* 1959. Reprint, Chicago: University of Chicago Press, 1976.
Washburne, E. B. *Sketch of Edward Coles, Second Governor of Illinois, and of the Slavery Struggle of 1823-4.* Chicago: Jansen, McClurg, 1882. Reprint, New York: Negro Universities Press, 1969.
Watts, Edward. *An American Colony: Regionalism and the Roots of Midwestern Culture.* Athens: Ohio University Press, 2002.

Watts, Steven. *The Republic Reborn: War and the Making of Liberal America, 1790–1820*. Baltimore: Johns Hopkins University Press, 1987.
Weaver, John. *The Great Land Rush and the Making of the Modern World, 1650–1900*. Montreal & Kingston: McGill-Queen's University Press, 2003.
Whitaker, Arthur. *The Mississippi Question 1795–1803: A Study in Trade, Politics, and Diplomacy*. 1934. Reprint, Gloucester, MA: Peter Smith, 1962.
———. *The Spanish-American Frontier 1783–1795*. 1927. Reprint, Gloucester, MA: Peter Smith, 1962.
White, Richard. *The Middle Ground: Indians, Empires, and Republics in the Great Lakes Region, 1650–1815*. Cambridge, UK: Cambridge University Press, 1991.
Wiebe, Robert H. *The Opening of American Society: From the Adoption of the Constitution to the Eve of Disunion*. 1984. Reprint, New York: Vintage Books, 1985.
Willig, Timothy D. *Restoring the Chain of Friendship: British Policy and the Indians of the Great Lakes, 1783–1815*. Lincoln: University of Nebraska Press, 2008.
Wilson, George R. *Early Indiana Trails and Surveys*. 1919. Reprint, Indianapolis: Indiana Historical Society Press, 2002.
Winch, Julie. *The Clamorgans: One Family's History of Race in America*. New York: Hill and Wang, 2011.
Witgen, Michael. *An Infinity of Nations: How the Native New World Shaped Early North America*. Philadelphia: University of Pennsylvania Press, 2012.
Woehrmann, Paul. *At The Headwaters of the Maumee: A History of the Forts of Fort Wayne*. Indianapolis: Indiana Historical Society, 1971.
Wood, W. Raymond. *Prologue to Lewis and Clark: The Mackay and Evans Expedition*. Norman: University of Oklahoma Press, 2003.
Wright, J. Leitch. *Britain and the American Frontier 1783–1815*. Athens: University of Georgia Press, 1975.
Yirush, Craig. *Settlers, Liberty, and Empire: The Roots of Early American Political Theory, 1675–1775*. Cambridge, UK: Cambridge University Press, 2011.

Articles

Angle, Paul. "Nathaniel Pope, 1784–1850, A Memoir." *Transactions of the Illinois State Historical Society*, XLIII (1936).
Bakalis, Michael. "Ninian Edwards and Territorial Politics in Illinois, 1775–1818."
Barnhart, John. "The Southern Influence in the Formation of Illinois." *JISHS* 32 (1939): 358–378.
Berkhofer, Robert Jr. "The Northwest Ordinance and the Principle of Territorial Evolution." In *The American Territorial System*. Edited by John Bloom. Athens: Ohio University Press, 1973.

Bestor, Arthur. "Constitutionalism and the Settlement of the West: The Attainment of Consensus, 1754–1784." In *The American Territorial System*. Edited by John Bloom. Athens: Ohio University Press, 1973.

———. "Patent-Office Models of the Good Society: Some Relationships between Social Reform and Westward Expansion." *American Historical Review* 58, no. 3 (April 1953): 505–26.

Bogue, Allan G., and Margaret Beattie Bogue. "'Profits' and the Frontier Land Speculator." *Journal of Economic History* 17 (1957): 1–24.

Briggs, Winstanley. "Le Pays de Illinois." *William and Mary Quarterly* 47, no. 1 (Jan. 1990): 30–56.

Cayton, Andrew. "'Noble Actors' upon 'The Theatre of Honour': Power and Civility in the Treaty of Greenville." In *Contact Points: American Frontiers from the Mohawk Valley to the Mississippi, 1750–1830*. Edited by Andrew Cayton and Frederika Teute. Chapel Hill: University of North Carolina Press, 1998.

———. "Race, Democracy, and the Multiple Meanings of the Indiana Frontier." In *Indiana Territory: A Bicentennial Perspective*. Edited by Darrel E. Bingham, 47–70. Indianapolis: Indiana Historical Society (2001).

———. "'Separate Interests' and the Nation-State: The Washington Administration and the Origins of Regionalism in the Trans-Appalachian West." *Journal of American History* 79, no. 1 (June 1992): 39–67.

Chapman, Carl. "The Indomitable Osage in Spanish Illinois, 1763–1840." In *The Spanish in the Mississippi Valley, 1762–1804*. Edited by John Francis McDermott, 287–301. Urbana: University of Illinois Press, 1974.

Davis, David Brion. "The Significance of Excluding Slavery from the Old Northwest in 1787." *Indiana Magazine of History* 84 (March 1988), 75–89.

Davis, James E. "'New Aspects of Men and New Forms of Society': The Old Northwest, 1790–1820." *JISHS* (August 1976).

Dillon, Merton. "Sources of Early Antislavery Thought in Illinois." *JISHS* 53 (Spring 1957): 389–403.

DuVal, Kathleen. "Debating Identity, Sovereignty, and Civilization: The Arkansas Valley after the Louisiana Purchase." *Journal of the Early Republic* 26 (Spring 2006): 25–58.

Edstrom, James. "'With . . . Candour and Good Faith.'" *Illinois Historical Journal* 88 (Winter 1995): 241–62.

Faragher, John Mack. "'More Motley than Mackinaw': From Ethnic Mixing to Ethnic Cleansing on the Frontier of the Lower Missouri, 1783–1833." In *Contact Points: American Frontiers from the Mohawk Valley to the Mississippi, 1750–1830*. Edited by Andrew Cayton and Frederika Teute. Chapel Hill: University of North Carolina Press, 1998.

Finkelman, Paul. "Evading the Ordinance: The Persistence of Bondage in Indiana and Illinois." *Journal of the Early Republic* 9 (Spring 1989): 21–51.

———. "Slavery, the 'More Perfect Union,' and the Prairie State," *Illinois Historical Journal* 80 (Winter 1987): 248–69.

———. "Slavery and the Northwest Ordinance: A Study in Ambiguity." *Journal of the Early Republic* 6 (Winter 1986): 343–70.
Fladeland, Betty. "Compensated Emancipation: A Rejected Alternative." *Journal of Southern History* 42, no. 2 (May 1976): 169–86.
Gates, Paul. "The Nationalizing Influence of the Public Lands: Indiana." In *This Land of Ours: The Acquisition and Disposition of the Public Domain*. Indianapolis: Indiana Historical Society, 1978.
———. "The Role of the Speculator in Western Development." In *The Jeffersonian Dream: Studies in the History of American Land Policy and Development*. Edited by Allan G. Bogue and Margaret Beattie Bogue. Albuquerque: University of New Mexico Press, 1996.
Gitlin, Jay. "On the Boundaries of Empire: Connecting the West to Its Imperial Past." In *Under an Open Sky: Rethinking America's Western Past*. Edited by William Cronon, George A. Miller, and Jay Gitlin, 71–89. New York: W.W. Norton, 1992.
Hammes, Raymond. "Land Transactions in Illinois Prior to the Sale of Public Domain." *JISHS* (Summmer 1984):101–14.
Horsman, Reginald. "Changing Images of the Public Domain: Historians and the Shaping of Midwest Frontiers." In *This Land of Ours: The Acquisition and Disposition of the Public Domain*. Indianapolis: Indiana Historical Society, 1978.
———. "The Northwest Ordinance and the Shaping of an Expanding Republic." *Wisconsin Magazine of History* (Autumn 1989), 21–32.
John, Richard R. "Governmental Institutions as Agents of Change: Rethinking American Political Development in the Early Republic, 1787–1835." *Studies in American Political Development* 11 (Fall 1997): 347–80.
North, Douglass, and Andrew Rutten. "The Northwest Ordinance in Historical Perspective." In *Essays on the Economy of the Old Northwest*. Edited by David Klingaman and Richard Vedder, 19–35. Athens: Ohio University Press, 1987.
Onuf, Peter. "The Expanding Union." In *Devising Liberty: Preserving and Creating Freedom in the New American Republic*. Edited by David Konig, 50–80. Stanford, CA: Stanford University Press, 1995.
———. "Federalism, Republicanism, and the Origins of American Sectionalism." In *All Over the Map: Rethinking American Regions*. Edited by Peter Onuf and Edward Ayers, 11–37. Baltimore: Johns Hopkins University Press, 1996.
———. "Liberty, Development, and Union: Visions of the West in the 1780s." *William and Mary Quarterly* 43, no. 2 (April 1986): 179–213.
———. "'The Strongest Government on Earth': Jefferson's Republicanism, the Expansion of the Union, and the New Nation's Destiny." In *The Louisiana Purchase and American Expansion, 1803–1898*. Edited by Sanford Levinson and Bartholomew Sparrow. Lanham, MD: Rowman & Littlefield, 2005. 41–68.

———. "Toward Federalism: Virginia, Congress, and the Western Lands." *William and Mary Quarterly* 34, no. 3 (July 1977): 353–74.

Rakove, Jack. "Ambiguous Achievement: The Northwest Ordinance." In *Northwest Ordinance: Essays on Its Formulation, Provisions, and Legacy*. Edited by Frederick D. Williams. East Lansing: Michigan State University Press, 1988.

Rhoden, Nancy. "Great Britain and America at 1800: Perspectives on the Frontier" In *Indiana Territory: A Bicentennial Perspective*. Edited by Darrel E. Bingham, 125–147. Indianapolis: Indiana Historical Society, 2001.

Rohrbough, Malcolm. "The Land Office Business in Indiana." In *This Land of Ours: The Acquisition and Disposition of the Public Domain*. Indianapolis: Indiana Historical Society, 1978.

Shoemaker, Floyd C. "The Louisiana Purchase, 1803, and the Transfer of Upper Louisiana to the United States, 1804." *Missouri Historical Review* 48 (October 1953): 1–22.

Simeone, James. "Ninian Edwards's Republican Dilemma." *Illinois Historical Journal* 90 (Winter 1997): 245–64.

Smith, Dwight L. "The Land Cession Treaty: A Valid Instrument of Transfer of Indian Title." In *This Land of Ours: The Acquisition and Disposition of the Public Domain*. Indianapolis: Indiana Historical Society, 1978.

Strickland, Arvarh E. "Aspects of Slavery in Missouri, 1821." *Missouri Historical Review* 65 (July 1971): 505–26.

Suppiger, Joseph. "Amity to Enmity: Ninian Edwards and Jesse B. Thomas." In *Journal of the Illinois State Historical Society*, 67 (April 1974): 201-211

Sutton, Robert. "Edward Coles and the Constitutional Crisis in Illinois, 1822–1824." *Illinois Historical Journal* 82 (Spring 1989): 33–46.

———. "The Northwest Ordinance: A Bicentennial Souvenir." *Illinois Historical Journal* 81 (Spring 1988): 13–24.

Taylor, Alan. "Land and Liberty on the Post-Revolutionary Frontier." In *Devising Liberty: Preserving and Creating Freedom in the New American Republic*. Edited by David Konig. Stanford, CA: Stanford University Press, 1995.

Thomas, Samuel W. "William Clark's 1795 and 1797 Journals and Their Significance." *Bulletin of the Missouri Historical Society* 25 (1969): 279–95.

Turner, Frederick Jackson. "The Problem of the West." In *Frontier and Section: Selected Essays of Frederick Jackson Turner*. Edited by Ray A. Billington. Englewood Cliffs, NJ: Prentice-Hall, 1964.

Way, Royal B. "The United States Factory System for Trading with the Indians, 1796–1822." *Mississippi Valley Historical Review* 6, no. 2 (Sept. 1919): 220–35.

Index

Abbadie, Jean-Jacques-Blas d', 20
Adams, John Quincy, 108–9, 136–37, 138, 140
American Bottom, 16, 25, 39, 122
American Fur Company, 96, 101, 103–6, 120, 122, 124, 125, 127, 131
Amherstburg conference, 79
Andrews, James, 37
annuities, 80, 131, 132, 133, 134, 135
Arikaras, 64, 66, 128, 129
Ashley, William, 117
Astor, John Jacob, 75, 80, 96, 101, 103–6, 120, 122, 127, 131
Atkinson, Henry, 127–28, 130
Austin, Moses, 36, 58

Backus, Elijah, 71
Barbour, John, 134, 135
Barton, David, 116, 117, 136
Bates, Edward, 116
Bates, Frederic, 64–65
Battle of Fallen Timbers (1794), 79, 167n34
Battle of Horseshoe Bend (1814), 85, 87, 167n34
Battle of New Orleans (1815), 88
Battle of the Thames (1813), 84
Battle of Tippecanoe (1811), 77
Baynton and Wharton, 20–21
Becknell, William, 125–26
Bellerive, Louis St. Ange de, 19
Bent, Silas, 63

Benton, Thomas Hart: on British activity in Pacific Northwest, 129; confirmation of land claims, 117, 171n44; elite's interests served by, 126, 172n6; on Missouri statehood, 117–18, 171n44; populist democracy adopted by, 142; presidential election of 1824, 136–37; and Santa Fe trade, 125, 126; on trading factories, 104–5, 126, 127
Birkbeck, Morris, 138, 140
Bissell, Daniel, 91
Blackhawk, 80, 84, 90, 133
Black Partridge, 82
Bond, Shadrach, 87, 108, 138
Boone, Daniel, 31, 36
Browne, Joseph, 58
Bryant, Guy, 25
Burr, Aaron, 58

Cahokia (Illinois), 14, 15, 22, 26, 38, 146
Calhoun, John C., 101, 105, 127–28, 134
Camden-Yorke opinion, 21
Cape Girardeau (Missouri), 31, 32, 101, 120
Carondelet, Francisco, 30, 32, 33, 34, 35, 36, 38, 155n47
Carr, William C., 52, 61, 62, 68
Cass, Lewis, 133, 134, 173n27
Cerré, Gabriel, 23, 26
Charless, Joseph, 82, 113, 116
Cherokee Indians, 95, 101, 102, 120
Chesapeake affair, 65, 78–79, 97

Chouteau, Auguste: in development of St. Louis, 9, 19, 20, 153n20; Fort Carondelet built, 35; Gratiot marries sister of, 145; Harrison stays at home of, 53; and Jefferson's meeting with Osage Indians, 51; Lewis and Clark assisted by, 48; at meeting over governance of Louisiana Purchase, 52; at Portage des Sioux treaty council, 89; presses his Spanish land claims, 117; Spanish Mines claim of, 54; in War of 1812, 86

Chouteau, Pierre, 12; as agent for Indian affairs, 51, 52, 54, 60, 64; Clark's treaty with Osage renegotiated by, 66; Gratiot marries sister of, 145; Lewis and Clark assisted by, 48–49; Madison administration criticizes, 69; Osage wife of, 12, 54, 60; in War of 1812, 85–86

Chouteau, Pierre, Jr., 131

Chouteau family: adjust to changing circumstances, 74; British goods smuggled, 60; on congressional bill for governing Louisiana, 50; and fur trade, 11, 12, 131; Indian treaties negotiated, 53–54; in land scramble, 11; and Lewis and Clark expedition, 48, 49; Lewis contracts with private company including, 68; maintain good relations with Indians during War of 1812, 86; Osage Indian connections, 9, 24, 35, 44, 54; under Spanish rule, 31; Stoddard as indebted to, 49

Clamorgan, Jacques, 53

Clark, George Rogers: British half of Illinois Country captured, 15, 21–23, 25, 144–45, 147, 154n26, 154n27; brother settles financial affairs of, 48; French legion against Upper Louisiana recruited, 30, 34–35; on Indian-settler violence in Illinois, 38; leaves Illinois, 26; Lorimier's trading post attacked, 31

Clark, Reuben, 68

Clark, William: and Ashley-Henry expedition, 127, 128, 129; Calhoun's instructions about American Fur Company, 105; in Cape Girardeau land conflict, 101; in construction of US sovereignty in Louisiana, 64; on controlling settlers after War of 1812, 95; efforts to acquire Indians lands by negotiation, 11; elected governor of Missouri, 116–17; federal policy executed by, 142; in Indian removal, 132–35, 173n20; and Jefferson's meeting with Osage Indians, 51; land speculation by, 103; Lewis contracts with private company including, 68; Madison administration criticizes, 69; as militia head and US Indian agent, 64; at Portage des Sioux treaty council, 89, 90, 91, 97, 117; in St. Louis, 47, 48, 73; treaty with Osage Indians, 66; in War of 1812, 84, 85, 86, 87, 88, 166n26. *See also* Lewis and Clark expedition

Clay, Henry, 96, 136
Coles, Edward, 137–38, 139, 140
Collot, Victor, 36
Cook, Daniel, 108–10, 135, 136, 138, 140, 142
Cook, Nathaniel, 117
Crawford, William, 94–95, 136
Crevecoeur, St. John de, 29
Croghan, George, 20–21
Crooks, Ramsay, 96, 127

Dallas, A. J., 90–91
Dearborn, Henry, 50, 57, 60, 65
Delassus, Carlos De Hault, 1, 44, 120, 144
Delaunay, David, 53
Delaware Indians, 31, 95, 132
Dickson, Robert, 79, 84, 87
District of Louisiana, 50, 53–54
Dodge, Henry, 116
Dodge, John, 26
Donaldson, James, 63, 71
Dorchester, Lord, 29
Dubuque, Julien, 54
Duncan, Joseph, 136
DuPont de Nemours, Pierre Samuel, 44–45, 47

Easton, Rufus, 57–58, 61, 62
Eddy, Henry, 138
Edgar, John, 25, 108
Edwards, Ninian: on British fur traders, 103; and Cook, 108, 109, 110; as governor of Illinois Territory, 67, 69–70; Illinois statehood sought by, 110; land speculation by, 103, 111; on management of Indian affairs, 92; in Missouri crisis, 135; political dynasticism attributed to, 136; at Portage des Sioux treaty council, 89; on second-stage government, 77,

164n4; seeks to acquire Indian lands, 102; as slaveholder, 108; in War of 1812, 81–82, 83, 85, 87–88
Elliot, Matthew, 79
Eustis, William, 68, 69

Flowers, George, 140–41
Floyd, John, 129
Ford, Thomas, 139–40
Fordham, Elias Pym, 138
Fort Carondelet, 35
Fromentin, Eligius, 52

Gallatin, Albert, 45, 51, 62, 71, 72
Gardoqui, Diego, 29, 32
Gayoso, Manuel, 35, 36
Genet, Edmond, 30, 34
Gibault, Father, 26
Gomo, 82
Gratiot, Charles, 23, 50, 53, 69, 144–45
Green, Duff, 116

Hamilton, Alexander, 34, 58, 112
Hammond, Samuel, 62, 116
Hamtramck, John F., 139
Hanks, Porter, 75
Harmar, Josiah, 27, 139
Harrison, William Henry: and Indians trading with British, 60; Indian treaties negotiated by, 7, 45–46, 55, 59, 66, 70, 74; and land claim problems, 61; Madison on land policy of, 94; militia organized by, 65; on Northwest Ordinance, 112, 113; Prophet and Tecumseh opposed, 65, 66; second stage of territorial government for Indiana Territory, 55, 58–59; sinking popularity in Indiana Territory, 54; visits St. Louis, 53–54; in War of 1812, 83–84
Henry, Andrew, 127–31
Henry, Patrick, 22
Howard, Benjamin, 81–82, 83, 84, 85, 96
Howard, Carlos, 36
Hull, William, 81, 82
Hunt, Seth, 58, 61

Illinois: admission to Union, 3, 10–11, 106–13, 121; civil government for, 28; competition with Missouri for settlers, 115, 171n40; constitution of 1818, 139, 140, 141; depression of early 1820s, 125, 137; explosion of immigration after War of 1812, 92, 95–96, 101, 119; idea of US evolves in, 74; Illinois Country gives rise to, 2, 4, 5; increasing hostility toward Indians in, 123–24, 131; indenture laws, 8, 11, 40, 100, 106, 107, 108, 110, 112, 121, 138; in Indiana Territory, 37, 42; land commissions in, 69–73; land on eve of statehood, 100–103; Missouri contrasted with, 106, 121, 146; multiracial communities absent in, 7; petitions to Congress from, 54–55, 60–61; political factionalism in, 10; politics in the new state, 135–43; presidential election of 1824, 136; public land sales in, 6, 61, 76, 92, 93, 97–98, 100, 101, 107, 121; shifting composition of settlers, 140; slavery convention of 1824, 8, 108, 198, 124, 137–41; slavery issue in, 8, 10, 11, 40, 41, 99–100, 106–13, 121, 124, 137–41, 143, 147; Tardiveau presents their grievances to Congress, 27–28; in War of 1812, 76
Illinois Company, 21
Illinois Territory: creation of, 67; second stage of territorial government for, 76–77, 164n4; on the way to statehood, 42. *See also* Illinois
indentures: in Illinois, 8, 11, 40, 100, 106, 107, 108, 110, 112, 121, 138; in Indiana, 8, 66; white settlers desire, 147
Indiana Territory: in division of Northwest Territory, 37, 42; indentures in, 8, 66; in Jefferson's imperial strategy, 45–46; militia organized in, 65; petitions to Congress from, 54–55, 66–67; second stage of territorial government, 55, 58–59; slavery prohibited in, 52, 53, 66; Upper Louisiana placed under, 50

Jackson, Andrew: Indian removal policy, 124, 142; military victories, 10, 85, 87, 88, 97, 167n34; and Portage des Sioux treaty council, 90–91; presidential election of 1824, 136–37; treaty to acquire Indian lands, 89, 167n34
Jay Treaty (1794), 36, 65, 72, 73, 78, 79, 157n62
Jefferson, Thomas: on Burr's treachery and western attachment, 58; Carr's criticism, 61; Chouteau and, 12;

embargo of British goods, 73, 78–79; on French retaking Louisiana, 44–45; on Indian assimilation, 133, 142; Indian policy, 46, 64; Louisiana Purchase, 47, 49, 50; Madison on land policy of, 94; meets with Arikara Indians, 64; and territorial assembly for Indiana, 59; and trading factories, 59–60, 66; on Virginia procuring Illinois, 22; and Wilkinson, 57, 62–63

Johnson v. M'Intosh (1823), 154n23

Jones, Michael, 69, 71

Kansas Indians, 134

Kaskaskia (Illinois): American merchants in, 25; during American Revolution, 21, 22, 26, 27, 147; British take control, 20; as capital of Illinois Territory, 42; founding, 14, 16; Harrison calls for federal garrison for, 46; land commission appointed for, 55; proximity to Indian villages, 38; state constitution signed in, 106; in War of 1812, 84

Keokuk, 90, 133

Kerlérec, Louis Billouart, comte de, 19–20

LaClède, Pierre, 9, 19, 20, 153n20

land commissions: citizens' frustration with, 77; colonial land grants investigated by, 6, 10, 43; complete their work, 92; in Illinois Territory, 69, 70–73; inability to resolve land claims problem, 60–63, 67, 94; for Kaskaskia and Vincennes, 55

Lassus de Luzières, Pierre-Charles de, 155n47

lead mining, 16, 36, 54, 57–58, 64–65, 94, 126, 172n6

Leavenworth, Henry, 129–30

Lewis, Meriwether: in construction of US sovereignty in Louisiana, 64; as governor of Louisiana Territory, 64, 66, 67–68; and Jefferson's meeting with Osage Indians, 51; as Jefferson's secretary, 49; in St. Louis, 47, 48, 73; takes his own life, 68; at transfer of Upper Louisiana to US, 1, 47, 144. *See also* Lewis and Clark expedition

Lewis and Clark expedition: Chouteau family assist, 48–49; diplomacy with Indians, 63–64, 73; good use of human resources by, 147; and Louisiana Purchase, 45; observations about people and places, 131–32; reunification of Illinois Country and, 42–43; and US projects of attachment and incorporation, 43

Lippincott, Thomas, 138

Lisa, Manuel, 44, 86, 127

Livingston, Robert, 45

Lorimier, Louis, 31–32, 35, 69, 133, 156n52

Louisiana Purchase, 47–54; American majority in Upper Louisiana by time of, 36; attachment of residents required in, 48; bill for governance of, 50, 52–53, 56; colonial land grants investigated after, 6, 10, 61–63, 70–73; division of Louisiana, 50; Harrison on Indians and, 59; idea of US evolves in, 74; Illinois Country on the eve of, 43–46; Illinois Country transformed by, 73; Indians in, 48, 49–50, 53, 59, 66, 69; Jefferson's plans for, 47, 49, 53; Napoleon decides to sell Louisiana, 37, 42; official transfer, 158n11; opposition to, 47, 48; residents' rights protected by, 47; signing of, 46; transfer of Upper Louisiana to United States, 1–2, 3, 47, 49, 144, 145; US sovereignty asserted in, 48, 56–58, 64

Lucas, John B. C., 62, 63, 71, 72, 116, 117

Mackay, James, 35, 51, 53

Madison, James: and Clark's appointments, 69; and Coles, 137; declaration of war in 1812, 77; embargo of British goods, 73, 78; and Lewis's private trading contract, 68; and Portage des Sioux treaty council, 89, 90, 91; pushes Indians to become more agricultural, 104; seeks peace with Indians, 94–96; threatens squatters with removal, 93–94; and trading factories, 66

Mason, George, 22

Maxent, Gilbert, 19, 20

McClean, John, 135

McClure, Samuel, 37

McKee, Andrew, 79

McKenney, Thomas, 105, 133

McNair, Alexander, 93–94, 116, 118

Menard, Pierre, 25–26, 86, 108, 111
métis, 12, 17, 39, 41, 43, 92, 103, 122, 124, 142
Miró, Esteban, 32–33
Mississippi River: British move into Upper Mississippi valley, 31; construction of effective sovereignty on both sides of, 9; federal government sees it as impassible, 55; as international boundary, 2, 23, 18, 39, 42, 146; New Orleans as depot for agricultural surplus of, 145; as organizational and conceptual dividing line, 5; Pike expedition up, 57; Portage des Sioux treaty council on, 89; profit as central element in transformation of valley, 12; pushing eastern Indians across, 42, 51, 100, 101–2, 132; Spanish close to American traders, 24, 31, 39; Spanish expeditions up, 35, 36; Treaty of San Lorenzo opens to American trade, 36; US gains control of both sides of, 6; white settlers demand access to, 39
Missouri: admission crisis, 3, 5, 8, 10–11, 99, 113–19, 121–22, 135, 141, 147; American officials find contentious environment in, 10; competition with Illinois for settlers, 115, 171n40; depression of early 1820s, 125; explosion of immigration after War of 1812, 92, 95–96, 101, 119; fur trade in, 11; in historical bifurcation of Illinois Country, 5; Illinois contrasted with, 106, 121, 146; Illinois Country gives rise to, 2, 4; increasing hostility toward Indians in, 123–24, 131; land on eve of statehood, 100–103; multiracial communities in, 7; politics in the new state, 135–37, 141–43; Portage des Sioux treaty council, 76, 88–91; presidential election of 1824, 136–37; public land sales in, 6, 61, 92, 93, 97–98, 100, 101, 102; slavery in, 7, 8, 11, 41, 99, 113–19, 121–22, 124, 137, 139, 143; Spanish rule, 18–20; in War of 1812, 76, 78, 81–88
Missouri Company, 35
Missouri Compromises, 5, 115–16, 118, 122, 135
Missouri River: Ashley-Henry expedition, 127–31; fur trade on, 35, 45, 48, 51, 54, 67; Lewis and Clark expedition up, 73, 131–32; Osage trading factory on, 80; Portage des Sioux treaty council on, 89, 90; US closes to British subjects, 57
Missouri Territory: creation of, 7, 42; second stage of territorial government for, 76–77. *See also* Missouri
Monroe, James: Astor and, 96; Bureau of Indian Affairs created, 133; Cook urges him to abolish slavery, 109; foreign traders banned, 104; Illinois statehood bill signed, 99; Indian policy, 104, 134, 142; land policy, 103; in Louisiana Purchase, 45; in Missouri statehood, 115–16, 118, 123; and Santa Fe trade, 126; on Treaty of Ghent, 89; and War of 1812, 82, 83, 87
Morales, Juan, 44
Morgan, George, 32–33
Morrison, William, 25, 108
Morse, Jedediah, 127
Moses, John, 171n40
Moustier, Count de, 28

Napoleon Bonaparte, 37, 42
New Madrid (Missouri), 30, 32
New Orleans: British blockade, 23; Clark on possession of, 34; as depot for agricultural surplus, 145; in division of Louisiana, 50; Gratiot in, 145; Jefferson on acquiring, 45; LaClède at, 19, 20; Spanish close to foreign traders, 44; Spanish rule resisted, 18; Tardiveau at, 29, 30; US acquisition, 47–48; white settlers need access to foreign markets via, 31
North West Company, 75
Northwest Ordinance: Crevecoeur on, 29; and effective sovereignty, 25, 28; Louisiana political system modeled on, 56; passage of, 27; self-government under, 50, 59; on slavery, 8, 9, 11, 28, 40, 46, 54, 66, 100, 106–13, 139–40, 141; as template for western land distribution, 6–7, 141
Northwest Territory: division of, 37, 42; Illinois as part of, 5, 8, 28, 106. *See also* Northwest Ordinance

O'Fallon, Benjamin, 128, 130
O'Fallon, James, 34
Orleans Territory, 50

Osage Indians: alliance with French, 17, 24; attempt to acculturate, 134; Cherokees clash with, 95; Pierre Chouteau's Osage wife, 12, 54, 60; Chouteaus' trade concession with, 44, 54; Clark's treaty with, 66; conflict with Upper Louisiana, 31, 32, 33, 35, 39, 66; in growth of St. Louis, 9; Harrison helps them negotiate treaty with their enemies, 59; as losers in postwar land grabs, 102; and Louisiana Purchase, 48, 50; meet with Jefferson, 51–52; military prowess, 15, 38, 78; objectives, 42; reject Tecumseh's pan-Indian confederation, 166n27; St. Louis attacked by, 66; settlers compete with, 3; splinter into two groups, 44; traders concerned about debts of, 60; trading factory for, 80; violence against white settlers, 38; in War of 1812, 85, 86

Peck, John Mason, 138
Penrose, Clement, 63, 71
Pérez, Manuel, 31
Perry, Oliver, 84
Piernas, Pedro, 19
Pike, Zebulon, 57, 64
Pilcher, Joshua, 130
Poindexter, George, 112, 113
Pollack, Oliver, 23
Pontiac's Rebellion, 18, 21
Pope, Nathaniel, 108, 110
Portage des Sioux treaty council, 76, 88–91, 92, 93, 117
Post, Justus, 125
Pothier, Touissant, 75
Prairie de Chien council, 133, 134
Prophet, The, 65, 66, 82

Reynolds, John, 82, 174n44
Ríu, Francisco, 18–19, 20
Roberts, Charles, 75
Russell, William, 87, 89

St. Ange de Bellerive, Louis, 19
St. Claire, Arthur, 28, 40, 139
St. Claire County (Illinois), 28
Ste. Genevieve (Missouri), 16, 18–19, 30, 36, 52, 53, 58
St. Louis: American Revolution and, 23; bill for governance of Louisiana Purchase opposed in, 50, 52–53; British-Indian attack of 1780, 31; as capital of Missouri Territory, 42; changing sovereignty in, 146; in construction of effective sovereignty on both sides of Mississippi River, 9; establishment of, 9, 19–20, 153n20; and foreign fur traders, 103; as French village, 15; Gratiot settles in, 145; Lewis and Clark in, 47, 48, 73; oaths of allegiance to US, 56; Osage Indians attack, 66; Ríu visits, 18–19; slavery in, 40; transfer of Upper Louisiana to United States, 1, 47, 49; and Treaty of Ghent, 89; in War of 1812, 83, 84, 85
Santa Fe trade, 124, 125–27, 172n67
Scott, John, 114, 116, 117, 136, 137, 142
Seven Years War, 14, 15, 17, 18, 19, 38
Shahaka, 64, 66, 68, 69
Shawnee Indians, 21, 31, 95, 120, 132
Sioux Indians, 64, 66, 95, 127, 128, 134
slavery: Cook urges plan to abolish, 109; in Illinois, 8, 10, 11, 40, 41, 99–100, 106–13, 121, 124, 137–41, 143, 147; Indiana Territory prohibits, 52, 53, 66; and Indians, 17, 41, 133; and land prices, 8–9; in Missouri, 7, 8, 11, 41, 99, 113–19, 121–22, 124, 137, 139, 143; Northwest Ordinance on, 8, 9, 11, 28, 40, 46, 54, 66, 100, 106–13, 139–40, 141; and property rights, 40; racial issue in Illinois Country, 37; in statehood process, 10–11, 99, 100, 106–19, 121–22; in Upper Louisiana, 30; white settlers desire, 67, 91, 147
Smith, Jedediah, 131
Smith T, John, 58
Soulard, Antoine, 48, 51, 53, 63, 69, 144
South West Company, 75, 104
squatters: on Indian lands, 72, 98; in Louisiana territory, 57; Madison threatens with removal, 93–94; rights, 7, 54, 93, 126; white settlers in Illinois Country, 25
Stirling, Thomas, 18
Stoddard, Amos, 1, 2, 49, 50, 52, 61, 144

Tallmadge, James, 99, 112–13, 114
Tardiveau, Barthelemi, 27–30, 40, 155n47, 27–30, 35, 155n47
Taylor, Zachary, 84

Tecumseh, 65, 66, 79, 82, 84, 166n27
Thomas, Jesse, 67, 108, 135
Todd, Andrew, 35
Todd, John, 23, 25, 26
trading factories, 59–60; abolition of, 105, 125, 126, 127; Astor and, 101, 104–6, 120, 127; banning foreign traders and, 93; British-Indian alliance as consequence of, 66, 73, 80, 97; Edwards on, 87–88; for limiting alcohol trade, 94
Treat, John, 60
Treaty of Fort Jackson (1814), 89, 167n34
Treaty of Ghent (1814), 88–89, 90, 92
Treaty of Greenville (1795), 7, 74, 79, 89
Treaty of Paris (1783), 2, 5, 72, 79, 146
Treaty of San Ildefonso (1800), 158n3
Treaty of San Lorenzo (Pinckney's Treaty) (1795), 35–36
Trudeau, Zenon, 32, 33, 34, 35

Ulloa, Antonio de, 18
Upper Louisiana: American Revolution in, 23; after American Revolution, 30–37; becomes District of Louisiana, 50; corruption in, 44; divided between Spain and Britain, 2, 14–15, 17, 24, 38; fur trade in, 24, 34, 39, 44, 48; Illinois Country contrasted with, 24–25, 29–30; Indians in, 7, 25, 30–32; Indian-white violence in, 38, 40–41; land in, 30, 32–33, 50, 53, 56; Osage conflict with, 31, 32, 33, 35, 39, 66; placed under Indiana Territory, 50; transfer to United States, 1–2, 3, 47, 49, 144, 145; US sovereignty solidifies in, 135–36; white settlers in, 30–31, 32–34, 36, 40–41. *See also* Louisiana Purchase

Vallé, Jean-Baptiste, 52
Vincennes (Indiana), 22, 26, 53, 55, 154n27

Wabash Company, 21
Warren, Hooper, 138
Washington, George, 40
Wayne, Anthony, 89, 167n34
White, James, 37
Whiteside, William, 38
Wilkinson, James: American interests undermined by, 32, 162n60; as governor of Louisiana Territory, 56–57, 60, 61–62, 64, 65, 69, 71; takes oath to Spanish, 35
Wythe, George, 22

EARLY AMERICAN PLACES

Cultivating Regionalism: Higher Education and the Making of the American Midwest
by Kenneth H. Wheeler

Race and Rights: Fighting Slavery and Prejudice in the Old Northwest, 1830–1870
by Dana E. Weiner

Confronting Slavery: Edward Coles and the Rise of Antislavery Politics in Nineteenth-Century America
by Suzanne Cooper Guasco

Parading Patriotism: Independence Day Celebrations in the Urban Midwest, 1826–1876
by Adam Criblez

Senator Benton and the People: Master Race Democracy on the Early American Frontiers
by Ken Mueller

"Remember Me To Miss Louisa": Hidden Black-White Intimacies in Antebellum America
by Sharony Green

www.ingramcontent.com/pod-product-compliance
Lightning Source LLC
Chambersburg PA
CBHW020124240426
43673CB00038B/584